EYEWITNESS 👁 HANDBOOKS

ROCKS
—AND—
MINERALS

EYEWITNESS ◉ HANDBOOKS

ROCKS
—AND—
MINERALS

CHRIS PELLANT

HELEN PELLANT
Editorial Consultant

Photography by
HARRY TAYLOR
(Natural History Museum)

DORLING KINDERSLEY
London • New York • Stuttgart

A DORLING KINDERSLEY BOOK

Editors Stella Vayne, James Harrison
Art Editor Clive Hayball
Technical Consultant Dr Robert Symes
(Natural History Museum, London)
Production Controller Caroline Webber

— ◆ —

First published in Great Britain in 1992
by Dorling Kindersley Limited,
9 Henrietta Street, London WC2E 8PS

549.
455869

A CIP catalogue record for this book is available from
the British Library

ISBN 0-7513-1000-X hardcover
ISBN 0-86318-810-9 flexibound

— ◆ —

Computer page make-up by
The Cooling Brown Partnership, Great Britain

Text film output by Creative Ace and
The Right Type, Great Britain

Reproduced by
Colourscan, Singapore

Printed and bound by
Kyodo Printing Co., Singapore

CONTENTS

COLLECTING ROCKS AND MINERALS

Rocks and minerals are a fundamental part of the earth's crust. Collecting and studying them can be both a rewarding and an absorbing hobby. This can involve travelling to wild and exciting places, much research, and some time spent cataloguing and displaying finds. As your collection grows, you can exchange material with other collectors, and purchase rare or exceptional specimens from mineral dealers.

A COLLECTING TRIP may take you to a site a kilometre away, or to the other side of the world. Wherever your exact destination is, you may find rock faces and surfaces in sea or river cliffs, or in man-made exposures such as quarries, road or rail cuttings, and artificial drainage channels. Seek permission to collect on private land, and remember to collect specimens in moderation. Always treat natural exposures with care, and don't quarry away natural rock faces. Collectors can also be conservationists.

FIELD SPECIMENS

You may come to explore an area where, millions of years ago, hot fluids – possibly associated with molten magma beneath the earth's surface – have deposited minerals in overlaying strata. In such an area, you can find many different specimens: rocks like granite and limestone, and minerals such as fluorite, may all occur within a short distance of each other.

SEASIDE CLIFF EXPOSURE
Search the shore below the cliffs for rocks and minerals. The dumps of abandoned mines, as on the cliff top here, are an excellent area to hunt for minerals.

CRINOIDAL
LIMESTONE

GRANITE

CRYSTALLINE
FLUORITE

• crystalline fluorite often found in old mine dumps

• granite is often found in disused quarries

• crinoidal limestone occurs on limestone cliffs

GEOLOGICAL MAPS

Geological maps show the surface distribution of rocks, their age relationships, and structural features. The coloured patterns of a geological map represent individual rock formations. Geological maps also give information about how the rocks behave below ground. Dip arrows provide clues to predict the structure, indicating the angle that a rock strata makes with the horizontal. Interpreting a geological map is a matter of experience and common sense. For instance, note that the mineral veins shown below occur near a metamorphic contact zone. Geological maps are obtainable from specialist map and museum shops.

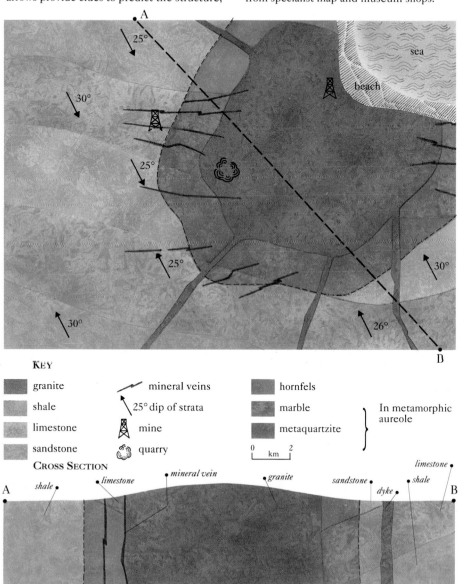

KEY

granite	mineral veins	hornfels	
shale	25° dip of strata	marble	In metamorphic aureole
limestone	mine	metaquartzite	
sandstone	quarry	0 km 2	

CROSS SECTION

FIELD EQUIPMENT

DO YOUR HOMEWORK before your field work: check your locality reference material, such as guide books and detailed maps, before setting out on any field trip. Geological maps are a great asset (see page 7) but, because overprinted colours may obscure features such as roads and quarries, you should also take a detailed, large-scale map to pinpoint the actual site. Take a compass for areas where there are few topographic features on the ground so that you can locate sites. Protective clothing is essential. When working below a high cliff or quarry face, a hard hat is a must. Put on goggles to shield your eyes from chips of rock flying off as you use your hammer, and wear strong gloves to protect your hands. Take a geological hammer to break up blocks of material already on the ground, but use it sparingly. Several hardened steel chisels are handy for extracting different minerals or for splitting rocks. Write notes, take pictures, or make a video of the location of your specimens. Without field notes, especially of a location, specimens are of little scientific value.

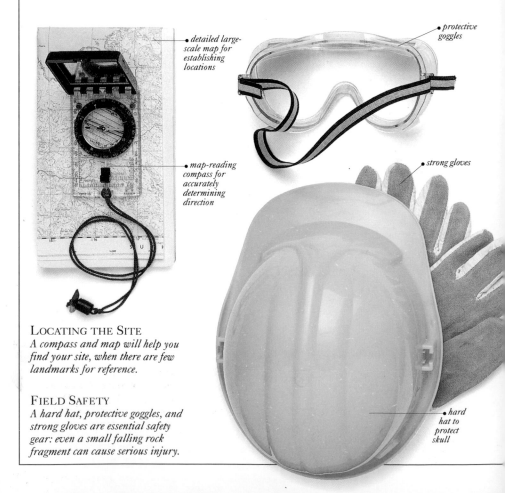

• detailed large-scale map for establishing locations

• map-reading compass for accurately determining direction

• protective goggles

• strong gloves

• hard hat to protect skull

LOCATING THE SITE
A compass and map will help you find your site, when there are few landmarks for reference.

FIELD SAFETY
A hard hat, protective goggles, and strong gloves are essential safety gear: even a small falling rock fragment can cause serious injury.

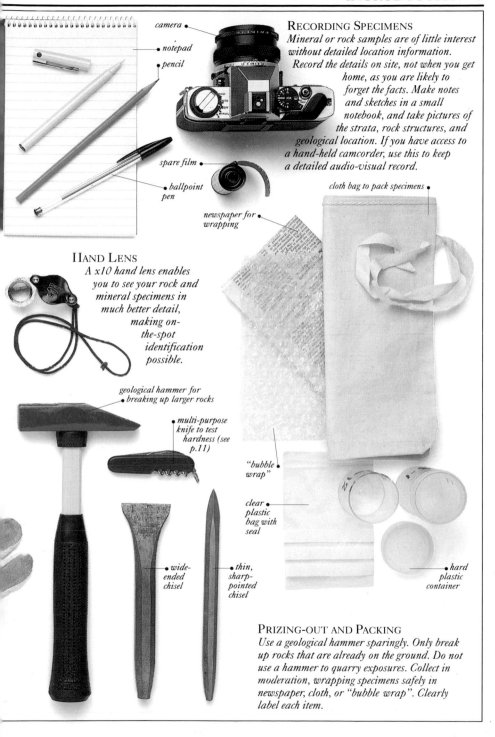

camera •

• notepad

• pencil

spare film •

• ballpont
pen

RECORDING SPECIMENS

*Mineral or rock samples are of little interest
without detailed location information.
Record the details on site, not when you get
home, as you are likely to
forget the facts. Make notes
and sketches in a small
notebook, and take pictures of
the strata, rock structures, and
geological location. If you have access to
a hand-held camcorder, use this to keep
a detailed audio-visual record.*

cloth bag to pack specimens •

newspaper for •
wrapping

HAND LENS

*A x10 hand lens enables
you to see your rock and
mineral specimens in
much better detail,
making on-
the-spot
identification
possible.*

geological hammer for
• breaking up larger rocks

• multi-purpose
knife to test
hardness (see
p.11)

"bubble •
wrap"

clear •
plastic
bag with
seal

• wide-
ended
chisel

• thin,
sharp-
pointed
chisel

• hard
plastic
container

PRIZING-OUT AND PACKING

*Use a geological hammer sparingly. Only break
up rocks that are already on the ground. Do not
use a hammer to quarry exposures. Collect in
moderation, wrapping specimens safely in
newspaper, cloth, or "bubble wrap". Clearly
label each item.*

HOME KIT

YOU HAVE COLLECTED your specimens and brought them home. Now you should prepare them carefully for identification, and then for display or storage. Your home kit must have the essential identification equipment shown here. Many specimens will have soil and/or rock matrix stuck to them which you will have to clean off. Use a soft brush to remove very loose soil and other rock debris. Avoid hammering at specimens with heavy or sharp tools, unless you want to reveal fresh surfaces. Hold the specimens in your hand while you brush away the loose material – a vice or metal clamp may cause damage.

If you are preparing a hard rock specimen, such as granite or gneiss, you can do very little damage even with a fairly coarse brush and running water. For delicate minerals, such as calcite crystals, use distilled water (which doesn't contain reactive chemical additives) and a very fine brush. For minerals that dissolve in water (the cubes of halite lose their sharp edges) use other liquids. Alcohol cleans nitrates, sulphates, and borates, and weak hydrochloric acid is a good cleaner for silicates but will dissolve carbonates. Soaking silicates overnight in acid will remove coatings of carbonate debris.

SCRAPING AND PRIZING TOOLS
Clean off loose debris from some specimens with sharp metal implements. A pointed tool like a bradawl is useful for prizing material off, but take great care not to damage the underlying rock. This is a preliminary stage of specimen preparation.

CLEANING BRUSHES
You can clean rocks and minerals using brushes of various sizes – from a soft paintbrush to a nailbrush – depending on the fragility of the specimen. A soft sable brush is best for removal of tiny sediment grains from minerals, while a nailbrush is best restricted to hard rocks, such as gneiss or gabbro, which it can't damage.

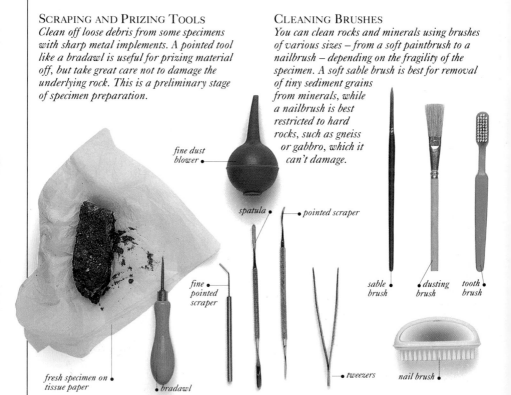

fine dust blower

spatula

pointed scraper

fine pointed scraper

fresh specimen on tissue paper

bradawl

tweezers

sable brush

dusting brush

tooth brush

nail brush

• *distilled water*

CLEANING LIQUIDS
Use distilled water, if possible, for cleaning, because tap water contains various chemicals that may react with minerals. Diluted hydrochloric acid will dissolve carbonate matrix. This acid is safe to use.

• *weak hydrochloric acid*

MINERAL TESTS
At home, basic chemistry tests are a good way of establishing a mineral's identity. Dilute acids will give consistent reactions on a given mineral: for example, carbonates effervesce in dilute hydrochloric acid. Always wear gloves when working with acids. A controlled flame is another test. Place a specimen on a charcoal block and concentrate a Bunsen flame onto it, using a blowpipe. The mineral may colour the flame, indicating chemical composition, or it may fuse, forming a small, globular, bead-like mass, or give off odours.

• *soft tissue paper for absorbing cleaning liquids*

cotton buds for reaching into cavities •

• *x10 hand lens for identifying specimens*

porcelain streak plate or tile •

IDENTIFICATION AIDS
A streak plate, hardness-testing tools, and hand lens are all indispensable identification aids. The properties of hardness and streak are explained on pages 25 and 26 respectively.

HARDNESS KIT
If you scratch a mineral with everyday objects in sequence – say a coin followed by a knife, followed by a piece of glass or quartz, you can •*determine the mineral's hardness.*

• *glass indicates hardness 6*

• *quartz indicates hardness 7*

• *specimen on "bubble wrap"*

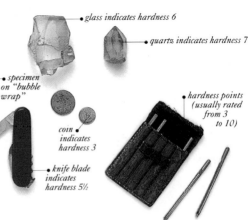

• *hardness points (usually rated from 3 to 10)*

coin indicates hardness 3 •

• *knife blade indicates hardness 5½*

ORGANIZING YOUR COLLECTION

A COLLECTION OF ROCKS and minerals is of no scientific value unless it is sensibly organized. Once you have collected and cleaned your specimens, they have to be organized for storage, and display, as well as catalogued and labelled. You'll probably want to display the more attractive specimens, and those which are fairly robust, in the home. Store these in a glass-fronted cabinet, otherwise dust will collect in the hollows and cavities. Keep delicate specimens in individual card trays or boxes, slightly larger than the specimens themselves, in a cabinet. Put a data card in the base of each specimen tray, with the specimen's name, location, date of collection, and catalogue number.

Enter each specimen in your catalogue – this can be a card index or home computer-based system. Number the catalogue entries to correspond with the numbers on the cards in the specimen trays. There will also be room for more detailed information in the catalogue than on the specimen tray. Write, or key-in, any map references, and any local geology such as other minerals or rocks at that location, and details of the rock structure, any large-scale formation and field features you saw there – perhaps a mineral vein and the rock in which the vein was running – along with key identifying features, which you can cross-refer to in the relevant rock or mineral entry in this book.

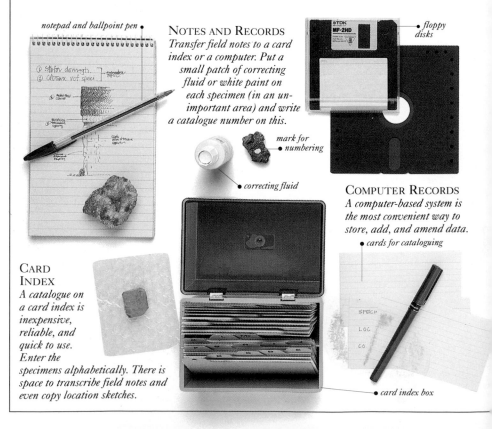

notepad and ballpoint pen

NOTES AND RECORDS
Transfer field notes to a card index or a computer. Put a small patch of correcting fluid or white paint on each specimen (in an unimportant area) and write a catalogue number on this.

floppy disks

mark for numbering

correcting fluid

COMPUTER RECORDS
A computer-based system is the most convenient way to store, add, and amend data.

cards for cataloguing

CARD INDEX
A catalogue on a card index is inexpensive, reliable, and quick to use. Enter the specimens alphabetically. There is space to transcribe field notes and even copy location sketches.

card index box

well-sorted
drawer

specimen labels

tissue-lined
cardboard trays

STORING YOUR SPECIMENS
*House your rocks and
minerals in card trays
within a drawer. You
can easily make the
trays at home, to fit
the drawer and the
specimens, or buy them
from a specialist
supplier. Pack the more
delicate items with tissue
paper to prevent them from
moving or rubbing against
each other. Small, plastic,
transparent-topped boxes are
also useful for storage.*

HOW THIS BOOK WORKS

THE BOOK IS ARRANGED in two parts: minerals, followed by rocks. The minerals, pages 46–179, are organized into eight main chemical groups (see pages 20–21 for an explanation). The mineral groups with the simplest chemistry come first, and are followed by the more complex varieties. Each separate group has a short introduction describing its general characteristics. The entries that follow give detailed information about the minerals found in the groups. The annotated example below shows how a typical entry is organized. The rocks, pages 180–249, are set out in the three large recognized classes (see pages 30–31). Typical annotated entries are shown opposite.

MINERALS

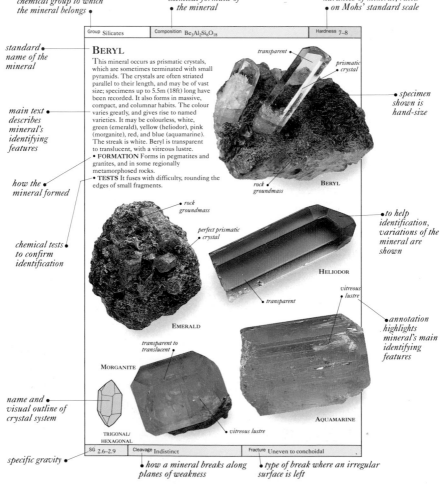

chemical group to which the mineral belongs •

chemical formula of • *the mineral*

hardness of mineral, rated • *on Mohs' standard scale*

standard • *name of the mineral*

| Group Silicates | Composition Be₃Al₂Si₆O₁₈ | Hardness 7–8 |

BERYL

This mineral occurs as prismatic crystals, which are sometimes terminated with small pyramids. The crystals are often striated parallel to their length, and may be of vast size; specimens up to 5.5m (18ft) long have been recorded. It also forms in massive, compact, and columnar habits. The colour varies greatly, and gives rise to named varieties. It may be colourless, white, green (emerald), yellow (heliodor), pink (morganite), red, and blue (aquamarine). The streak is white. Beryl is transparent to translucent, with a vitreous lustre.
• FORMATION Forms in pegmatites and granites, and in some regionally metamorphosed rocks.
• TESTS It fuses with difficulty, rounding the edges of small fragments.

main text • *describes mineral's identifying features*

how the • *mineral formed*

chemical tests • *to confirm identification*

transparent •

prismatic • *crystal*

• *specimen shown is hand-size*

rock groundmass

BERYL

rock groundmass •

perfect prismatic • *crystal*

•*to help identification, variations of the mineral are shown*

HELIODOR

transparent •

vitreous lustre

•*annotation highlights mineral's main identifying features*

EMERALD

transparent to translucent •

MORGANITE

AQUAMARINE

name and • *visual outline of crystal system*

vitreous lustre •

TRIGONAL/ HEXAGONAL

| SG 2.6–2.9 | Cleavage Indistinct | Fracture Uneven to conchoidal |

specific gravity •

• *how a mineral breaks along planes of weakness*

• *type of break where an irregular surface is left*

IGNEOUS ROCKS

classification of the rock • • *material from which rock has formed* • • *size of grains in rock* *crystal shape: euhedral is well formed, anhedral is* • *poorly formed*

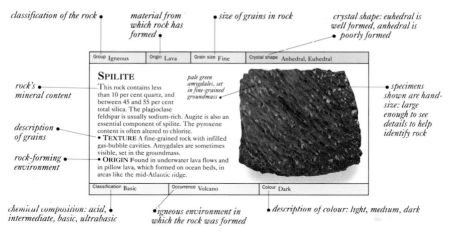

Group Igneous	Origin Lava	Grain size Fine	Crystal shape Anhedral, Euhedral

rock's • *mineral content*

SPILITE
This rock contains less than 10 per cent quartz, and between 45 and 55 per cent total silica. The plagioclase feldspar is usually sodium-rich. Augite is also an essential component of spilite. The pyroxene content is often altered to chlorite.

pale green amygdales, set in fine-grained groundmass •

description • *of grains*

rock-forming • *environment*

• **TEXTURE** A fine-grained rock with infilled gas-bubble cavities. Amygdales are sometimes visible, set in the groundmass.
• **ORIGIN** Found in underwater lava flows and in pillow lava, which formed on ocean beds, in areas like the mid-Atlantic ridge.

• *specimens shown are hand-size: large enough to see details to help identify rock*

Classification Basic	Occurrence Volcano	Colour Dark

chemical composition: acid, • *intermediate, basic, ultrabasic* • *igneous environment in which the rock was formed* • *description of colour: light, medium, dark*

METAMORPHIC ROCKS

• *type of metamorphism*

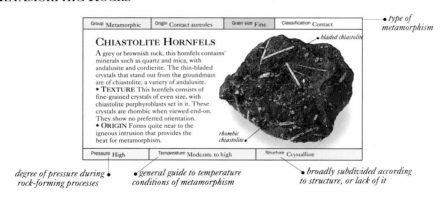

Group Metamorphic	Origin Contact aureoles	Grain size Fine	Classification Contact

• bladed chiastolite

CHIASTOLITE HORNFELS
A grey or brownish rock, this hornfels contains minerals such as quartz and mica, with andalusite and cordierite. The thin-bladed crystals that stand out from the groundmass are of chiastolite, a variety of andalusite.
• **TEXTURE** This hornfels consists of fine-grained crystals of even size, with chiastolite porphyroblasts set in it. These crystals are rhombic when viewed end-on. They show no preferred orientation.
• **ORIGIN** Forms quite near to the igneous intrusion that provides the heat for metamorphism.

rhombic chiastolite •

Pressure High	Temperature Moderate to high	Structure Crystalline

degree of pressure during • *rock-forming processes* • *general guide to temperature conditions of metamorphism* • *broadly subdivided according to structure, or lack of it*

SEDIMENTARY ROCKS

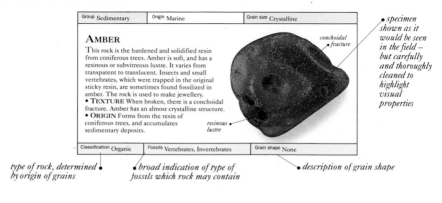

Group Sedimentary	Origin Marine	Grain size Crystalline

• *specimen shown as it would be seen in the field – but carefully and thoroughly cleaned to highlight visual properties*

AMBER
This rock is the hardened and solidified resin from coniferous trees. Amber is soft, and has a resinous or subvitreous lustre. It varies from transparent to translucent. Insects and small vertebrates, which were trapped in the original sticky resin, are sometimes found fossilized in amber. The rock is used to make jewellery.
• **TEXTURE** When broken, there is a conchoidal fracture. Amber has an almost crystalline structure.
• **ORIGIN** Forms from the resin of coniferous trees, and accumulates sedimentary deposits.

conchoidal • *fracture*

resinous • *lustre*

Classification Organic	Fossils Vertebrates, Invertebrates	Grain shape None

type of rock, determined • *by origin of grains* • *broad indication of type of fossils which rock may contain* • *description of grain shape*

MINERAL OR ROCK?

ROCKS ARE aggregates of minerals – usually several, but sometimes only one or two. Similarly, minerals are either free, uncombined native elements, or elemental compounds. Gold, silver, and copper are metallic native elements. Feldspars, pyroxenes, amphiboles, and micas are rock-forming silicates – compounds in which metallic elements combine with linked Si-O tetrahedra.

WHAT IS A MINERAL?

With a few notable exceptions (water, mercury, opal), minerals are solid, inorganic elements or elemental compounds. They have definite atomic structures and chemical compositions which vary within fixed limits. Each and every quartz crystal, whether crystallized in a sandstone vein, or in volcanic lava, possesses the same chemical and physical properties.

bubbles of carbon dioxide

PHYSICAL PROPERTY
All specimens of the same mineral will have a similar atomic structure.

calcite always effervesces with cold, dilute hydrochloric acid

calcite cleaves into rhombs, proving its consistent physical structure

CHEMICAL PROPERTY
Every mineral has a definite composition which varies within fixed limits.

cleavage plane

CLEAVED
CALCITE
RHOMBS

NATURAL
OCCURRENCE
Minerals often crystallize from fluids associated with volcanic lava (left). Crusts of minerals may also form around the volcano's vent as other fluids dissipate.

WHAT IS A ROCK?

Rocks are the essential components of our planet. They are classified into three major groups, determined by how the rocks were formed: igneous, metamorphic, and sedimentary (see pages 30–31). Rocks are aggregates of many different mineral grains, which are fused, cemented, or bound together.

GRANITE

ROCK: A MINERAL AGGREGATE

Granite is a rock composed essentially of three minerals: quartz, mica, and feldspar. Their crystals interlock as a result of crystallization during the cooling of molten magma. The quartz is grey and glassy, the feldspar is light, often in prismatic crystals, and the mica is glittery, and dark or silvery.

mica

quartz

feldspar

QUARTZ
A common mineral in granite, quartz is lightly coloured and hard.

FELDSPAR
Two types of feldspar occur in granite. In the rock, they are often very well formed crystals.

MICA
Forming as small glittery crystals in granite, mica can be both dark biotite and light muscovite.

MICROSCOPIC CLOSE-UP
This granite is shown at about x30 magnification. Notice how the crystals making up the rock are interlocked.

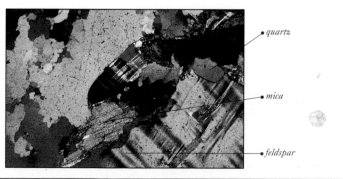

quartz

mica

feldspar

MINERAL FORMATION

THE EARTH'S CRUST is made of rocks, which themselves are aggregates of minerals. The finest mineral specimens usually occur in hydrothermal veins. These are fractures in the earth's crust through which very hot fluids circulate. These fluids contain the elements from which many minerals form. Mineral specimens also occur in igneous rocks, crystallizing directly from cooling magma (molten rock beneath the earth's surface) or lava (molten rock ejected at the earth's surface). A range of minerals forms in metamorphic rocks when pre-existing rocks are crystallized. In some sedimentary rocks, such as limestones, evaporites, and ironstones, minerals will crystallize from low temperature solutions often very near the surface of the earth.

MINERAL VEINS

These are sheet-like areas of minerals which often cut through existing rock structures. Originally, they may have been faults where rocks have been broken, and one rock mass has moved in relation to another; or joints, where fractures occur without movement. In the vein there can be a complete mineral filling, or crystallization around fragmented masses (breccias).

CASSITERITE

• typical mineral from a hydro-thermal vein

common vein • mineral formed from hot chemical solutions beneath the earth's crust

MILKY QUARTZ

QUARTZ VEIN
A vein of white milky quartz (left), cutting through dark slates (far left). Originally formed at great depth, this has been exposed by both weathering and erosion.

IGNEOUS ROCKS

Minerals develop in igneous rocks (see page 32) when molten magma solidifies. The densest minerals, ferro-magnesian silicates like olivine and pyroxene, form at the highest temperatures, whereas less dense minerals, like feldspar and quartz, occur later in the cooling sequence. Minerals forming in molten rock often grow unrestricted, and can have a fine crystal form.

ORTHOCLASE
FELDSPAR

• silicate mineral
commonly found in
many igneous rocks

GRANITE EXPOSURE
An exposure of the igneous rock, granite, showing large feldspar crystals set in the rock groundmass (above).

GARNET

• almandine, a garnet
commonly found in
metamorphic rocks

METAMORPHIC ROCKS

A range of minerals, including garnet, mica, and kyanite, develop in metamorphic rocks (see page 34). Temperature and pressure may re-arrange chemicals in the existing rocks to create new minerals; or chemically potent fluids circulating through the rock may add extra elements.

MUSCOVITE MICA

• shiny mineral found in
many metamorphic rocks,
especially schist

SCHIST OUTCROP
Schist forms where rocks have been folded deep in the earth's crust, due to intense pressures (left).

MINERAL COMPOSITION

MINERALS ARE free, uncombined elements, or elemental compounds. Their compositions are given as chemical formulae. The formula for fluorite is CaF_2. This indicates that calcium (Ca) atoms have combined with fluorine (F) atoms. The subscripted number ($_2$) shows there are twice as many fluorine atoms as there are of calcium. Minerals are arranged into groups according to their chemical composition, and their crystal structure.

NATIVE ELEMENTS
These are free, uncombined elements. This relatively small group consists of around 50 members, some of which (gold, silver) are commercially valuable.

SILVER

HALIDES
All minerals in this group contain one of the halogens: fluorine, chlorine, bromine, or iodine. Atoms of these elements combine with metallic atoms to form minerals like halite (sodium and chlorine) or fluorite (calcium and fluorine). This is a small group of minerals, with around 100 members in all.

HALITE

SULPHUR

OXIDES AND HYDROXIDES
This group has over 250 minerals. Oxides are compounds in which one or two metallic elements combine with oxygen. A metallic element combining with water and hydroxl forms a hydroxide.

HEMATITE

SULPHIDES
A common group of over 300 minerals, sulphides are chemical compounds in which sulphur has combined with metallic and semi-metallic elements. Pyrite and realgar are examples of this group.

PYRITE

REALGAR

OPAL

CALCITE

CARBONATES

A group of 200 minerals, carbonates are compounds in which one or more metallic elements combine with the $(CO_3)^{-2}$ carbonate radical. Calcite, the commonest carbonate, forms when calcium combines with the carbonate radical.

SULPHATES

These are compounds in which one or more metallic elements combine with the sulphate $(SO_4)^{-2}$ radical.

GYPSUM

PYROMORPHITE

PHOSPHATES

A brightly coloured group of minerals, phosphates are compounds in which one or more metallic elements combine with the phosphate $(PO_4)^{-3}$ radical. Arsenates and vanadates are associated with this group.

SILICATES

A significant and common group of over 500 minerals, silicates are compounds in which metallic elements combine with either single, or linked Si-O (silicon-oxygen) tetrahedra Si_{4+}. Silicates are divided into six structural classes.

HORNBLENDE

GROSSULAR GARNET

CHEMICAL ELEMENTS

Symbol	Name	Symbol	Name
Ac	Actinium	Mn	Manganese
Ag	Silver	Mo	Molybdenum
Al	Aluminium	N	Nitrogen
Am	Americium	Na	Sodium
Ar	Argon	Nb	Niobium
As	Arsenic	Nd	Neodymium
At	Astatine	Ne	Neon
Au	Gold	Ni	Nickel
B	Boron	No	Nobelium
Ba	Barium	Np	Neptinium
Be	Beryllium	O	Oxygen
Bi	Bismuth	Os	Osmium
Bk	Berkelium	P	Phosphorus
Br	Bromine	Pa	Protactinium
C	Carbon	Pb	Lead
Ca	Calcium	Pd	Palladium
Cd	Cadmium	Pm	Promathium
Ce	Cerium	Po	Polonium
Cf	Californium	Pr	Praseodymium
Cl	Chlorine	Pt	Platinum
Cm	Curium	Pu	Plutonium
Co	Cobalt	Ra	Radium
Cr	Chromium	Rb	Rubidium
Cs	Cesium	Re	Rhenium
Cu	Copper	Rh	Rhodium
Dy	Dysprosium	Rn	Radon
Er	Erbium	S	Sulphur
Es	Einsteinium	Sb	Antimony
F	Fluorine	Sc	Scandium
Fe	Iron	Se	Selenium
Fm	Fermium	Si	Silicon
Fr	Francium	Sm	Samarium
Ga	Gallium	Sn	Tin
Gd	Gadolinium	Sr	Strontium
Ge	Germanium	Ta	Tantalum
H	Hydrogen	Tb	Terbium
He	Helium	Tc	Technetium
Hf	Hafinium	Te	Tellurium
Hg	Mercury	Th	Thorium
Ho	Holmium	Ti	Titanium
I	Iodine	Tl	Thallium
In	Indium	Tu	Thulium
Ir	Iridium	U	Uranium
K	Potassium	V	Vanadium
Kr	Krypton	W	Tungsten
La	Lanthanum	Xe	Xenon
Li	Lithium	Y	Yttrium
Lu	Lutetium	Yb	Ytterbium
Lw	Lawrencium	Zn	Zinc
Md	Mendelevium	Zr	Zirconium
Mg	Magnesium		

MINERAL CHARACTERISTICS

MINERALS EXHIBIT a number of properties that are used for identification. It is essential to take a scientific approach when testing a mineral. First, observe the colour (see page 26), lustre (page 27), and habit (page 23). Then test for hardness (page 25), specific gravity (page 25), and streak (page 26). Fracture and cleavage (page 24) may be obvious, or you may have to break the mineral.

CRYSTAL SYSTEMS

The geometrical shapes in which minerals crystallize are organized, according to their symmetry, into six main groups called crystal systems. Within each of these systems, many different forms are possible, but all the forms in a crystal system can be related to the symmetry of that system. From a study of mineral habits, it may be possible to say to which crystal system the mineral belongs. The small blue diagram that appears with each mineral represents its crystal system.

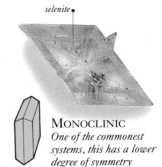

selenite

MONOCLINIC
One of the commonest systems, this has a lower degree of symmetry than the cubic system.

iron pyrite

CUBIC
Essentially cube-shaped crystals, though this category also includes octahedral-shaped (8-sided) or dodecahedral-shaped (12-sided) crystals.

TRICLINIC
The least symmetrical of the crystal systems.

axinite

idocrase

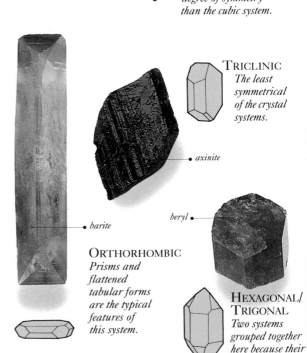

barite

beryl

TETRAGONAL
A form that is usually more elongated than the cube.

ORTHORHOMBIC
Prisms and flattened tabular forms are the typical features of this system.

HEXAGONAL/ TRIGONAL
Two systems grouped together here because their symmetry is similar.

HABIT

The habit is the characteristic appearance of a crystal that is determined by its predominant form. Several descriptive terms to identify a crystal's habit are defined below.

DENDRITIC
Plant-like shape.

copper

actinolite

BLADED
Looks like the blade of a knife.

barite

beryl

PRISMATIC
Shows a uniform cross-section.

scolecite

ACICULAR
Slender needle-like masses.

PRISMATIC
Terminated prisms.

hematite

limonite

MASSIVE
Indicates no definitive shape.

RENIFORM
Rounded kidney-shaped masses.

TWINNING

Twinning refers to a non-parallel, symmetrical intergrowth of two or more crystals of the same species. Twinning can occur by contact or interpenetration. Multiple and polysynthetic twins involve more than two individual crystals.

cerussite

staurolite

CONTACT TWIN
Radiating mass of touching, contact crystals.

PENETRATION TWIN
Showing two parts of a crystal that have intergrown.

CLEAVAGE

Cleavage is the way that a mineral breaks along well-defined planes of weakness. Often these planes are between layers of atoms or other places where the atomic bonding is weakest. Cleavage surfaces are not perfectly smooth like crystal faces, though they are very consistent and reflect light evenly. Cleavage is described as perfect, distinct, indistinct, or none.

PERFECT BASAL CLEAVAGE

• breaks parallel to base of lepidolite crystal

Iceland spar • displays perfect rhombohedral cleavage

PERFECT RHOMBIC CLEAVAGE

PERFECT CUBIC CLEAVAGE

• cube-shaped break in galena

PERFECT PRISMATIC CLEAVAGE

• surfaces parallel to a prism in cerussite

FRACTURE

If you strike a mineral with a geologist's hammer and it breaks, leaving surfaces that are rough and uneven, it is said to fracture. (Cleavage surfaces are usually flat, and exactly the same shape may be produced by repeated hammer blows.) Most minerals fracture and cleave, but some will only fracture. Common fracture terms are uneven, conchoidal (shell-like), hackly (jagged), and splintery.

CONCHOIDAL

curved fracture • in opal

UNEVEN FRACTURE

• rough, uneven surfaces of rock crystal

HARDNESS

A useful aid for identifying a mineral is the hardness test. The hardness of a mineral is its resistance to being scratched. The scale of hardness from 1 (talc) to 10 (diamond) was devised by Friedrich Mohs. Minerals with higher Mohs' numbers will scratch those lower in the scale. Thus calcite will scratch gypsum, but not fluorite. Minerals can also be tested with everyday objects: a mineral scratched with a coin will have a hardness of less than 3½.

FINGER NAIL: 2½

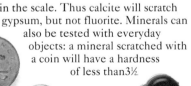

COINS: 3½

KNIFE BLADE: 5½

GLASS: 6

QUARTZ: 7

MOHS' SCALE OF HARDNESS

TALC: 1 GYPSUM: 2 CALCITE: 3 FLUORITE: 4 APATITE: 5 ORTHOCLASE: 6 QUARTZ: 7 TOPAZ: 8 CORUNDUM: 9 DIAMOND: 10

SPECIFIC GRAVITY

Comparing the weight of a mineral with the weight of an equal volume of water, gives a mineral's specific gravity. This is shown numerically : an SG of 2.5 indicates that the mineral is two-and-a half times as heavy as water. The quartz specimen (right) is larger than the galena but weighs less as it has a lower SG.

QUARTZ SG: 2.65

GALENA SG: 7.5

COLOUR

The colour of a mineral – as seen in natural light – is an obvious and useful identification feature. Although it helps to identify those minerals with characteristic colours, there are pitfalls in relying solely on this feature. Many minerals – quartz, for example – occur in a variety of colours, while a large number of minerals are white or colourless. The selection of quartz below, indicates the range of colours found in minerals.

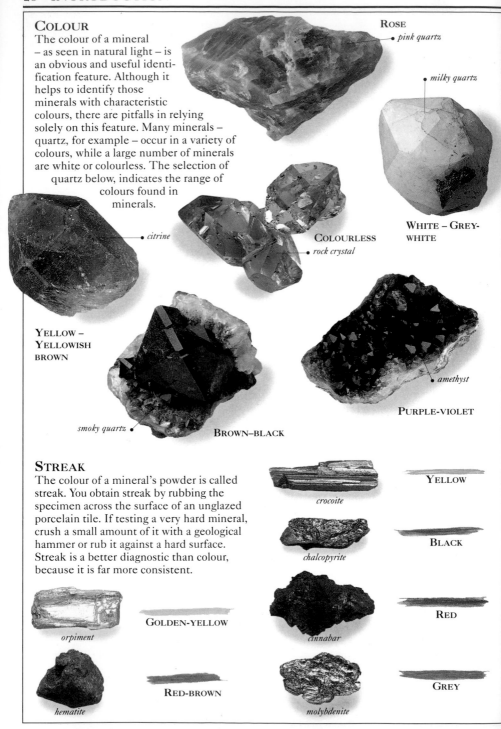

ROSE
• *pink quartz*

• *milky quartz*

• *citrine*

COLOURLESS
• *rock crystal*

WHITE – GREY-WHITE

YELLOW – YELLOWISH BROWN

• *amethyst*

PURPLE-VIOLET

smoky quartz •

BROWN–BLACK

STREAK

The colour of a mineral's powder is called streak. You obtain streak by rubbing the specimen across the surface of an unglazed porcelain tile. If testing a very hard mineral, crush a small amount of it with a geological hammer or rub it against a hard surface. Streak is a better diagnostic than colour, because it is far more consistent.

crocoite

YELLOW

chalcopyrite

BLACK

orpiment

GOLDEN-YELLOW

cinnabar

RED

hematite

RED-BROWN

molybdenite

GREY

TRANSPARENCY

Transparency refers to the way in which light passes through a mineral specimen. It depends on the way mineral atoms are bonded. Mineral specimens that allow objects to be seen through them are transparent. If light passes through, but the object cannot be clearly seen, then the specimen is translucent. When light does not pass through a specimen, even when cut very thin, it is opaque.

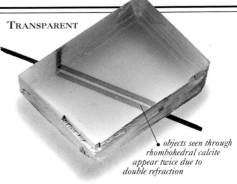

TRANSPARENT

objects seen through rhombohedral calcite appear twice due to double refraction

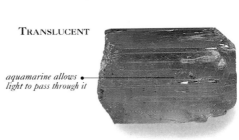

TRANSLUCENT

aquamarine allows light to pass through it

OPAQUE

gold allows no light to pass through it

LUSTRE

Lustre describes the way light is reflected off a mineral's surface. The type and intensity of lustre vary according to the nature of the mineral surface and the amount of light absorbed. Well-recognized, mainly self-explanatory terms are used to describe lustre. They include dull, metallic, pearly, vitreous (glassy), greasy, and silky.

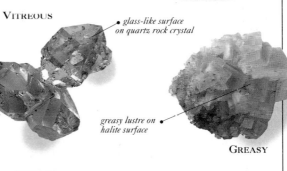

VITREOUS

glass-like surface on quartz rock crystal

greasy lustre on halite surface

GREASY

SILKY

metallic lustre on galena surface

silky surface on "satin spar" gypsum

DULL, METALLIC

dull and metallic lustre on hematite

METALLIC

MINERAL IDENTIFICATION

To HELP with mineral identification, the minerals are listed according to hardness, and then obvious, reliable properties are included alongside.

KEY TO ABBREVIATIONS:
av-average; con.-conchoidal; dis.-distinct; h-heavy; imp.-imperfect; ind.-indistinct; not det.-not determined; oct.-octahedral; per.-perfect; pin.-pinachoidal; prism.-prismatic; rhom.-rhombohedral; subcon.-subconchoidal; un.-uneven; vh-very heavy; vl-very light; <-less than or equal to; >-more than.

MINERAL	SG	CLEAVAGE	FRACTURE
HARDNESS <2½			
Acanthite	vh	none	uneven
Annabergite	h	perfect	uneven
Artinite	av	perfect	uneven
Aurichalcite	h	perfect	uneven
Autunite	h	perfect basal	uneven
Bismuth	vh	perfect basal	uneven
Bismuthinite	vh	perfect	uneven
Borax	vl	. perfect	con.
Brucite	av	perfect	uneven
Carnallite	vl	none	con.
Carnotite	h	perfect basal	uneven
Chalcanthite	av	imperfect	con.
Chlorargyrite	vh	none	un. - subcon.
Chrysotile	av	none	uneven
Cinnabar	vh	perfect prism.	con. - un.
Clinochlore	av	perfect	uneven
Covellite	h	perfect basal	uneven
Cryolite	av	none	uneven
Cyanotrichite	av	none	uneven
Epsomite	vl	perfect	con.
Erythrite	h	perfect	uneven
Galena	vh	perfect cubic	subcon.
Glauconite	av	perfect basal	uneven
Graphite	av	perfect basal	uneven
Gypsum	av	perfect	splintery
Halite	av	perfect cubic	un. - con.
Hydrozincite	h	perfect	uneven
Jamesonite	vh	good basal	un. - con.
Kaolinite	av	perfect basal	uneven
Linarite	vh	perfect	con.
Molybdenite	av	perfect basal	uneven
Muscovite	av	perfect basal	uneven
Nitratine	av	perfect rhom.	con.
Orpiment	h	perfect	uneven
Phlogopite	av	perfect basal	uneven
Proustite	vh	distinct rhom.	con. - un.
Pyrargyrite	vh	distinct rhom.	con. - un.
Pyrophyllite	av	perfect	uneven
Realgar	h	good	con.
Sepiolite	av	not det.	uneven
Stephanite	vh	imperfect	un. - subcon.
Stibnite	h	perfect	un. - subcon.
Sulphur	av	imp. basal	un. - con.
Sylvanite	vh	perfect	uneven
Sylvite	vl	perfect cubic	uneven
Talc	av	perfect	uneven
Torbernite	h	perfect basal	uneven
Tungstite	vh	perfect	uneven
Tyuyamunite	h	perfect basal	uneven
Ulexite	vl	perfect	uneven
Vermiculite	av	perfect	uneven
Vivianite	av	perfect	uneven
Wad	h	none	uneven
HARDNESS <3½			
Adamite	h	good	subcon. - un.
Anglesite	vh	good basal	con.
Anhydrite	av	perfect	un.- splintery
Antigorite	av	perfect basal	con. - splintery
Antimony	vh	perfect basal	uneven
Astrophyllite	h	perfect	uneven
Atacamite	h	perfect	con.

MINERAL	SG	CLEAVAGE	FRACTURE
Barite	h	perfect	uneven
Bauxite	av	none	uneven
Biotite	av/h	perfect basal	uneven
Boleite	vh	perfect	uneven
Bornite	vh	very poor	un. - con.
Boulangerite	vh	good	uneven
Bournonite	vh	imperfect	subcon - un.
Calcite	av	perfect	subcon.
Celestine	h	perfect	uneven
Cerussite	vh	dis. prismatic	con.
Chalcosine	vh	indistinct	con.
Chamosite	h	not det.	uneven
Clinoclase	h	perfect	uneven
Copiapite	av	perfect	uneven
Copper	vh	none	hackly
Crocoite	vh	dis. prismatic	con. - un.
Descloizite	vh	none	un. - con.
Enargite	h	perfect	uneven
Gibbsite	av/h	perfect	uneven
Glauberite	av	perfect	con.
Gold	vh	none	hackly
Greenockite	h	distinct	con.
Jarosite	av/h	distinct	uneven
Leadhillite	vh	perfect basal	con.
Lepidolite	av/h	perfect basal	uneven
Millerite	vh	perfect rhom.	uneven
Olivenite	h	indistinct	un. - con.
Polybasite	vh	imp. basal	uneven
Polyhalite	av	perfect	uneven
Silver	vh	none	hackly
Strontianite	h	per. prismatic	uneven
Thenardite	av	perfect	uneven
Trona	av	perfect	uneven
Vanadinite	vh	none	con. - un.
Volborthite	h	perfect basal	uneven
Witherite	h	distinct	uneven
Wulfenite	vh	dis. pyramidal	subcon.
HARDNESS <5½			
Alunite	av	distinct basal	con.
Analcime	av	very poor	subcon.
Ankerite	av	perfect rhom.	subcon.
Apatite	h	poor	con. - un.
Apophyllite	av	perfect	uneven
Aragonite	av	distinct pin.	subcon.
Azurite	h	perfect	con.
Bayldonite	vh	none	uneven
Brochantite	h	perfect	con. - un.
Chabazite	av	indistinct	uneven
Chalcopyrite	h	poor	un. - con.
Chromite	h	none	uneven
Cobaltite	vh	perfect	uneven
Colemanite	av	perfect	un. - con.
Chrysocolla	av/h	none	un. - con.
Cuprite	vh	poor oct.	con. - un.
Datolite	av	none	un. - con.
Dioptase	h	perfect	un. - con.
Dolomite	av	per. rhom.	subcon.
Eudialyte	av	indistinct	uneven
Fluorite	h	per. oct.	con.
Glaucodot	vh	perfect	uneven
Goethite	h	perfect	uneven
Gyrolite	av	perfect	uneven

MINERAL	SG	CLEAVAGE	FRACTURE
Harmotome	av	distinct	un. - subcon.
Hauerite	h	perfect	subcon. - un.
Hausmannite	h	good	uneven
Hemimorphite	h	perfect	un. - con.
Herderite	av/h	poor	subcon.
Heulandite	av	perfect	uneven
Kyanite	h/vh	perfect	uneven
Laumontite	av	perfect	uneven
Lazurite	av	imperfect	uneven
Lepidocrocite	h	perfect	uneven
Limonite	h	none	uneven
Magnesite	h	perfect rhom.	con. - un.
Malachite	h	perfect	subcon. - un.
Manganite	h	perfect	uneven
Mesolite	av	perfect	uneven
Mimetite	vh	none	subcon. - un.
Monazite	h/vh	distinct	con. - un.
Natrolite	av	perfect	uneven
Nickeline	vh	none	uneven
Nosean	av	indistinct	un. - con.
Pectolite	av	perfect	uneven
Pentlandite	h	none	con.
Perovskite	h	imperfect	subcon. - un.
Phillipsite	av	distinct	uneven
Pyrochlore	h	distinct	subcon. - un.
Pyromorphite	vh	v. poor prism	un. - subcon.
Pyrrhotite	h	none	subcon. - un.
Rhodochrosite	h	perfect rhom.	uneven
Riebeckite	h	perfect	uneven
Scheelite	vh	distinct	subcon. - un.
Scolecite	av	perfect	uneven
Scorodite	h	imperfect	subcon.
Siderite	h	perfect rhom.	uneven
Smithsonite	h	perfect rhom.	subcon. - un.
Sphalerite	h	perfect	con.
Sphene	h	distinct	con.
Stilbite	av	perfect	uneven
Tennantite	h	none	un. - subcon.
Tetrahedrite	h/vh	none	un. - subcon.
Thomsonite	av	perfect	un. - subcon.
Wavellite	av	perfect	subcon. - un.
Willemite	h	basal	uneven
Wolframite	vh	perfect	uneven
Wollastonite	av/h	perfect	splintery
Xenotime	h/vh	per. prismatic	uneven
Zincite	vh	perfect	con.
HARDNESS <6			
Actinolite	h	good	un. - subcon.
Aegirine	h	good	uneven
Akermanite	av	distinct	un. - con.
Amblygonite	h	perfect	uneven
Anatase	h	perfect basal	subcon.
Anthophyllite	av/h	perfect	uneven
Arfvedsonite	h	perfect	uneven
Arsenopyrite	vh	indistinct	uneven
Augite	h	good	un. - con.
Brookite	h	poor	subcon. - un.
Cancrinite	av	perfect	uneven
Chloanthite	vh	distinct	uneven
Enstatite	h	good	uneven
Gehlenite	h	distinct	un. - con.
Glaucophane	h	perfect	un. - con.
Grunerite	h	good	uneven
Hauyne	av	indistinct	un. - con.
Hedenbergite	h	good	un. - con.
Hematite	vh	none	un. - subcon.
Hornblende	h	perfect	uneven
Humite	h	poor	uneven
Hypersthene	h	good	uneven
Ilmenite	h	none	con. - un.
Ilvaite	h	distinct	uneven

MINERAL	SG	CLEAVAGE	FRACTURE
Lazulite	h	indis. - pris.	un.- splintery
Leucite	av	very poor	con.
Milarite	av	none	con. - un.
Nepheline	av	indistinct	con.
Neptunite	h	perfect	con.
Richterite	av/h	perfect	uneven
Romanechite	vh	not det.	uneven
Samarskite	vh	indistinct	con.
Scapolite	av	distinct	un. - con.
Skutterudite	vh	distinct	uneven
Smaltite	vh	distinct	uneven
Sodalite	av	poor	un. - con.
Tremolite	av/h	good	un. - subcon.
Turquoise	av	good	con.
HARDNESS <7			
Albite	av	distinct	uneven
Andesine	av	perfect	un. - con.
Anorthite	av	perfect	con. - un.
Anorthoclase	av	perfect	uneven
Axinite	h	good	un. - con.
Bytownite	av	perfect	un. - con.
Cassiterite	vh	poor	subcon. - un.
Chloritoid	h	perfect	uneven
Chondrodite	h	poor	uneven
Clinozoisite	h	perfect	uneven
Columbite	vh	distinct	subcon. - un.
Diaspore	h	perfect	con.
Diopside	h	good	uneven
Epidote	h	perfect	uneven
Franklinite	vh	none	un. - subcon.
Gadolinite	h	none	con.
Jadeite	h	good	splintery
Labradorite	av	perfect	un. - con.
Magnetite	vh	none	subcon. - un.
Marcasite	h	distinct	uneven
Microcline	av	perfect	uneven
Oligoclase	av	perfect	un. - con.
Opal	av	none	con.
Orthoclase	av	perfect	un. - con.
Petalite	av	perfect	subcon.
Prehnite	av	distinct	uneven
Pyrite	h	indistinct	con. - un.
Pyrolusite	vh	perfect	uneven
Quartz	av	none	con. - un.
Rhodonite	h	perfect	con. - un.
Rutile	h	distinct	con. - un.
Sanidine	av	perfect	con. - un.
Stibiconite	h/vh	not det.	uneven
Tourmaline	h	very ind.	un. - con.
Vesuvianite	h	indistinct	un. - con.
Zoisite	h	perfect	un. - con.
HARDNESS >7			
Andalusite	h	dis. prismatic	un. - subcon.
Beryl	av	indistinct	un. - con.
Chalcedony	av	none	con.
Chrysoberyl	h	dis. prismatic	con. - un.
Cordierite	av	distinct	con.
Corundum	h	none	con. - un.
Diamond	h	per. oct.	con.
Dumortierite	h	good	uneven
Euclase	h	perfect	con.
Garnet	h	none	un. - con.
Olivine	h	imperfect	con.
Phenakite	av	distinct	con.
Ruby	h	none	con. - un.
Sillimanite	h	perfect	uneven
Spinel	h	none	con. - un.
Spodumene	h	perfect	uneven
Staurolite	h	distinct	un. - subcon.
Topaz	h	perfect	subcon. - un.
Zircon	h	imperfect	un. - con.

HOW ROCKS ARE FORMED

ROCK FORMS in cycles. Molten magma inside the earth's crust slowly rises towards the surface. This may form from large masses, plutons (**1**); smaller intrusions, dykes (**2**); or lava flows and volcanoes. On cooling, igneous rocks such as granite are formed. Rocks are brought to the surface by earth

ROCK CYCLE
The rock-making cycle, shown below, spans over millions of years.

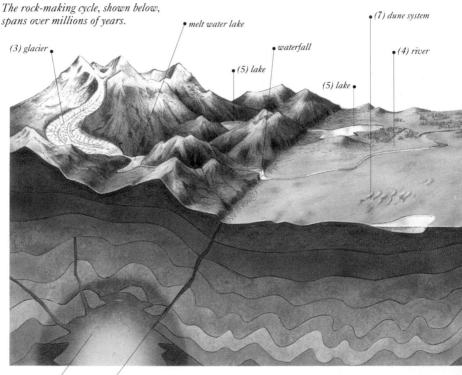

melt water lake

(7) dune system

(3) glacier

waterfall

(4) river

(5) lake

(5) lake

(1) plutons   *(2) dykes*

granite

schist

IGNEOUS
Molten magma forces its way through other rocks. On cooling, it can form granite dykes (left).

METAMORPHIC
Heat and pressure in mountain-building change sedimentary and igneous rocks to metamorphic rocks.

movements, and they are exposed by erosion and weathering. Further erosion by ice, water, wind, and weathering breaks down the rocks into particles, which are transported by glaciers (**3**), rivers (**4**), and wind. The particles are deposited as sedimentary layers in lakes (**5**), deltas (**6**), dunes (**7**), and on the sea bed to form sedimentary rocks such as clay or shale (**8**). Much sediment is deposited on the continental shelf (**9**),

and some is carried to the greater depths of the ocean floor by dense currents channelled by ocean canyons (**10**). When sedimentary and igneous rocks are subjected to intense heat and pressure during large-scale mountain-building, they become metamorphic rocks, such as schist and gneiss. Further increases in temperature and pressure may cause the rock to become molten, and the rock cycle is completed.

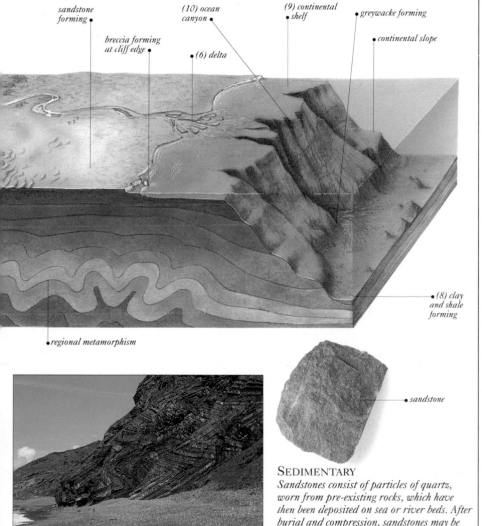

sandstone forming

breccia forming at cliff edge

(10) ocean canyon

(6) delta

(9) continental shelf

greywacke forming

continental slope

(8) clay and shale forming

regional metamorphism

sandstone

SEDIMENTARY
Sandstones consist of particles of quartz, worn from pre-existing rocks, which have then been deposited on sea or river beds. After burial and compression, sandstones may be folded, as seen on the sea cliff (left).

IGNEOUS ROCK CHARACTERISTICS

IGNEOUS ROCKS crystallize from molten magma or lava. The starting composition of the magma, the manner in which it travels towards the earth's surface, and the rate at which it cools, all help to determine its composition and resultant characteristics. These characteristics include grain size, crystal shape, mineral content, and overall colour.

coarse-grained gabbro, a plutonic-igneous rock with large crystals

ORIGIN
Origin indicates whether the rock is intrusive (magma crystallized beneath the earth's surface) or extrusive (lava crystallized at the earth's surface).

augite, a ferro-magnesian

OCCURRENCE
This describes the form of the molten mass when it cooled. A pluton, for instance, is a very large, deep intrusion that can measure many kilometres across; a dyke is a narrow, discordant sheet of rock; a sill is a concordant sheet.

labradorite, a feldspar

INTRUSIVE BASIC DYKE
A dolerite dyke is an igneous rock which has intruded sedimentary shale.

MINERAL CONTENT
Rocks are aggregates of minerals. Feldspars (right), micas, quartz, and ferro-magnesians (above) make up the bulk of igneous rocks. "Composition" describes how minerals affect the rock's chemistry.

GRAIN SIZE

This indicates whether a rock is plutonic (coarse-grained) or extrusive (fine-grained). Coarse-grained igneous rocks such as gabbro have crystals over 5mm (³⁄₁₆in) in diameter; medium-grained rocks such as dolerite have crystals 0.5–5mm (¹⁄₄₈–³⁄₁₆in) in size; and fine-grained rocks, such as basalt, have crystals that are less than 0.5mm (¹⁄₄₈in) in size.

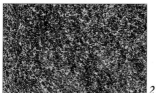

SEEING THE GRAINS

Individual grains of gabbro (1) can be seen with the naked eye, but you need a hand lens to see the separate grains in dolerite (2). Basalt (3) is fine-grained, requiring the use of a microscope.

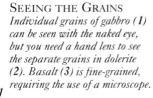
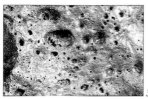

CRYSTAL SHAPE

Slow cooling gives the minerals time to develop well-formed (euhedral) crystals. Fast cooling allows time only for poorly formed (anhedral) crystals to grow.

TEXTURE

Texture refers to the way the grains or crystals are arranged, and their size relative to one another.

EUHEDRAL CRYSTALS

Highly magnified section of dolerite (left) with well-formed crystals.

COLOUR

Colour is generally an accurate indicator of chemistry, reflecting a mineral's content. Light colour indicates an acid rock, with over 65 per cent silica. Basic rocks are dark coloured, with low silica, and a high proportion of dark, dense ferro-magnesian minerals such as augite.

COMPOSITION

Igneous rocks are arranged into groups according to chemical composition: acid rocks, with over 65 per cent total silica content (including over 10 per cent modal quartz); intermediate rocks with 55–65 per cent silica content; basic rocks with 45–55 per cent total silica content (less than 10 per cent modal quartz). Ultrabasic rocks have less than 45 per cent total silica content.

LIGHT COLOUR
Rhyolite, an acid lava, has over 65 per cent silica and over 10 per cent quartz.

MEDIUM COLOUR
Andesite, an intermediate rock with 55–65 per cent total silica content.

DARK COLOUR
Basalt, a basic rock with 45–55 per cent silica content.

TYPES OF METAMORPHISM

METAMORPHIC ROCKS are rocks that have been changed considerably from their original igneous, sedimentary, or earlier metamorphic structure and composition. The rocks are formed by the application of heat and pressure (greatest near mountain-building) to a pre-existing rock.

REGIONAL METAMORPHISM
When rock in a mountain-building region is transformed by both heat and pressure, it becomes regionally metamorphosed rock. The metamorphosed area can cover thousands of square kilometres. The sequence below demonstrates how the nature of a rock changes as the heat and pressure intensify.

METAMORPHIC LANDSCAPE
Gneiss, a rock altered by a high degree of regional metamorphism, forms a rugged landscape.

SHALE

1. NO PRESSURE
Fossiliferous shale, a fine-grained sedimentary rock rich in clay minerals and quartz, with fossil brachiopod shells, unaffected by metamorphism.

2. LOW PRESSURE
When fossiliferous shale is subjected to low pressure, the fossils may be distorted or destroyed. The resulting rock is slate.

SLATE

SCHIST

4. HIGH PRESSURE
At the highest pressures and temperatures, and where active fluids may be circulating through the rocks, gneiss, a coarse-grained rock, is formed. Any rock can be altered by these conditions.

3. MODERATE PRESSURE
Slate, as well as many other rocks, forms medium-grained schist when subjected to moderate increases in temperature and pressure.

GNEISS

CONTACT METAMORPHISM

Rocks in the metamorphic aureole, the area surrounding an igneous intrusion or near a lava flow, may be altered by direct heat alone. These rocks are called contact metamorphic rocks. The heat may change the minerals in the original rock so that the resulting metamorphic rock is more crystalline, and features such as fossils may disappear. The extent of the metamorphic aureole is determined by the magma's or lava's temperature and the size of the intrusion.

SANDSTONE

• grains loosely held together

MAGMA INTRUSION
A mass of dark coloured dolerite (at the base of the cliff), has intruded and heated layers of originally black shale, metamorphosing them to a lighter rock (hornfels).

• interlocking quartz crystals

HEAT ALONE
When heated, sandstone (above) – a porous, sedimentary rock – becomes metaquartzite (right), a crystalline, non-porous rock, composed of an interlocking mosaic of quartz crystals.

METAQUARTZITE

DYNAMIC METAMORPHISM

When large scale movements take place in the earth's crust, especially along fault lines, dynamic metamorphism occurs. Great masses of rock are forced over other rocks. Where these rock masses come into contact with each other, a crushed and powdered metamorphic rock called mylonite forms.

MYLONITE

• highly altered and distorted by forces of thrust movement

MOVEMENT OF ROCK MASSES
A low-angled thrust fault, half way up the cliff.

METAMORPHIC ROCK CHARACTERISTICS

METAMORPHIC ROCKS exhibit certain typical features. The minerals of which they are made usually occur as crystals. Crystal orientation is determined by whether the rock formed as a result of both heat and pressure, or heat alone. Their size reflects the degree of heat and pressure to which they were subjected. Thus, examination of the crystals in a metamorphic rock can help to establish its origin and its identity.

foliated gneiss shows bands of dark biotite mica

STRUCTURE
This indicates the way minerals are oriented in a rock. Contact metamorphic rocks have a crystalline structure: the minerals are usually randomly arranged. Regional metamorphic rocks, however, are foliated: the pressure forces certain minerals to become aligned.

FOLIATED

CRYSTALLINE

mass of randomly organized, fused crystals in blue-veined marble

kyanite schist has foliated structure, but alignment here is less evident than in gneiss

GRAIN SIZE

Grain size indicates the temperature and pressure conditions to which the rock was subjected: generally, the higher the pressure and temperature, the coarser the grain size. Thus slate, which forms under low pressure, is fine-grained. Schist, formed by moderate temperature and pressure, is medium-grained, and gneiss formed at high temperatures and pressures is coarse-grained.

COARSE-GRAINED

• schist

gneiss •

black slate •

MEDIUM-GRAINED

FINE-GRAINED

PRESSURE AND TEMPERATURE

Medium- to high-grade metamorphism occurs at a minimum temperature of approximately 250° C (temperatures in some metamorphic rocks can be much lower), and a maximum temperature of 800° C; above this, the rock melts to become magma or lava. Intensity of pressure ranges from 2,000 kilobars to 10,000 kilobars.

quartz •

mica •

MINERAL CONTENT

The presence of certain minerals in metamorphic rocks can help the identification process. Garnet and kyanite occur in gneiss and schists, while crystals of pyrite are frequently set into the cleavage surfaces of slate. Minerals such as brucite can occur in marble.

GNEISS
Under a microscope, gneiss reveals quartz and mica (left).

MILKY QUARTZ
• *found in meta-quartzite and gneiss*

• *found in gneiss and schist*

ORTHOCLASE
FELDSPAR
• *found in gneiss and schist*

MUSCOVITE

SEDIMENTARY ROCK CHARACTERISTICS

As SEDIMENTARY ROCKS form in layers, or strata, they can be distinguished from igneous and metamorphic rocks in the field. A hand specimen usually breaks along layered surfaces. Another key feature that sets them apart is their fossil content – fossils are never found in crystalline igneous rocks and only rarely in metamorphic rocks. The origins of the particles that make up sedimentary rocks determine their appearance, and give clues to their identity.

ORIGIN
Sedimentary rocks form at, or very near, the earth's surface where rock particles transported by wind, water, and ice are deposited on dry land, on the beds of rivers and lakes, and in marine environments: beaches, deltas, and the sea.

• *quartz conglomerate*

LAYERS OF SEDIMENT
The pebbles and sand collecting on this beach may eventually form sedimentary rocks.

FOSSIL CONTENT
Fossils mainly occur in sedimentary rocks. They are the remains of animals and plants preserved in layers of sediment. The type of fossil found in a rock gives an indication of the rock's origin: a marine fossil, for instance, suggests that the rock formed from sediments deposited in the sea. Rocks especially rich in fossils include limestone.

• *brachiopod fossils in shelly limestone*

GRAIN SIZE

Although the classification of grain size in sedimentary rocks can be complex, the terms coarse-, medium-, and fine-grained are usually used. Grains may range in size from boulders to minute particles of clay. Coarse-grained rocks composed of fragments easily seen with the naked eye include conglomerate, breccia, and some sandstones. Medium-grained rocks, the grains of which can be seen with a hand lens, include other sandstones. Fine-grained rock, includes shale, clay, and mudstone.

COARSE-GRAINED

• *quartz conglomerate*

shale •

FINE-GRAINED

MEDIUM-GRAINED

• *sandstone*

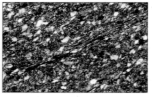

MAGNIFIED GRAINS

Highly magnified rock specimens reveal the shape of the grains in the sediment. These can vary from rounded (above left) to angular (above right).

GRAIN SHAPE

The way the grains that make up sedimentary rocks are transported influences their shape. Wind erosion creates round sand particles, but angular pebbles. Water-based erosion gives rise to angular, sand-sized particles, but smooth, round pebbles.

CLASSIFICATION

This explains the source of the rock's grains. Detrital rocks contain particles from pre-existing rocks; the term, biogenic, indicates that the rock is made of shells or other fossil fragments; and the term, chemical, indicates that the minerals were produced by chemical precipitation.

CHEMICAL

• *rock gypsum*

CHEMICAL

• *oolitic limestone*

• *breccia*

DETRITAL

• *pink orthoquartzite*

DETRITAL

ROCK IDENTIFICATION KEY

THIS KEY IS DESIGNED to help identify your rock specimens. In Stage 1 decide whether the rock is igneous, metamorphic, or sedimentary. In Stage 2, determine the grain size – follow the key to direct you to the correct category: an eye represents coarse-grained; a hand lens represents medium-grained; and a microscope suggests fine-grained. In Stage 3 (see pages 42–5), you have to take into consideration other rock properties (colour, structure, and mineral content) to lead you finally to specific rock entries in this book.

STAGE 1

IGNEOUS?

If you have an igneous rock, it will show a crystalline structure; that is, it will be composed of an interlocking mosaic of mineral crystals. These crystals may be randomly set into the rock, or they may show some form of alignment. They lack structures like bedding planes (sedimentary rocks) and foliation (metamorphic rocks). Some lavas may be full of small gas-bubble hollows. No fossils will be evident.

• randomly oriented crystals

• interlocking crystals cannot be easily broken from the rock

METAMORPHIC?

If you have a metamorphic rock, it will be one of two major types. A regionally metamorphosed rock will have a characteristic structure, or foliation. This foliation is often wavy; not flat like the bedding planes of a sedimentary rock. Contact metamorphism produces a more random arrangement.

• foliated gneiss with wavy bands

SEDIMENTARY?

If your sample is a sedimentary rock, layers may be evident in it. Grains can be poorly held together, and you may be able to rub them off with your fingers. Quartz is a dominant mineral in many sediments, and calcite is present in limestones. The presence of fossils also helps to distinguish sedimentary rocks from igneous or metamorphic specimens.

• grains of quartz, weakly cemented together

STAGE 2

Once you have established the formation of the rock, the next step is to categorize it by grain size. This refers to the size of the grains in the body of rock, not to the odd large crystal that may be set into it.

 VISIBLE TO NAKED EYE

 HAND LENS NEEDED

 MICROSCOPE NEEDED

IGNEOUS

 Coarse-grained

 Medium-grained

Fine-grained

METAMORPHIC

 Coarse-grained

Medium-grained

Fine grained

SEDIMENTARY

 Coarse-grained

 Medium-grained

Fine-grained

STAGE 3

You have decided whether the rock is igneous, sedimentary, or metamorphic; and you have identified its grain size. If you have an igneous rock, look at its colour, next. Acid rocks, rich in low density, pale silicates, are light coloured. Basic and ultrabasic rocks, rich in heavy ferromagnesian minerals, are dark. The

IGNEOUS	COARSE-GRAINED	MEDIUM-GRAINED

LIGHT COLOUR
Pink granite **180**, *White granite* **180**, *Porphyritic granite* **181**, *Graphic granite* **181**, *Adamellite* **182**, *Pegmatite* **185**, *White granodiorite* **187**, *Syenite* **188**, *Anorthosite* **191**.

MEDIUM COLOUR
Hornblende granite **181**, *Granodiorite* **187**, *Diorite* **187**, *Syenite* **188**, *Nepheline syenite* **188**, *Agglomerate* **204**.

DARK COLOUR
Gabbro **189**, *Larvikite* **189**, *Olivine gabbro* **190**, *Bojite* **191**, *Serpentinite* **194**, *Pyroxenite* **194**, *Kimberlite* **195**, *Peridotite* **195**.

METAMORPHIC	COARSE-GRAINED	MEDIUM-GRAINED

FOLIATED
Gneiss **213**, *Folded gneiss* **213**, *Augen gneiss* **214**, *Granular gneiss* **214**, *Migmatite* **214**, *Amphibolite* **215**, *Eclogite* **215**.

UNFOLIATED
Granulite **215**, *Marbles* **216–217**, *Skarn* **220**.

intermediate rocks, as the description implies, lie between the above two categories in mineral content and, therefore, colour. If you have a metamorphic rock, examine whether it is foliated (some min- erals align) or unfoliated (crystalline, with no apparent structure). Decide which of these categories your specimen falls into, and then refer to the pages indicated for further identification information.

FINE-GRAINED		

 LIGHT COLOUR
Microgranite 183,
Quartz porphyry 184,
Granophyre 186, *Leuco gabbro* 190.

 LIGHT COLOUR
Rhyolite 196, *Ignimbrite*
206, *Volcanic bomb* 206.

 MEDIUM COLOUR
Lamprophyre 199,
Rhomb porphyry 201.

 MEDIUM COLOUR
Dacite 197, *Lamprophyre*
199, *Andesite* 199, *Trachyte*
201, *Pumice* 205, *Tuff* 205,
Ignimbrite 206.

 DARK COLOUR
Dolerite 192, *Norite*
192, *Troctolite* 193.

 DARK COLOUR
Venolith 184, *Dunite* 193,
Obsidian 197, *Pitchstone* 198,
Basalt 202, *Spilite* 203, *Tuff*
204, *Volcanic bomb* 206,
Ropy lava 207.

FINE-GRAINED		

 FOLIATED
Phyllite 210,
Folded schist 211,
Garnet schist 211,
Muscovite schist 211,
Biotite schist 212,
Kyanite schist 212.

 FOLIATED
Green slate 208, *Black slate*
208, *Slate with pyrite* 209,
Slate with distorted fossils
209, *Phyllite* 210.

 UNFOLIATED
Marbles 216–217,
Hornfels 218–219,
Chiastolite hornfels 218,
Spotted slate 219,
Metaquartzite 220,
Skarn 220.

 UNFOLIATED
Marbles 216–217, *Spotted
rock* 219, *Skarn* 220,
Halleflinta 221,
Mylonite 221.

STAGE 3 *continued*

If you have a sedimentary rock, look at its mineral composition. Is it made up mainly of rock fragments, in effect miniature rocks? Or is it composed mainly of quartz? Quartz is easily recognizable, as it is usually grey in colour and very hard.

SEDIMENTARY	COARSE-GRAINED	MEDIUM-GRAINED
	MAINLY ROCK FRAGMENTS *Polygenetic conglomerate* **222**, *Breccia* **223**.	
	MAINLY QUARTZ FRAGMENTS *No rocks in this category.*	
	CALCIUM CARBONATE DOMINANT *Limestone breccia* **223**, *Pisolitic limestone* **236**, *Crinoidal limestone* **238**.	
	OTHER MINERALS *No rocks in this category.*	

You may have a limestone, rich in calcium carbonate, identifiable by its pale colour and its effervescing reaction with dilute hydrochloric acid. Or your sedimentary rock specimen may be composed mainly of minerals other than calcium carbonate and quartz. Decide which of these four categories your specimen falls into, and then refer to the pages indicated for further identification information.

FINE-GRAINED	

 MAINLY ROCK
FRAGMENTS
Greywacke **229**.

 MAINLY ROCK
FRAGMENTS
No rocks in this category.

 MAINLY QUARTZ
FRAGMENTS
Sandstone **225**, *Green sandstone* **226**, *Milletseed sandstone* **226**, *Micaceous sandstone* **227**, *Limonitic sandstone* **227**, *Orthoquartzite (pink and grey)* **228**, *Arkose* **229**.

 MAINLY QUARTZ
FRAGMENTS
Loess **224**, *Shale* **231**, *Siltstone* **232**, *Mudstone* **232**, *Clay* **233**.

 CALCIUM
CARBONATE
DOMINANT
Oolitic limestone **236**, *Shelly limestone* **239**, *Tufa* **241**, *Stalactite* **242**, *Travertine* **242**.

 CALCIUM CARBONATE
DOMINANT
Calcareous mudstone **233**, *Marl* **234**, *Chalk* **237**, *Coral limestone* **238**, *Bryozoan limestone* **239**, *Shelly limestone* **239**, *Nummulitic limestone* **240**.

 OTHER MINERALS
Rock salt **235**, *Rock gypsum* **235**, *Potash rock* **235**, *Dolomite* **241**, *Ironstone* **243**.

 OTHER MINERALS
Boulder clay **224**, *Loess* **224**, *Clay* **233**, *Dolomite* **241**, *Ironstone* **243**, *Anthracite* **244**, *Coal* **244**, *Lignite* **244**, *Peat* **245**, *Jet* **245**, *Amber* **246**, *Chert* **246**, *Flint* **246**.

MINERALS

NATIVE ELEMENTS

NATIVE ELEMENTS are free, un-combined elements which are classified into three groups: Metals such as gold, silver, and copper; semimetals such as arsenic and antimony; and nonmetals, including carbon and sulphur. Metallic elements are very dense, soft, malleable, ductile, and opaque. Massive dendritic, wire-like habits are common. Distinct crystals are rare. Unlike metals, semimetals are poor conductors of electricity and they usually occur in nodular masses. Nonmetallic elements are transparent to translucent, do not conduct electricity, and tend to form distinct crystals.

Group Native elements	Composition Au		Hardness 2½–3

GOLD

Crystals form as cubes or octahedra, but are rare. The usual habits are as grains, flakes, nuggets, and dendritic masses. The bright, rich yellow colour is resistant to tarnishing. Gold is often rich in silver, when it is paler in colour. The streak is golden-yellow. Gold is opaque, and its lustre is metallic.

• **FORMATION** Forms mainly in hydrothermal veins, often associated with quartz and sulphides. It also occurs in placer deposits of unconsolidated sand, and in sandstone and conglomerate. It is possible to find alluvial gold in grains or nuggets, in stream beds. Panning for gold by sifting the sediment is an age-old method of looking for this rare and valuable mineral. Gold can be confused with pyrite and chalcopyrite at first, but only a few tests are needed to identify it.

• **TESTS** Insoluble in all single acids; soluble in aqua regia.

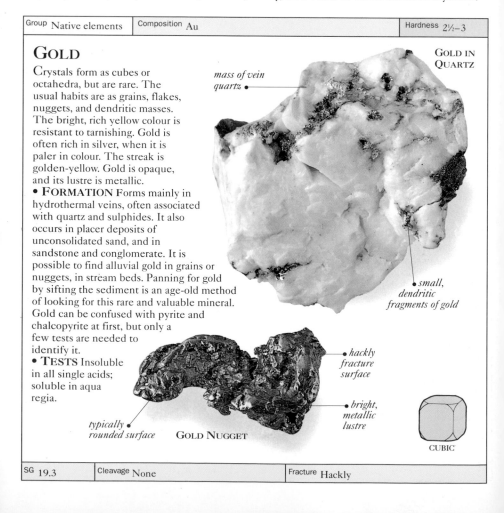

GOLD IN QUARTZ

mass of vein quartz

small, dendritic fragments of gold

hackly fracture surface

bright, metallic lustre

typically rounded surface

GOLD NUGGET

CUBIC

SG 19.3	Cleavage None		Fracture Hackly

Group Native elements	Composition Ag		Hardness 2½–3

SILVER

Crystals are rare. They form as cubes and octahedra, sometimes in parallel bands. The usual habits are wires, scales, dendrites, and massive. Silver is silver-white in colour, though it tarnishes on exposure to the atmosphere. It produces a silvery white streak. Silver is opaque, and the lustre is metallic.
• **FORMATION** Forms in hydrothermal veins, and in the oxidized regions of ore deposits, with gold, and other silver minerals, and metallic sulphides. Silver forms 20 to 25 per cent of the gold and silver alloy, called electrum.
• **TESTS** Silver is soluble in nitric acid, and is fusible. It tarnishes if exposed to the fumes of hydrogen sulphide. It is the best conductor of electricity and heat.

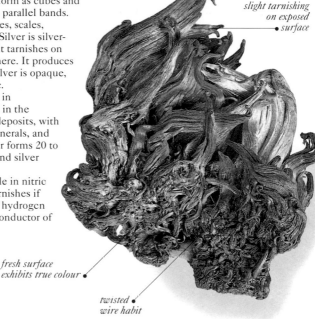

slight tarnishing on exposed surface

fresh surface exhibits true colour

CUBIC

twisted wire habit

SG 10.5	Cleavage None		Fracture Hackly

Group Native elements	Composition Pt		Hardness 4–4½

PLATINUM

Crystals take the form of cubes, but are uncommon. Usually found as grains, nuggets, and scales, platinum is silvery grey to white in colour. The streak is white to silvery grey. Platinum is opaque, and has a metallic lustre. This lustre is not altered by tarnishing if the mineral is exposed to the atmosphere.
• **FORMATION** Originally formed in basic and ultrabasic igneous rocks, and rarely in contact aureoles, platinum also occurs in placer sediments because of its very high specific gravity.
• **TESTS** When there are iron impurities present, platinum can be weakly magnetic. It is insoluble in all acids, except aqua regia.

uneven surface

rounded nugget

CUBIC

SG 21.4	Cleavage None		Fracture Hackly

Group Native elements	Composition Cu		Hardness 2½–3

COPPER

It is rare for copper to form crystals; when it does, they take the form of cubes, octahedra, or dodecahedra. The usual habits are dendritic and massive. Copper can also form in wires. Colour is a key identification feature, and is copper-red or pale rose-red on fresh surfaces. It tarnishes to copper-brown. The streak is copper-red. Copper is an opaque mineral. Its lustre is metallic.
• **FORMATION** Forms chiefly in the regions where veins containing copper sulphides have been altered.
• **TESTS** It is soluble in nitric acid.

dendritic copper

COPPER ON LIMONITE

• copper

• limonite groundmass

metallic lustre on fresh surfaces

DENDRITIC COPPER

CUBIC

SG 8.9	Cleavage None	Fracture Hackly

Group Native elements	Composition Bi		Hardness 2–2½

BISMUTH

some iridescence •

This mineral forms indistinct crystals, which are often twinned. Habits are usually massive, foliated, dendritic, reticulated, lamellar, and granular. It is silvery white, with a reddish or iridescent tarnish. The streak is silvery white. Bismuth is opaque, with a metallic lustre.
• **FORMATION** Forms in hydro-thermal veins, and pegmatites.
• **TESTS** Fuses at low temperature, and dissolves easily in nitric acid.

TRIGONAL / HEXAGONAL

lamellar habit •

metallic lustre •

SG 9.7–9.8	Cleavage Perfect basal	Fracture Uneven

Group Native elements	Composition As	Hardness 3½

ARSENIC

On rare occasions, arsenic forms rhombohedral crystals. It commonly occurs as granular, botryoidal, or stalactitic masses. It is pale grey, and tarnishes to dark grey. The streak is pale grey. Arsenic is an opaque mineral, and it has a metallic lustre.
• **FORMATION** Forms mainly in hydrothermal veins.
• **TESTS** Heated, arsenic gives off fumes smelling of garlic.

metallic lustre

TRIGONAL /
HEXAGONAL

botryoidal habit

SG 5.7	Cleavage Perfect basal	Fracture Uneven

Group Native elements	Composition Sb	Hardness 3–3½

ANTIMONY

Crystals though rare, are pseudocubic, or tabular, and often twinned. Usual habits are massive, lamellar, granular, or acicular. It is pale silvery grey, with a grey streak. It is opaque, and the lustre is brilliant metallic.
• **FORMATION** Forms in hydrothermal veins with arsenic and silver, as well as galena, sphalerite, pyrite, and stibnite.
• **TESTS** Burns white fumes in the air; turns flame greenish blue.

massive habit

crystal apparent

TRIGONAL /
HEXAGONAL

SG 6.6–6.7	Cleavage Perfect basal	Fracture Uneven

Group Native elements	Composition S	Hardness 1½–2½

SULPHUR

The crystal forms of this mineral are tabular, and bipyramidal. Sulphur also occurs in massive, encrusting, powdery, and stalactitic habits. It is bright lemon-yellow to yellowish brown, and the streak is white. Sulphur is transparent to translucent, and has a resinous to greasy lustre.
• **FORMATION** Forms around volcanic craters and hot springs.
• **TESTS** Fuses at low temperature, giving off sulphur dioxide.

tabular crystal

resinous lustre

bipyramidal crystal

ORTHORHOMBIC

SG 2.0–2.1	Cleavage Imperfect basal	Fracture Uneven to conchoidal

Group Native elements	Composition Hg		Hardness Liquid

MERCURY

This mineral is classified in the trigonal/hexagonal system, but it shows a rhombohedral crystal habit only below –39 °C. It occurs as a liquid at normal temperatures, forming as small globules. It is pale silvery white. There is no streak. Mercury is opaque, and has a brilliant metallic lustre.
• **FORMATION** Around volcanic vents, often with cinnabar.
• **TESTS** Mercury dissolves when placed in nitric acid.

opaque

mercury in cavities in rock groundmass

MERCURY IN CLOSE-UP

rock groundmass

TRIGONAL/ HEXAGONAL

SG 13.6–14.4	Cleavage None	Fracture None

Group Native elements	Composition Ni,Fe		Hardness 4–5

NICKEL-IRON

This uncommon mineral forms in massive and granular habits. It is steel-grey, dark grey, or blackish in colour. The streak is steel-grey. Nickel-iron is opaque, and has a metallic lustre on fresh surfaces.
• **FORMATION** Nickel-iron forms in some altered basalts. It occurs when iron-rich minerals in the basalt are chemically reduced. Some varieties occur in ultrabasic rocks that have been altered by serpentinization. Nickel-iron is very common in meteorites as kamacite-taenite masses; it is a rare terrestrial material, though it is believed that much of the earth's core contains both iron and nickel.
• **TESTS** Nickel-iron is strongly magnetic.

weathered iron meteorite

NICKEL-IRON IN CLOSE-UP

opaque

hackly fracture

CUBIC

SG 7.3–8.2	Cleavage Poor cubic	Fracture Hackly

Group Native elements	Composition C		Hardness 10

DIAMOND

The crystals form as octahedra, cubes, dodecahedra, and tetrahedra, often with curved faces. Diamond also occurs in rounded masses with a radiating structure (bort), and as micro-crystalline masses (carbonado). It may be colourless, white, grey, orange, yellow, brown, pink, red, blue, green, or black. The streak is white. Diamond is transparent to opaque, and has an adamantine to greasy lustre. It is used chiefly as an industrial abrasive, and is also a highly-valued and sought-after gem.
• **FORMATION** Found in ultrabasic rocks (kimberlites), forming pipe-like intrusions.
• **TESTS** The hardest of all the known minerals – it cannot be scratched by any other mineral.

transparent crystal •

TRANSPARENT DIAMOND

rock • groundmass

yellowish octahedral • crystal in rock groundmass

YELLOW DIAMOND

• adamantine lustre

CUBIC

SG 3.52	Cleavage Perfect octahedral	Fracture Conchoidal

Group Native elements	Composition C		Hardness 1–2

GRAPHITE

The crystals form as flattened, tabular, hexagonal plates. Graphite also occurs in massive, foliated, granular, and earthy habits. It is dark grey to black, and has a dark grey or black streak. This is an opaque mineral. Its lustre is dull metallic.
• **FORMATION** Forms in metamorphic rocks, including slate and schist.
• **TESTS** Feels greasy. If rubbed on paper, a grey mark is left.

perfect cleavage •

metallic lustre •

TRIGONAL/ HEXAGONAL

• massive habit

SG 2.1–2.3	Cleavage Perfect basal	Fracture Uneven

SULPHIDES AND SULPHO-SALTS

S ULPHIDES ARE chemical compounds in which sulphur has combined with metallic and semi-metallic elements. When tellurium sulphide substitutes for sulphur, the resultant compound is a telluride; if arsenic substitutes, arsenide is formed. The properties of sulphides, tellurides, and arsenides are somewhat variable.

———— • ————

Many sulphides have metallic lustres, and are soft and dense (e.g. galena and molybdenite). Some are non-metallic

(orpiment, realgar), or relatively hard (marcasite, cobaltite). Well-formed, highly symmetrical crystals are the rule.

———— • ————

Sulphides are very important ores of lead, zinc, iron, and copper. They form in hydrothermal veins below the water table as they are easily oxidized to sulphates. Sulpho-salts are compounds in which metallic elements combine with sulphur plus a semi-metallic element (e.g. antimony and arsenic). Their properties are similar to sulphides.

Group Sulphides	Composition PbS		Hardness 2½

GALENA

This very common ore mineral forms cubes, octahedra, or cubo-octahedral crystals, and also occurs in massive, granular, and fibrous habits. Both the colour and streak are lead-grey. Galena is opaque, with a metallic lustre.
• FORMATION Galena forms in hydrothermal veins, when hot fluids find their way to higher levels in the earth's crust. It can occur with several other minerals, including fluorite, quartz, calcite, sphalerite, and pyrite.
• TESTS This mineral is soluble in hydrochloric acid, producing the "bad eggs" smell of hydrogen sulphide.

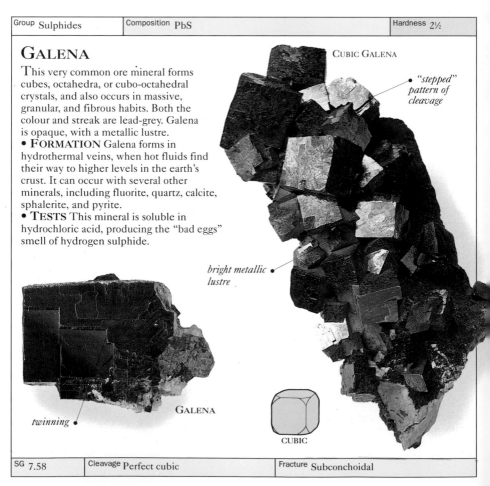

CUBIC GALENA

• "stepped" pattern of cleavage

bright metallic • lustre

twinning •

GALENA

CUBIC

SG 7.58	Cleavage Perfect cubic	Fracture Subconchoidal

Group Sulphides	Composition HgS	Hardness 2–2½

CINNABAR

This mineral forms as thick tabular, rhombohedral, and prismatic crystals, which are commonly twinned. It also occurs in massive, encrusting, or granular habits. The colour is typically brownish red or scarlet. The streak is scarlet. Cinnabar is transparent to opaque, and has an adamantine, submetallic, or dull lustre.
- **FORMATION** Forms with realgar and pyrite, around volcanic vents, and hot springs. Other associated minerals include native mercury, marcasite, opal, quartz, stibnite, and calcite. It may also occur in mineral veins, and in sedimentary rocks associated with recent volcanic activity.
- **TESTS** Does not alter when exposed to the atmosphere.

adamantine lustre

TRIGONAL/ HEXAGONAL

mass of small crystals

SG 8.0–8.2	Cleavage Perfect prismatic	Fracture Conchoidal to uneven

Group Sulphides	Composition CdS	Hardness 3–3½

GREENOCKITE

This mineral occurs as tabular, pyramidal, and prismatic crystals, but more often as earthy coatings on other minerals. It is yellow, orange-yellow, orange, or red in colour, and the streak is orange-yellow to brick-red. It is a transparent to translucent mineral. It has a resinous or adamantine lustre.
- **FORMATION** Greenockite occurs as a replacement and alteration product of sphalerite, when the sphalerite is cadmium-rich. Although it is not a common mineral, greenockite sometimes forms as minute crystals with other minerals, including prehnite, and zeolites.
- **TESTS** Greenockite is soluble in hydrochloric acid, producing hydrogen sulphide, which gives off a "bad eggs" smell.

resinous lustre

coating of greenockite on rock surface

conchoidal fracture

TRIGONAL/ HEXAGONAL

SG 4.7–4.8	Cleavage Distinct	Fracture Conchoidal

Group Sulphides	Composition Ag_2S		Hardness 2–2½

ACANTHITE

This mineral forms as prismatic crystals. Acanthite is typically grey to iron-black, and has a black streak. The mineral is opaque, and has a metallic lustre. It is dimorphous with argentite; this means that, over a certain temperature, acanthite alters from a single mineral into another mineral form, which is known as argentite.

• **FORMATION** Forms in hydrothermal mineral veins, associated with native silver, proustite, pyrargyrite, and other sulphides, such as galena.

• **TESTS** Acanthite is soluble in dilute nitric acid. It fuses easily, releasing sulphurous fumes.

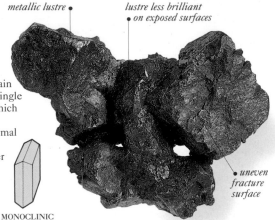

metallic lustre

lustre less brilliant on exposed surfaces

uneven fracture surface

MONOCLINIC

SG 7.22	Cleavage None	Fracture Uneven

Group Sulphides	Composition CoAsS		Hardness 5½

COBALTITE

This mineral commonly forms as octahedral or pseudo-cubic crystals. Crystal faces are usually striated. Other habits include massive, granular, and compact. The colour varies from greyish black to silvery white. When tested for streak, a greyish black powder is produced. Cobaltite is opaque; light is unable to pass through it, even when it is in thin pieces. It has a metallic lustre on fresh crystal, or broken, surfaces.

• **FORMATION** Forms in hydrothermal veins (fractures in the earth's crust through which hot fluids circulate, depositing minerals as they cool) and also in metamorphic rocks, with other arsenides and sulphides.

• **TESTS** Fuses quite easily, forming a globule which is slightly magnetic. Cobaltite is soluble in nitric acid.

chalcopyrite, an associated mineral

metallic lustre

striations on crystal face

ORTHORHOMBIC

pseudo-cubic cobaltite crystal

SG 6.3	Cleavage Perfect	Fracture Uneven

Group Sulphides	Composition ZnS	Hardness 3½–4

SPHALERITE

This mineral, known also as blende, or black jack, forms tetrahedral and dodecahedral crystals; it often exhibits curved crystal faces. Other habits include massive, granular, concretionary, and botryoidal. The colour ranges from black, brown, yellow, and red, to green, grey, and white. It can also be colourless. The streak is pale brown to colourless. Sphalerite varies from translucent to transparent. It has a resinous to adamantine lustre.

• **FORMATION** Common in hydrothermal veins, it occurs with minerals such as dolomite, quartz, pyrite, galena, fluorite, barite, and calcite.

• **TESTS** The addition of dilute hydrochloric acid to sphalerite produces a smell reminiscent of hydrogen sulphide ("rotten eggs"). If pure, it is infusible, but as the iron content of sphalerite rises, the mineral specimen melts with increasing ease.

typical resinous lustre

MASSIVE SPHALERITE

adamantine lustre on sphalerite crystal face

groundmass of rock and pale dolomite

CUBIC

CRYSTALLINE SPHALERITE

SG 3.9–4.1	Cleavage Perfect	Fracture Conchoidal

Group Sulphides	Composition Sb₂S₃	Hardness 2

STIBNITE

This mineral forms as prismatic crystals, which often have longitudinal striations. Other habits are columnar, granular, compact, and bladed. Both colour and streak are lead-grey. Stibnite is opaque. It has a metallic lustre.

• **FORMATION** Forms in hydrothermal veins, and deposits where a preformed rock is wholly or partly replaced with new material from circulating fluids.

• **TESTS** Stibnite is fusible in a match flame, and it is soluble in hydrochloric acid.

quartz and barite groundmass

longitudinal striations

prismatic stibnite crystals in radiating groups

ORTHORHOMBIC

SG 4.63-4.66	Cleavage Perfect	Fracture Uneven to subconchoidal

Group Sulphides	Composition Cu_5FeS_4	Hardness 3

BORNITE

The crystals formed by bornite are cubic, octahedral, or dodecahedral, and they often have curved or rough faces. More usually, it forms in compact, granular, or massive habits. Bornite can be coppery red, coppery brown, or bronze, tarnishing to iridescent blue, purple, and red – leading to its common name "peacock ore". The streak is greyish black. Bornite is opaque, with a metallic lustre.

• **FORMATION** Forms in hydrothermal veins, with minerals such as quartz, chalcopyrite, and galena. It also forms in some igneous rocks. The oxidation zone of copper veins can contain bornite.

• **TESTS** Bornite is soluble in nitric acid.

iridescence

uneven fracture

metallic lustre

rough crystal faces

CUBIC

SG 5.0–5.1	Cleavage Very poor	Fracture Uneven to conchoidal

Group Sulphides	Composition $CuFeS_2$	Hardness 3½–4

CHALCOPYRITE

Forming pseudotetrahedral crystals, often with striated faces and commonly twinned, chalcopyrite can also occur in compact, massive, reniform, or botryoidal habits. It is brassy yellow in colour, often with an iridescent tarnish. There is a greenish black streak. The mineral has a metallic lustre, and is opaque.

• **FORMATION** One of the most important ores of copper, chalcopyrite forms in sulphide ore deposits. These are often hydrothermal veins, where it may occur with pyrrhotite, quartz, calcite, pyrite, sphalerite, and galena. It is also present where copper deposits have been altered.

• **TESTS** It is soluble in nitric acid, and colours a flame green.

quartz crystals

twinned chalcopyrite crystals

metallic lustre

TETRAGONAL

SG 4.3–4.4	Cleavage Poor	Fracture Uneven to conchoidal

Group Sulphides	Composition Cu_2S	Hardness $2\frac{1}{2}$–3

CHALCOSINE

On rare occasions, chalcosine occurs as pseudohexagonal prisms formed by twinning. It may also form in short, prismatic, or tabular crystals, but the usual habit is massive. Both the colour and streak are dark grey. It is an opaque mineral, and it has a metallic lustre.
• **FORMATION** Forms in hydrothermal veins with other minerals, such as bornite, quartz, calcite, covellite, chalcopyrite, galena, and sphalerite.
• **TESTS** This mineral is soluble in nitric acid, and is also fusible. When it is burnt, chalcosine colours a flame green, and also produces sulphur dioxide fumes.

• *dolomite groundmass*
• *metallic lustre*
twinning •
MONOCLINIC
pseudohexagonal crystals •

SG 5.5–5.8	Cleavage Indistinct	Fracture Conchoidal

Group Sulphides	Composition CuS	Hardness $1\frac{1}{2}$–2

COVELLITE

This mineral occurs as thin, tabular, hexagonal plates, but more usually it forms in a massive, foliated habit. It is indigo-blue in colour, often tinged with purple iridescence. There is a dark grey to black streak. Covellite is an opaque mineral, and has a submetallic to dull lustre. If broken, a perfect basal cleavage into thin, flexible laminae is produced.
• **FORMATION** Occurs in the parts of copper veins that have been altered – often by secondary enrichment, due to fluids seeping through the vein.
• **TESTS** Covellite fuses very easily, producing a blue-coloured flame. It dissolves in hydrochloric acid.

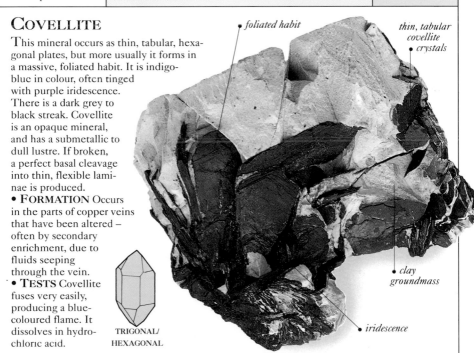

• *foliated habit*
thin, tabular covellite • *crystals*
• *clay groundmass*
TRIGONAL/ HEXAGONAL
• *iridescence*

SG 4.6–4.8	Cleavage Perfect basal	Fracture Uneven

Group Sulphides	Composition As_2S_3	Hardness 1½–2

ORPIMENT

uneven fracture

This mineral forms small, prismatic crystals, though only rarely. More frequently, it occurs as thin, foliated masses, or in massive, or columnar habits. The colour is usually a rich lemon-yellow, though it can be brownish yellow. The streak is pale yellow. Orpiment is transparent to translucent. On fresh surfaces the lustre is resinous, but the cleavage surfaces are pearly.

• **FORMATION** This mineral is found in low temperature hydrothermal veins, often with stibnite, and realgar. Orpiment also forms in the crusts deposited around hot springs.

• **TESTS** This mineral fuses quite easily. When heated, it gives off a very strong smell of garlic, typical for a mineral rich in arsenic. Orpiment also dissolves in nitric acid, leaving behind traces of yellow sulphur on the liquid surface.

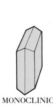

MONOCLINIC

pearly lustre on cleavage surface

typical foliated appearance

SG 3.4–3.5	Cleavage Perfect	Fracture Uneven

Group Sulphides	Composition AsS	Hardness 1½–2

REALGAR

grey quartz

rock groundmass

This mineral forms as short, prismatic, striated crystals, and also as massive, compact, and granular aggregates. The colour is bright red to orange-red. The streak is orange-yellow to orange-red. Realgar is transparent to translucent. It has a resinous to greasy lustre.

• **FORMATION** Forms in hydrothermal veins, and also around hot springs. It can be found with stibnite and orpiment, as well as with minerals of lead, silver, and antimony.

• **TESTS** As with other arsenic minerals, realgar gives off a strong smell of garlic when heated.

MONOCLINIC

prismatic realgar crystals

SG 3.56	Cleavage Good	Fracture Conchoidal

Group Sulphides	Composition MoS_2	Hardness $1-1\frac{1}{2}$

MOLYBDENITE

This mineral usually forms as tabular or barrel-shaped crystals. It can also occur as foliated masses, scales, or grains. The colour is grey. There is also a grey streak. Molybdenite is an opaque mineral, and it has a metallic lustre.
• **FORMATION** Forms in hydrothermal veins. This mineral also forms in granitic rocks.
• **TESTS** Molybdenite can feel quite greasy to the touch.

hexagonal foliated mass

TRIGONAL/ HEXAGONAL

granite groundmass

metallic lustre

SG 4.62–5.06	Cleavage Perfect basal	Fracture Uneven

Group Sulphides	Composition MnS_2	Hardness 4

HAUERITE

Crystals are octahedral to cubo-octahedral. It can also occur in a massive habit, or as globular aggregates. The colour is reddish brown to brownish, or black, and hauerite has a brownish red streak. This mineral is opaque, with a metallic to dull lustre.
• **FORMATION** Forms in caps of salt domes by alteration in evaporites.
• **TESTS** It is soluble in hydrochloric acid.

octahedral habit

CUBIC

dull lustre

opaque

SG 3.46	Cleavage Perfect	Fracture Subconchoidal to uneven

Group Sulphides	Composition Bi_2S_3	Hardness 2

BISMUTHINITE

Crystals are prismatic, or acicular. Bismuthinite also occurs in massive, fibrous, or foliated habits. The colour is lead-grey to silvery white, and the streak is lead-grey. It is opaque, with a metallic lustre.
• **FORMATION** Forms in high temperature hydrothermal veins and in granitic rocks. It occurs with native bismuth, and various sulphides.
• **TESTS** It is soluble in nitric acid, leaving flaky particles of sulphur on the surface.

mass of small, bismuthinite, acicular crystals

ORTHORHOMBIC

rock groundmass

SG 6.8	Cleavage Perfect	Fracture Uneven

Group Sulphides	Composition FeS_2		Hardness 6–6½

PYRITE

This mineral forms as cubic, pyritohedral, or octahedral crystals; twinning is common. The crystal faces are frequently striated. Pyrite can be massive, granular, reniform, stalactitic, botryoidal, and nodular. The pale yellow colour gives rise to its nickname, "fool's gold". It has a greenish black streak. Pyrite is opaque, and has a metallic lustre.
• FORMATION Pyrite is a common accessory mineral in igneous, sedimentary, and metamorphic rocks.
• TESTS Gives off sparks if struck with a hard metal object. Fuses quite easily.

perfect octahedral pyrite crystal

striated pyrite crystal face

OCTAHEDRAL
PYRITE

quartz crystal

CUBIC

NODULAR PYRITE

SG 5.0	Cleavage Indistinct	Fracture Conchoidal to uneven

Group Sulphides	Composition FeS		Hardness 3½–4½

PYRRHOTITE

This mineral forms as tabular or platy crystals. Other habits are massive and granular. The colour varies from bronze-yellow to a coppery bronze-red; the mineral tarnishes to brown, often with iridescence. The streak is dark grey to black. Pyrrhotite is an opaque mineral, and has a metallic lustre.
• FORMATION Commonly forms in magmatic igneous deposits, especially those of basic and ultrabasic composition. It occurs with pyrite, galena, sphalerite, and other sulphides.
• TESTS Pyrrhotite is magnetic.

horizontal striations on crystal face

metallic lustre

mass of twinned crystals

MONOCLINIC

tabular, six-sided crystal

SG 4.53–4.77	Cleavage None	Fracture Subconchoidal to uneven

Group Sulphides	Composition FeAsS	Hardness 5½–6

ARSENOPYRITE

This mineral forms as prismatic crystals, often twinned. It also exhibits massive, columnar, and granular habits. Typically silvery white, arsenopyrite tarnishes to pink, brown, and copper shades, with iridescence. The streak is black to grey. It is opaque, and has a metallic lustre.
• **FORMATION** Forms in hydrothermal veins, in metamorphic rocks, and in basic igneous rocks.
• **TESTS** When a specimen is heated, or if it is struck with a hard object, arsenopyrite produces a smell reminiscent of garlic.

striated crystal face

metallic lustre on crystal face

MONOCLINIC

SG 5.9–6.2	Cleavage Indistinct	Fracture Uneven

Group Sulphides	Composition FeS$_2$	Hardness 6–6½

MARCASITE

This mineral forms crystals in a variety of shapes, including tabular and pyramidal. These crystals commonly have curved faces, and form spear-shaped or cockscomb aggregates, as a result of twinning. Marcasite also occurs in massive, stalactitic, and reniform habits. Nodules of marcasite have a radiating internal structure. Its brassy yellow colour is paler than that of pyrite, and darkens with exposure. The streak is greenish black. It is an opaque mineral, and it has a metallic lustre.
• **FORMATION** Commonly forms from acidic solutions permeating beds of shale, clay, limestone, and chalk.
• **TESTS** Decomposes readily on exposure to the air. Pyrite, which is chemically identical to marcasite, does not decompose as easily. It will dissolve in nitric acid, but with difficulty.

metallic lustre

marcasite colour change due to exposure

chalk groundmass

ORTHORHOMBIC

marcasite crystal aggregates with a spear-shaped habit

SG 4.92	Cleavage Distinct	Fracture Uneven

Group Sulphides	Composition NiS		Hardness 3–3½

MILLERITE

Crystals are usually very thin, often hair-like, and in radiating groups. Millerite can occur in a massive habit. It is brass-yellow, and the streak is greenish black. It is opaque, with a metallic lustre.
• **FORMATION** Often forms by replacing other nickel minerals. Occurs in limestones, dolomites, serpentines, and veins of carbonate minerals.
• **TESTS** A good conductor of electricity, millerite fuses easily.

TRIGONAL /
HEXAGONAL

radiating mass of thin millerite crystals

calcite groundmass

SG 5.3–5.6	Cleavage Perfect rhombohedral	Fracture Uneven

Group Sulphides	Composition (Co,Fe)AsS		Hardness 5

GLAUCODOT

This mineral occurs as prismatic, striated crystals, which may be twinned. It also occurs in a massive habit. The colour is grey to white. There is a black streak. Glaucodot is an opaque mineral, with a metallic lustre.
• **FORMATION** Forms in hydrothermal veins, with minerals such as pyrite.
• **TESTS** Glaucodot is soluble in nitric acid, and gives off a smell of garlic when heated.

ORTHORHOMBIC

metallic lustre on striated face

prismatic habit

SG 5.9-6.1	Cleavage Perfect	Fracture Uneven

Group Sulphides	Composition (Fe,Ni)$_9$S$_8$		Hardness 3½–4

PENTLANDITE

This mineral forms as massive or granular specimens. It is bronze-yellow, and has a brown streak. Pentlandite is an opaque mineral, with a metallic lustre.
• **FORMATION** Forms in basic igneous rocks, such as norite, as a result of magmatic segregation. It is associated with minerals such as chalcopyrite, pyrrhotite, and arsenides of nickel.
• **TESTS** Fuses very easily, producing a bead of lead-grey.

CUBIC

uneven fracture

massive habit

SG 4.6–5.0	Cleavage None	Fracture Conchoidal

Group Tellurides	Composition $AuAgTe_4$	Hardness $1\frac{1}{2}-2$

SYLVANITE

This mineral forms short, prismatic crystals, which are commonly twinned. Sylvanite also occurs as bladed, columnar, and granular masses. The colour is silvery white, grey, or yellow. The streak is silvery white to steel-grey. Sylvanite is opaque, and it has a metallic lustre.

• **FORMATION** Forms in hydrothermal veins with fluorite, other tellurides, sulphides, carbonates, gold, tellurium, and quartz. Very fine crystals, up to 1cm (⅜in) long, have been found with native gold.

• **TESTS** It is soluble in nitric acid, leaving a yellow-gold residue. When heated in concentrated sulphuric acid, the solution becomes reddish in colour.

calcite groundmass

twinned sylvanite crystals

brilliant metallic lustre

MONOCLINIC

SG 8.1–8.2	Cleavage Perfect	Fracture Uneven

Group Arsenides	Composition $NiAs$	Hardness $5-5\frac{1}{2}$

NICKELINE

Crystals rarely form in nickeline; when they occur it is as small pyramidal specimens. The usual habits are massive, reniform, and columnar. It is very pale copper-red, tarnishing to blackish. When tested for streak, a brownish black powder is produced. It is an opaque mineral, and has a metallic lustre.

• **FORMATION** Forms in hydrothermal veins, and in norites, and is associated with ores of silver, nickel, and cobalt.

• **TESTS** Nickeline is soluble in nitric acid, staining the solution green. It smells of garlic when heated. It fuses very easily.

massive habit

copper-red when fresh

TRIGONAL / HEXAGONAL

SG 7.7–7.8	Cleavage None	Fracture Uneven

Group Arsenides	Composition $(Co,Ni)As_{2-3}$	Hardness 5½–6

SMALTITE

cubo-octahedral smaltite crystals

An arsenic-deficient variety of skutterudite, this mineral forms as cubic, octahedral, or cubo-octahedral crystals. Other habits are massive, granular, or reticulated. It is tin-white in colour, and the streak is black. Smaltite is opaque, and it has a metallic lustre.

• **FORMATION** This mineral forms in hydrothermal veins.
• **TESTS** Gives off fumes that smell of garlic when heated.

metallic lustre

CUBIC

rock groundmass

SG 6.1–6.9	Cleavage Distinct	Fracture Uneven

Group Arsenides	Composition $(Ni,Co)As_{2-3}$	Hardness 5½–6

CHLOANTHITE

octahedral crystals on groundmass

An arsenic-deficient variety of nickel-skutterudite, chloanthite forms either as cubic or octahedral crystals, and in massive or granular habits. The colour is tin-white and the streak black. It is opaque and has a metallic lustre.

• **FORMATION** Forms in hydrothermal veins.
• **TESTS** Chloanthite is nickel-rich. It gives off fumes that smell strongly of garlic when heated.

CUBIC

opaque

metallic lustre

SG 6.1–6.9	Cleavage Distinct	Fracture Uneven

Group Arsenides	Composition $CoAs_{2-3}$	Hardness 5½–6

SKUTTERUDITE

octahedral habit

This is an intermediate member of the chloanthite-skutterudite-smaltite series. It forms mainly as cubic crystals. Octahedral crystals may occur, but are rare. Other habits are massive and granular. The colour is tin-white, and the streak black. It is opaque, and has a metallic lustre.

• **FORMATION** It forms in hydrothermal veins.
• **TESTS** Fumes smelling strongly of garlic are given off when it is heated.

CUBIC

opaque

metallic lustre

SG 6.1–6.9	Cleavage Distinct	Fracture Uneven

Group Sulpho-salts	Composition Cu_3AsS_4	Hardness 3

ENARGITE

Crystals are prismatic or tabular, and often twinned. The crystal faces show vertical striations. Enargite may also form in massive or granular habits. The colour and streak are dark grey to black. It is opaque, with a metallic lustre.
• **FORMATION** Found in hydrothermal veins, or replacement deposits. These mineral veins are formed when hot fluids circulating in the earth's crust move upwards, where the elements held in them are precipitated. Enargite is associated with many minerals, such as quartz, and sulphides, including galena, bornite, sphalerite, pyrite, and chalcopyrite. It also occurs in the cap rocks of salt domes, with minerals such as anhydrite.
• **TESTS** When heated, it smells of garlic. It is soluble in nitric acid, and melts in a match flame.

twinned crystals with striations

uneven fracture

metallic lustre

ORTHORHOMBIC

SG 4.4–4.5	Cleavage Perfect	Fracture Uneven

Group Sulpho-salts	Composition $Pb_4FeSb_6S_{14}$	Hardness 2½

JAMESONITE

This mineral forms as acicular to fibrous crystals, and in massive and plumose habits. The colour and streak are both dark grey. Jamesonite is an opaque mineral, and has a metallic lustre.
• **FORMATION** Forms in hydrothermal veins, where hot, chemically-rich fluids have permeated joints and fault lines, depositing minerals in the process of cooling. Jamesonite is associated with other sulpho-salts, with sulphides, carbonates, and also with the common mineral quartz.
• **TESTS** Jamesonite is soluble in hydrochloric acid.

rock groundmass

metallic lustre

mass of fibrous, twisted jamesonite crystals

MONOCLINIC

SG 5.63	Cleavage Good basal	Fracture Uneven to conchoidal

Group Sulpho-salts	Composition Ag_5SbS_4	Hardness $2-2\frac{1}{2}$

STEPHANITE

This mineral forms as short, prismatic, or tabular crystals, which are sometimes twinned. The habit can also be massive. Stephanite is typically iron-black in colour, with a black streak. It is an opaque mineral, and the lustre is metallic.
• **FORMATION** Forms in veins, with native silver, and with sulphides and other sulpho-salts, such as acanthite, tetrahedrite, polybasite, proustite, and argentite.
• **TESTS** Stephanite is soluble in nitric acid, and produces arsenic and sulphur oxide when this test is carried out. This mineral fuses very easily.

short, tabular crystal

hexagonal crystal outline

metallic lustre on fresh faces

twinned crystals

ORTHORHOMBIC

SG 6.25	Cleavage Imperfect	Fracture Uneven to subconchoidal

Group Sulpho-salts	Composition Ag_3SbS_3	Hardness $2\frac{1}{2}$

PYRARGYRITE

This mineral forms as prismatic or scalenohedral crystals, which may be twinned. Other habits include massive, compact, and disseminated particles. Pyrargyrite is typically dark red to black. The streak is dark red. This is a translucent mineral; the lustre is adamantine to submetallic.
• **FORMATION** Forms in hydrothermal veins, where it is associated with other sulpho-salts; with silver; and with other minerals, such as pyrite, galena, quartz, dolomite, and calcite.
• **TESTS** This mineral is soluble in nitric acid, and fuses easily.

adamantine lustre

twinned crystals

prismatic crystal showing six sides

TRIGONAL / HEXAGONAL

submetallic lustre

SG 5.8–5.9	Cleavage Distinct rhombohedral	Fracture Conchoidal to uneven

Group Sulpho-salts	Composition $(Ag)_{16}Sb_2S_{11}$	Hardness 2–3

POLYBASITE

This mineral forms as tabular, pseudo-hexagonal crystals, which often have triangular striations on their faces. It can occur in a massive habit. Polybasite is iron-black in colour, and has a black streak; thin splinters may be dark red. It is an opaque mineral, and has a metallic lustre on fresh surfaces.
• **FORMATION** Forms in hydrothermal veins with native silver, as well as with other sulpho-salts and sulphides, such as galena, argentite, and other silver and lead minerals.
• **TESTS** When it is heated in a flame, this mineral fuses very easily at low temperature.

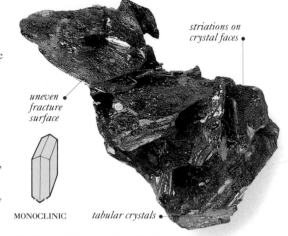

striations on crystal faces •

uneven • fracture surface

MONOCLINIC   tabular crystals •

SG 6.0–6.3	Cleavage Imperfect basal	Fracture Uneven

Group Sulpho-salts	Composition $PbCuSbS_3$	Hardness 2½–3

BOURNONITE

This mineral forms as short, prismatic or tabular crystals, which are commonly twinned and striated. It can also occur in massive, granular, and compact habits. The colour is typically steel-grey to black. The streak is grey or black. Bournonite is opaque, and has a metallic lustre.
• **FORMATION** Forms with tetrahedrite, galena, silver, chalcopyrite, siderite, quartz, sphalerite, and stibnite in hydrothermal veins; these are fractures in the earth's crust, through which hot fluids circulate, depositing minerals as they cool.
• **TESTS** When heated in a flame, bournonite fuses very easily. It is readily soluble in nitric acid. The presence of copper in bournonite's chemical composition is suggested by the fact that the resultant nitric acid solution is coloured green.

metallic lustre on crystal faces •

uneven • fracture

prismatic • bournonite crystal, showing orthorhombic symmetry

quartz • groundmass

ORTHORHOMBIC

SG 5.7–5.9	Cleavage Imperfect	Fracture Subconchoidal to uneven

Group Sulpho-salts	Composition $Cu_{12}Sb_4S_{13}$	Hardness 3–4½

TETRAHEDRITE

This mineral forms tetrahedral-shaped crystals, from which it gets its name. The crystals are often twinned, and have a mass of triangular faces. Other habits are granular, massive, and compact. The colour is grey to black, and the streak is variable, from black or brown to red. It is opaque, and has a metallic lustre. Tetrahedrite is grouped chemically with tennantite (below).
• **FORMATION** Forms in hydrothermal veins with sulphides, carbonates, quartz, fluorite, and barite.
• **TESTS** Tetrahedrite is soluble in nitric acid.

triangular crystal face

quartz crystals

CUBIC

twinned, tetrahedral crystals

SG 4.6–5.1	Cleavage None	Fracture Uneven to subconchoidal

Group Sulpho-salts	Composition $(Cu,Fe)_{12}As_4S_{13}$	Hardness 3–4½

TENNANTITE

The tetrahedral crystals formed by tennantite are often modified by other forms. The crystals are frequently twinned. Other habits are massive, granular, and compact. This mineral is dark grey to black in colour, and the streak is black, brown, or dark red. Tennantite is opaque. It has a metallic lustre, which sometimes can be very bright.
• **FORMATION** Forms in hydrothermal veins, in association with many other minerals, such as barite, fluorite, quartz, galena, sphalerite, pyrite, chalcopyrite, calcite, and dolomite. This mineral may also form in high temperature veins, and in contact metasomatic deposits.
• **TESTS** It is soluble in nitric acid, and fuses easily.

tetrahedral crystal

iridescent crystals

CUBIC

SG 4.59–4.75	Cleavage None	Fracture Uneven to subconchoidal

Group Sulpho-salts	Composition $Pb_5Sb_4S_{11}$	Hardness 2½–3

BOULANGERITE

This mineral forms long, prismatic crystals, which may be acicular. Other habits are massive, fibrous, or plumose. The colour is lead-grey to bluish grey, and the streak is brownish. Boulangerite is opaque, and has a dull or metallic lustre.
• **FORMATION** Forms in hydrothermal veins, together with galena, pyrite, and sphalerite; with sulpho-salts, including tetrahedrite, tennantite, and proustite; and with other minerals, such as quartz, and various carbonates.
• **TESTS** When it is heated in a flame, boulangerite fuses very easily. It does not react with cold, dilute acids, but is soluble in hot, strong acids

massive habit •

dull lustre •

• *uneven fracture*

• *metallic lustre*

MONOCLINIC

SG 5.8–6.2	Cleavage Good	Fracture Uneven

Group Sulpho-salts	Composition Ag_3AsS_3	Hardness 2–2½

PROUSTITE

The crystals formed by proustite are prismatic, rhombohedral, and scalenohedral. This mineral also forms in massive or compact habits. It is a rich scarlet colour, and also has a scarlet streak, though it blackens on exposure to light. It is translucent to transparent. The lustre of proustite ranges from adamantine to submetallic.
• **FORMATION** Forms in hydrothermal veins, where it is associated with other sulpho-salts, including tetrahedrite and tennantite; with sulphides, such as galena; and with quartz.
• **TESTS** Soluble in nitric acid. Fuses easily.

twinned, prismatic crystals •

adamantine lustre on crystal faces •

translucent edge •

TRIGONAL / HEXAGONAL

• *striated face*

SG 5.55–5.64	Cleavage Distinct rhombohedral	Fracture Conchoidal to uneven

HALIDES

HALIDES ARE compounds in which metallic elements combine with halogens (the elements chlorine, bromine, fluorine, and iodine). Halides are common in a number of geological environments. Some, such as halite, are found in evaporite sequences. These are alternating layers of sedimentary rock, which contain evaporites, such as gypsum, halite, and potash rock in a strict sequence, interbedded with rocks such as marl and limestone.

————— • —————

Other halides, like fluorite, occur in hydrothermal veins. The halides are usually very soft minerals, and many have cubic crystal symmetry. Their specific gravity tends to be low.

Group Halides	Composition NaCl		Hardness 2

HALITE

The crystals formed by halite are cube-shaped and frequently have concave faces. They are called hopper crystals. Very rarely, halite occurs as octahedral crystals. Other habits include massive, granular, and compact. In a compact habit, the mineral is known as rock salt. It can be white, colourless, orange, yellow, reddish, blue, purple, and black. The streak, however, is consistently white. Halite is transparent to translucent, and has a vitreous lustre.

• **FORMATION** This is an evaporite mineral, formed by precipitation, as the water in a salt lake, or a lagoon dries out. Halite is associated with other evaporite minerals, such as sylvite, gypsum, dolomite, and anhydrite.

• **TESTS** There are several very easy tests that can be applied to halite. It has a salty taste. It is also readily soluble in cold water; if some of the resulting solution is left to dry out, small hopper crystals will form by precipitation. Halite feels greasy when handled. It colours a flame yellow. It can contain impurities, which may produce green, orange, or reddish fluorescence.

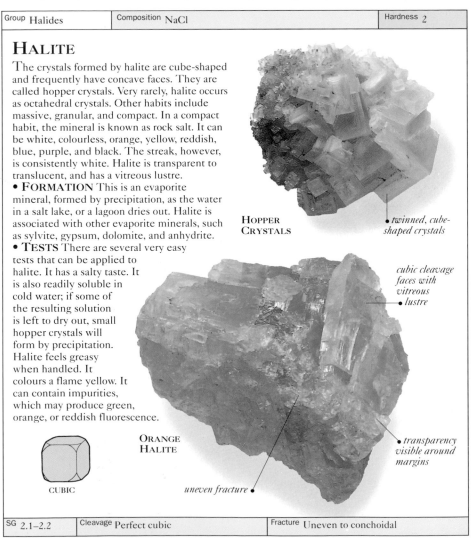

HOPPER CRYSTALS

• *twinned, cube-shaped crystals*

cubic cleavage faces with vitreous lustre

ORANGE HALITE

• *transparency visible around margins*

CUBIC

uneven fracture •

SG 2.1–2.2	Cleavage Perfect cubic	Fracture Uneven to conchoidal

Group Halides	Composition KCl	Hardness 2

SYLVITE

The crystals usually form as cubes and, rarely, as octahedra. Sylvite can also occur in crusts, and in massive or granular habits. It can be colourless, whitish, grey, bluish, yellow, purple, or red. The streak is white. This is a transparent mineral, which has a vitreous lustre.

• **FORMATION** Forms as an evaporite mineral, by precipitation from salt solutions. It is associated with minerals such as halite, gypsum, polyhalite, carnallite, and anhydrite.

• **TESTS** Like halite, sylvite is soluble in cold water. It has a bitter taste.

CUBIC

interlocking cubic crystals

vitreous lustre on crystal faces

transparency around crystal margins

well formed, cube-shaped crystals

SG 1.99	Cleavage Perfect cubic	Fracture Uneven

Group Halides	Composition AgCl	Hardness 2½

CHLORARGYRITE

Crystals are rare. This mineral usually occurs in massive or flaky habits, or as crusts and waxy coatings. Chlorargyrite is colourless when fresh, but varies from grey to green or yellow on exposure to light, eventually turning purple-brown. It ranges from transparent to nearly opaque. The lustre is resinous to adamantine.

• **FORMATION** Forms as a secondary mineral in oxidation zones of silver deposits.

• **TESTS** Chlorargyrite is malleable at ordinary temperatures, and melts in a candle flame. It is soluble in ammonia, but not in nitric acid.

crusty chlorargyrite

CUBIC

limonite groundmass

SG 5.55	Cleavage None	Fracture Uneven to subconchoidal

Group Halides	Composition $KMgCl_3.6H_2O$	Hardness 2

CARNALLITE

This mineral rarely forms crystals. When crystals occur, they are pseudohexagonal, and have a pyramidal shape. The usual habits are granular or massive. Carnallite is white or colourless, though it can be reddish in colour due to minute inclusions of the iron oxide mineral, hematite. Carnallite varies between transparent and translucent. The lustre is greasy, and has a shiny appearance.

• **FORMATION** Forms in thick sequences of evaporites, including gypsum, anhydrite, halite (rock salt), and sylvite, in association with sedimentary rocks, such as marl, clay, and dolomite.

• **TESTS** Carnallite has a bitter, salty taste, and is deliquescent. It fuses easily, turning the flame violet, which indicates the presence of potassium.

granular surface

massive habit

ORTHORHOMBIC

reddish colour due to inclusions of hematite

greasy lustre, with shiny, reflective surfaces

SG 1.6	Cleavage None	Fracture Conchoidal

Group Halides	Composition Na_3AlF_6	Hardness 2½

CRYOLITE

This mineral forms pseudocubic and short, prismatic crystals; twinning is common. It can also occur in massive or granular habits. Cryolite can be colourless, white, yellowish, brown, or reddish. The streak is white. The mineral is transparent to translucent, and has a vitreous or greasy lustre.

• **FORMATION** Forms in igneous rocks, especially acid pegmatites.

• **TESTS** It is almost invisible in water because it has a similar refractive index. It fuses very easily, the flame being coloured yellow, which indicates the presence of sodium. The transparent globule produced by melting becomes opaque as it cools down.

cuboidal outline

MONOCLINIC

vitreous lustre

transparency at edges

SG 2.97	Cleavage None	Fracture Uneven

Group Halides	Composition $Pb_{26}Ag_{10}Cu_{24}Cl_{62}(OH)_{48}.3H_2O$	Hardness 3–3½

BOLEITE

This mineral forms cubic and octahedral crystals in the cubic system. (Some mineralogists put boleite into the tetragonal system.) The colour is a deep, rich indigo blue, and the streak is blue with a greenish tinge. Boleite is a translucent mineral. Although the crystal faces have a vitreous lustre, the cleavage surfaces are pearly.

• **FORMATION** Forms with a number of other secondary lead minerals, in the leached zone of lead deposits. These minerals include cumengite, and pseudoboleite.

• **TESTS** Boleite is soluble in nitric acid. A further aid to identification is that the mineral fuses easily.

gypsum groundmass

uneven fracture on broken surfaces

twinned boleite crystals

cubic boleite crystals

CUBIC

SG 5.0–5.1	Cleavage Perfect	Fracture Uneven

Group Halides	Composition $Cu_2Cl(OH)_3$	Hardness 3–3½

ATACAMITE

This mineral forms thin, prismatic and tabular crystals, which are often twinned. The crystal faces are frequently striated. Atacamite can also occur in massive, fibrous, and granular habits. The colour varies from bright green to very dark green, and the streak is apple green. This is a transparent to translucent mineral. It has a vitreous to adamantine lustre.

• **FORMATION** Forms in the oxidized regions of copper deposits, as a secondary mineral, in association with malachite, azurite, and quartz. Atacamite also forms around volcanic vents.

• **TESTS** Atacamite is soluble in hydrochloric acid, without any effervescence. It fuses in a flame easily, colouring the flame blue.

pale quartz, an associated mineral

dark green, prismatic atacamite crystals

bright green malachite, an associated mineral

ORTHORHOMBIC

SG 3.76	Cleavage Perfect	Fracture Conchoidal

Group Halides	Composition CaF_2		Hardness 4

FLUORITE

The crystals formed by this mineral are cubes and octahedra, and are often twinned. Fluorite may also be in massive, granular, and compact habits. It occurs in a great variety of colours, ranging from purple, green, colourless, white, and yellow, to pink, red, blue, and black. The streak is white. Fluorite is a transparent to translucent mineral, and has a vitreous lustre. If broken, its perfect octahedral cleavage produces triangular shapes on the corners of the cubic crystals.

• **FORMATION** Forms in hydrothermal veins, and around hot springs. Fluorite is a fairly common mineral, and is associated with quartz, calcite, dolomite, galena, pyrite, chalcopyrite, sphalerite, barite, and various other hydrothermal-vein minerals.

• **TESTS** As its name suggests, it can be strongly fluorescent in ultra-violet light.

PURPLE FLUORITE

• *octahedral crystal, showing translucency*

GREEN FLUORITE

• *transparent*

• *twinned cubes*

YELLOW FLUORITE

• *twinning*

vitreous lustre •

• *striations on crystal faces*

octahedral crystal •

BLUE JOHN

alternating light and dark bands •

• *vitreous lustre*

PINK FLUORITE

CUBIC

SG 3.18	Cleavage Perfect octahedral	Fracture Conchoidal

Group Halides	Composition $Pb_2CuCl_2(OH)_4$	Hardness $2\frac{1}{2}$

DIABOLEITE

This mineral forms as tabular crystals, which often have a square outline, and which are usually very small. Diaboleite can also occur in a massive or granular habit, and as aggregates of thin plates. It is deep blue in colour, and has a pale blue-coloured streak. It is a transparent to translucent mineral, and it has a vitreous lustre on fresh surfaces.

• **FORMATION** Diaboleite forms where original minerals have been secondarily altered. This may occur when fluids from the earth's surface, or rising from below, react with existing rocks and minerals. Its formation is associated with several other similar minerals, such as linarite, boleite and cerussite.

• **TESTS** Gives off water if heated in a closed tube.

vitreous lustre

rock groundmass

aggregates of very small diaboleite crystals

weathered rock

TETRAGONAL

SG 5.42	Cleavage Perfect basal	Fracture Conchoidal

Group Halides	Composition $NaSr_3Al_3(F,OH)_{16}$	Hardness $4–4\frac{1}{2}$

JARLITE

This mineral can sometimes form as very small tabular crystals. More commonly, however, the habit is massive. Jarlite is usually white in colour, but it can also be brown, grey, or colourless. The streak is white. It is a transparent to translucent mineral, and has a vitreous lustre on crystal faces.

• **FORMATION** This unusual mineral forms in two main geological situations. It occurs with another halide, cryolite, in pegmatites, and can also be found in mica schists. These rocks are formed by medium grade regional metamorphism, and are produced at considerable depth in the earth's crust. In this situation, jarlite is most likely to be found with topaz and fluorite.

• **TESTS** Gives off water if heated in a closed tube.

small, jarlite crystals

barite, an associated mineral

MONOCLINIC

SG 3.87	Cleavage Not determined	Fracture Uneven

OXIDES AND HYDROXIDES

OXIDES are composed of elements combined with oxygen. A particularly common example is the iron oxide, hematite, which is iron combined with oxygen (O). Oxides form a variable group, occurring in many geological environments and in most rock types. Some, such as hematite, magnetite (another iron oxide), cassiterite (tin oxide), and chromite (chromium oxide), are important ores of metals. Others, like corundum (aluminium oxide), have gemstone varieties, such as ruby and sapphire. The properties of the oxides are varied. The gem varieties, and metallic ores, are very hard, and of high specific gravity. They also vary considerably in colour, from the rich red of ruby, the blue of sapphire, and the red, green, and blue of spinel (magnesium, aluminium oxide), to the black of magnetite.

———— • ————

Hydroxides form when a metallic element combines with water and hydroxyl (OH). A common example is brucite (magnesium hydroxide). Hydroxides, formed through a chemical reaction between an oxide and water, are usually of low hardness: brucite, for example, has a hardness of 2½; gibbsite (aluminum hydroxide) is 2½–3½.

Group Oxides	Composition $MgAl_2O_4$	Hardness 7½–8

SPINEL

This mineral forms as octahedral and sometimes cubic or dodecahedral crystals. Other habits are massive, granular, and compact. The colour ranges from red, to green, blue, brown, and black. The streak is white. Spinel is transparent to opaque, and has a vitreous lustre.

• **FORMATION** Forms in a variety of metamorphic rocks, including serpentinites, gneiss, and marble, as well as in igneous rocks of basic chemistry.

• **TESTS** A characteristic of this mineral is that it is infusible. Picotite is the chromium-rich variety, and pleonaste is the dark, iron-rich variety of spinel.

dark octahedral pleonaste crystal in groundmass

PLEONASTE

octahedral crystal •

CUBIC

RUBY SPINEL

quartz groundmass

SG 3.5–4.1	Cleavage None	Fracture Conchoidal to uneven

Group Oxides	Composition ZnO	Hardness 4–4½

ZINCITE

Pyramidal, hemimorphic crystals are formed by this mineral, but only rarely. Usually, zincite occurs in massive, granular, and foliated habits. The colour is dark red to orange-yellow. The streak is orange-yellow. Zincite is translucent to transparent, and it has a subadamantine lustre.

• FORMATION Forms in contact metamorphic rocks, and is associated with minerals such as calcite, willemite, franklinite, and tephrite. Zincite is an important zinc mineral, prized by collectors and mineralogists for its rarity.

• TESTS Zincite is soluble in hydrochloric acid, but shows no effervescence. It is fluorescent, and infusible when placed in a flame.

subadamantine lustre

mass of foliated zincite crystals

calcite groundmass

TRIGONAL / HEXAGONAL

SG 5.68	Cleavage Perfect	Fracture Conchoidal

Group Oxides	Composition $(Zn,Mn^{+2},Fe^{+2})(Fe^{+3},Mn^{+3})_2O_4$	Hardness 5½–6½

FRANKLINITE

This mineral is in the spinel group. It occurs as octahedral crystals, frequently with rounded edges, and in granular or massive habits. The colour is black, with a reddish brown to black streak. Franklinite is opaque, and it has a metallic lustre.

• FORMATION Forms in zinc deposits in metamorphosed limestones and dolomites. It is associated with a number of other minerals, including calcite, willemite, zincite, rhodonite, and garnet.

• TESTS This mineral is weakly magnetic. When heated in a flame, it becomes strongly magnetic, and is infusible. It is soluble in hydrochloric acid, with no effervescence.

octahedral franklinite crystal

uneven fracture

calcite groundmass

CUBIC

SG 5.07–5.22	Cleavage None	Fracture Uneven to subconchoidal

Group Oxides	Composition Cu_2O	Hardness 3½–4

CUPRITE

Crystals are octahedral, cubic, and dodecahedral; twinning is uncommon. Cuprite also occurs in massive, compact, and granular habits. The colour is red, and the streak a brownish red. Cuprite is a translucent to transparent mineral. When exposed to the air, it tarnishes to semi-opaque. It has an adamantine, submetallic, or earthy lustre.

• **FORMATION** This widespread mineral forms in the oxidized parts of copper deposits, where it is associated with native copper, malachite, azurite, chalcocine, and oxides of iron.

• **TESTS** It is soluble in nitric and other acids. It fuses, turning the flame green.

cubo-octahedral crystal

submetallic lustre

CUBIC

twinned crystals

adamantine lustre on crystal faces

SG 6.14	Cleavage Poor octahedral	Fracture Conchoidal to uneven

Group Oxides	Composition $FeCr_2O_4$	Hardness 5½

CHROMITE

The crystals are octahedral, but rarely occur. The usual habits are massive, granular, or nodular. Chromite is black to brownish black, and the streak is dark brown. This mineral is opaque, and has a metallic lustre.

• **FORMATION** Forms in igneous rocks, especially ultrabasic and basic rocks; placer deposits often contain chromite.

• **TESTS** Chromite is insoluble in acids, and is weakly magnetic. It is infusible when placed in a flame.

weathered, individual chromite crystals

CUBIC

nodular chromite

metallic lustre not seen on unbroken surfaces

serpentinite groundmass

SG 4.5–4.8	Cleavage None	Fracture Uneven

Group Oxides	Composition Fe_3O_4	Hardness 5½–6½

MAGNETITE

This common oxide mineral forms octahedral and dodecahedral crystals, and also occurs in massive and granular habits. The colour is black, and so is the streak. Magnetite is an opaque mineral. The lustre may be either metallic or dull.
• **FORMATION** Magnetite forms in igneous rocks, and also in veins and replacement deposits.
• **TESTS** As the name suggests, this mineral is highly magnetic, attracting iron filings. It will also deflect a compass needle.

granular habit of small particles

OCTAHEDRAL CRYSTAL

CUBIC

triangular crystal face

GRANULAR MAGNETITE

SG 5.2	Cleavage None	Fracture Subconchoidal to uneven

Group Oxides	Composition $FeTiO_3$	Hardness 5–6

ILMENITE

This mineral usually forms thick, tabular crystals; sometimes it forms rhombohedral crystals. Twinning is common. Other habits are lamellar, massive, compact, and granular. It is black or brownish black, with a black to brownish red streak. It is opaque. Ilmenite has a lustre ranging from metallic to dull.
• **FORMATION** Forms in many igneous rocks as an accessory mineral, including pegmatites, and in mineral veins. It is also found as a placer in black sands.
• **TESTS** Soluble in concentrated hydrochloric acid if powdered first. Weakly magnetic when cold.

twinned ilmenite crystals

TRIGONAL / HEXAGONAL

lamellar ilmenite

oligoclase feldspar groundmass

SG 4.72	Cleavage None	Fracture Conchoidal to uneven

Group Oxides	Composition Fe_2O_3		Hardness 5–6

HEMATITE

The crystals of this mineral are tabular, or rhombohedral, and occasionally prismatic or pyramidal. Tabular crystals may form as rosettes, when they are called iron roses. Other habits are massive, compact, columnar, fibrous, reniform, botryoidal, stalactitic, foliated, and granular. When hematite forms in a reniform habit, it is known as kidney ore. Its colour ranges from brownish, bright red, blood-red, and brownish red, to steel-grey, and iron-black. The streak is brownish red. It is an opaque mineral, with a metallic to dull lustre.

• **FORMATION** Occurs as a hydrothermal and replacement mineral. It also forms in igneous rocks as an accessory mineral.

• **TESTS** This mineral may become magnetic when heated.

HEXAGONAL HEMATITE

hexagonal outline

tabular habit

metallic lustre

KIDNEY ORE

specularite centres

rounded shapes

SPECULAR HEMATITE

prismatic quartz crystals

mass of specular hematite crystals

kidney ore groundmass

specular cavities

bright metallic lustre

weathered specimen, showing massive habit

TRIGONAL/ HEXAGONAL

MASSIVE HEMATITE

SG 5.26	Cleavage None	Fracture Uneven to subconchoidal

Group Oxides	Composition $BeAl_2O_4$	Hardness $8\frac{1}{2}$

CHRYSOBERYL

The chrysoberyl crystals are tabular or prismatic, and commonly twinned. Other habits are granular and massive. The colour varies from green or yellow to brownish, or grey. The gem variety, alexandrite, is green in daylight but is red in tungsten light. Chrysoberyl is a transparent to translucent mineral, and it has a vitreous lustre.

• **FORMATION** Forms in many rocks, including pegmatites, schists, gneisses, and marbles. Chrysoberyl also occurs in placer sands, which are alluvial deposits. Its occurrence here is largely due to its great hardness and resistance to weathering and erosion.

• **TESTS** It is an insoluble mineral.

vitreous lustre •

striations on • *crystal faces*

crystals are • *transparent to translucent*

tabular crystal •

• *twinned crystals*

ORTHORHOMBIC

SG 3.7–3.8	Cleavage Distinct prismatic	Fracture Conchoidal to uneven

Group Oxides	Composition SnO_2	Hardness 6 7

CASSITERITE

This mineral may form as short or slender prismatic, or bipyramidal, crystals. Other habits are massive, granular, botryoidal, and reniform. Typically, it is brown to black, but it may also be yellowish or colourless. The streak is white, grey, or brownish. Cassiterite is transparent to nearly opaque. The lustre is adamantine on crystal faces, and greasy when fractured.

• **FORMATION** Forms in high temperature hydrothermal veins, where associated minerals include quartz, chalcopyrite, and tourmaline. It also forms in some contact metamorphic rocks.

• **TESTS** This mineral is insoluble in acids. Cassiterite is also infusible.

adamantine lustre on crystal faces •

twinned • *crystals*

• *opaque*

short, prismatic • *crystals*

TETRAGONAL

SG 7.0	Cleavage Poor	Fracture Subconchoidal to uneven

Group Oxides	Composition Al_2O_3		Hardness 9

CORUNDUM

This mineral forms steep bipyramidal, prismatic, tabular, or rhombohedral crystals. It also occurs in massive and granular habits. Corundum can be many colours, but always has a white streak. It is transparent to translucent, with a vitreous to adamantine lustre.
• **FORMATION** Forms in silica-poor igneous rocks, and metamorphic rocks rich in aluminium.
• **TESTS** It is insoluble.

TRIGONAL/
HEXAGONAL

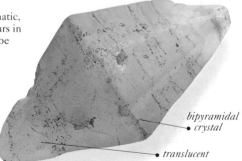

bipyramidal crystal

translucent

SG 4.0–4.1	Cleavage None	Fracture Conchoidal to uneven

Group Oxides	Composition Al_2O_3		Hardness 9

RUBY

A variety of corundum, ruby forms as bipyramidal, prismatic, tabular, or rhombohedral crystals. It is red in colour, and has a white-coloured streak. Ruby is translucent to transparent, with a vitreous or adamantine lustre.
• **FORMATION** Forms in igneous and metamorphic rocks. Because of its hardness and density, ruby also occurs in river gravels.
• **TESTS** Insoluble in acids.

TRIGONAL/
HEXAGONAL

vitreous lustre

ruby crystals in groundmass

ruby crystal

SG 4.0–4.1	Cleavage None	Fracture Conchoidal to uneven

Group Oxides	Composition Al_2O_3		Hardness 9

SAPPHIRE

The blue-coloured variety of corundum, sapphire forms as bipyramidal, prismatic, tabular, or rhombohedral crystals. Other habits are massive and granular. The streak is white. Sapphire is transparent to translucent, with a vitreous or adamantine lustre.
• **FORMATION** Sapphire forms in certain igneous and metamorphic rocks. It also occurs in sedimentary alluvial deposits.
• **TESTS** It is insoluble in acids, and infusible.

TRIGONAL/
HEXAGONAL

sapphire crystals in rock groundmass

bipyramidal crystal

SG 4.0–4.1	Cleavage None	Fracture Conchoidal to uneven

Group Oxides	Composition MnO_2	Hardness $2-6\frac{1}{2}$

PYROLUSITE

Crystals are prismatic, but very rare. The usual habits are massive, compact, columnar, or fibrous. Dendritic coatings are common. It is black to dark grey in colour, and has a black or bluish black streak. Pyrolusite is an opaque mineral, and it has a metallic to dull, or earthy lustre.

• **FORMATION** Forms as a precipitate in lakes and bogs, and also in nodules on the deep ocean bed. Pyrolusite is a secondary mineral in manganese veins.

• **TESTS** Soluble in hydro-chloric acid. It will leave sooty marks if touched.

dendritic habit on a rock surface

DENDRITIC PYROLUSITE

TETRAGONAL

• *dull lustre*

• *uneven fracture*

MASSIVE PYROLUSITE

SG 5.06	Cleavage Perfect	Fracture Uneven

Group Oxides	Composition $CaTiO_3$	Hardness $5\frac{1}{2}$

PEROVSKITE

This mineral forms pseudocubic crystals, with striations parallel to the edges. It also occurs as reniform masses. The colour is yellow, amber, dark brown, or black, and there is a colourless to pale grey streak. Perovskite is a transparent to opaque mineral, and it has a metallic to adamantine lustre.

• **FORMATION** Forms in certain basic and ultrabasic igneous rocks, schists rich in talc and chlorite, and in some marbles. Perovskite is also an accessory mineral in some rocks. An accessory mineral is not an important rock-former, and its presence does not influence the bulk chemistry or classification of the rock.

• **TESTS** It is soluble only in hot, sulphuric acid. Perovskite is infusible.

• *pseudocubic crystal*

striated crystal

ORTHORHOMBIC

SG 4.01	Cleavage Imperfect	Fracture Subconchoidal to uneven

Group Oxides	Composition TiO_2	Hardness 6–6½

RUTILE

Together with brookite an anatase, rutile forms a trimorphous series. The crystals are prismatic, and are often striated. Rutile also forms as very slender acicular crystals in quartz (rutilated quartz). Twinning is common. It can also be massive in habit. The colour is reddish brown, red, yellow, or black, and there is a pale brown to yellowish streak. Rutile is a transparent to opaque mineral, and it has a submetallic to adamantine lustre.
• **FORMATION** Forms as an accessory mineral in many igneous rocks, and also in metamorphic schists and gneisses. Thin needles sometimes form as inclusions ("cat's eye" and "star" asterism) in quartz, and corundum, and other transparent host minerals.
• **TESTS** This mineral is insoluble in various acids.

acicular crystals in quartz

RUTILATED QUARTZ

massive rutile

uneven fracture

rock groundmass

TETRAGONAL

MASSIVE RUTILE

SG 4.23	Cleavage Distinct	Fracture Conchoidal to uneven

Group Oxides	Composition TiO_2	Hardness 5½–6

BROOKITE

This mineral forms as tabular crystals, striated vertically, and also as prismatic crystals. The colour is brown, reddish brown, or brownish black. The streak can be white, grey, or yellowish. It is a transparent to opaque mineral, with an adamantine to submetallic lustre.
• **FORMATION** This mineral occurs in a number of geological situations. It forms in certain metamorphic rocks, especially high grade schists and gneisses, in veins cutting through the rock. It is often associated with quartz, rutile, and feldspars. It can also occur in sedimentary rocks as a detrital mineral, after being eroded from its original location and then being redeposited.
• **TESTS** It is insoluble in acids and infusible.

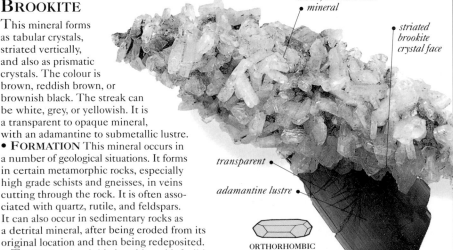

albite, an associated mineral

striated brookite crystal face

transparent

adamantine lustre

ORTHORHOMBIC

SG 4.1–4.2	Cleavage Poor	Fracture Subconchoidal to uneven

Group Oxides	Composition TiO_2	Hardness $5\frac{1}{2}$–6

ANATASE

The pyramidal crystals formed by anatase are often striated. Crystals may also be tabular, and these are often highly modified. The colour may be brown, deep blue, or black, and the streak is colourless, white, or pale yellow. Anatase is a transparent to nearly opaque mineral, and it has an adamantine to submetallic lustre.
• **FORMATION** This particular type of titanium dioxide forms in certain metamorphic rocks, especially schist and gneiss. It can also occur in some igneous rocks, such as diorite and granite, where it is an accessory mineral. Anatase is also found in placer deposits, after it has been removed from its original location and then redeposited alluvially.
• **TESTS** This mineral is insoluble in all acids.

small, bipyra-midal anatase crystal

albite, an associated mineral

opaque crystal

ORTHORHOMBIC

SG 3.82–3.97	Cleavage Perfect basal	Fracture Subconchoidal

Group Oxides	Composition UO_2	Hardness 5–6

URANINITE

Occurs as cubic, cubo-octahedral, octahedral, or dodecahedral crystals. More often, it forms in massive (when it is known as "pitchblende"), botryoidal, or granular habits. The colour and streak can be black to brownish black, or greyish black. Uraninite is an opaque mineral and it has a submetallic, greasy, dull, or pitchlike lustre.
• **FORMATION** It forms in hydrothermal veins. It also occurs in stratified sediment-ary rocks, such as sandstone and conglomerate, and in some igneous rocks, including pegmatites and granites.
• **TESTS** Uraninite is highly radioactive. It is infusible, and insoluble in hydrochloric acid. It does dissolve slowly, however, if put in nitric acid.

botryoidal habit

opaque

CUBIC

submetallic to dull lustre

SG 6.5–10.0	Cleavage Indistinct	Fracture Conchoidal to uneven

Group Oxides	Composition SiO_2	Hardness 7

QUARTZ

One of the most common minerals, quartz forms hexagonal prisms, terminated by rhombohedra, or pyramidal shapes. Quartz faces are often striated, and the crystals twinned and distorted. It also occurs in massive, granular, concretionary, stalactitic, and cryptocrystalline habits. The colouring is amazingly variable, and quartz may be white, grey, red, purple, pink, yellow, green, brown, and black, as well as being colourless. It is also the source of a wide variety of semi-precious gemstones – many of which are shown here. The streak is white. Quartz is a transparent to translucent mineral, and it has a vitreous lustre on fresh surfaces.

• **FORMATION** This mineral occurs commonly in igneous, metamorphic, and sedimentary rocks, and can be frequently found in mineral veins with metal ores.

• **TESTS** Quartz is insoluble, unless placed in hydrofluoric acid.

TRIGONAL/
HEXAGONAL

*milky quartz
groundmass*

SMOKY QUARTZ

vitreous lustre

ROSE QUARTZ

uneven fracture

*vitreous
lustre*

translucent

*mass of
pyramidal
crystals*

AMETHYST

SG 2.65	Cleavage None	Fracture Conchoidal to uneven

prismatic crystal

MILKY QUARTZ

transparent
specimens

ROCK CRYSTAL

vitreous lustre

prismatic
crystal habit

hexagonal
crystal

CITRINE

conchoidal
fracture

vitreous lustre
on crystal face

uneven
fracture at
base of crystal

Group Oxides	Composition SiO_2	Hardness 7

CHALCEDONY

A microcrystalline variety of silicon dioxide,
chalcedony usually occurs as mammillary or
botryoidal masses. The colour is highly variable,
and may be white, blue, red, green, brown, or
black. Varieties of chalcedony include jasper,
an opaque form; agate, a form with concentric
banding of different colours; moss agate, with
dark dendritic patterns; chrysoprase, a green
variety; and onyx, in which the banding is
parallel. Carnelian is red to reddish brown,
and sard is light to dark brown. There is a
white streak. Chalcedony is a transparent
to translucent, or opaque mineral, and it
has a vitreous to waxy lustre.
• **FORMATION** This mineral forms
in cavities in rocks of different types,
especially lavas. Much chalcedony
develops at relatively low temperatures, as a precipitate from silica-
rich solutions. It can also be
formed as a dehydration
product of opal.
• **TESTS** Its higher
specific gravity can help
to distinguish chalce-
dony from opal.

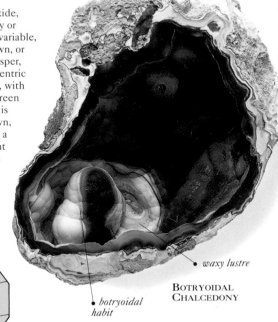

waxy lustre

*botryoidal
habit*

**BOTRYOIDAL
CHALCEDONY**

*TRIGONAL/
HEXAGONAL*

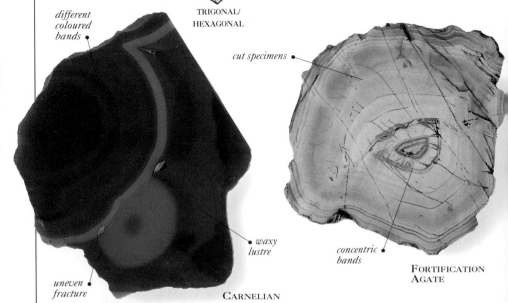

*different
coloured
bands*

cut specimens

*waxy
lustre*

*concentric
bands*

**FORTIFICATION
AGATE**

*uneven
fracture*

CARNELIAN

SG 2.65 ·	Cleavage None	Fracture Conchoidal

waxy lustre

mammillary
habit

JASPER

CHRYSOPRASE

bands of different
colours

uneven fracture

vitreous lustre

ONYX

parallel
bands

Group Oxides	Composition $(Fe,Mn)(Nb,Ta)_2O_6$	Hardness 6–6½

COLUMBITE

This mineral forms a series with tantalite. The crystals are tabular or prismatic, and commonly twinned. It also occurs in a massive habit. It is grey-black to brownish black, and may have an iridescent tarnish. The streak is dark red to black. This series is translucent to opaque, with a submetallic to resinous lustre.
• **FORMATION** Forms in granitic pegmatites.
• **TESTS** The specific gravity increases with tantalum content.

translucent to opaque

submetallic to resinous lustre

tabular crystal

ORTHORHOMBIC

SG 5.1–8.2	Cleavage Distinct	Fracture Subconchoidal to uneven

Group Oxides	Composition $(Y,Ce,U,Fe)_3(Nb,Ta,Ti)_5O_{15}$	Hardness 5–6

SAMARSKITE

This mineral occurs as prismatic crystals, which have a rectangular cross-section, and in massive or compact habits. The colour is black or brownish, and the streak is undetermined. Samarskite is a translucent to opaque mineral, and it has a resinous, vitreous, or submetallic lustre on fresh surfaces.
• **FORMATION** Forms in granitic pegmatites.
• **TESTS** It is soluble in hot acids, and radioactive.

iridescence

opaque

conchoidal fracture

ORTHORHOMBIC

SG 5.15–5.69	Cleavage Indistinct	Fracture Conchoidal

Group Oxides	Composition Mn_3O_4	Hardness 5½

HAUSMANNITE

The pseudo-octahedral and pyramidal crystals formed by hausmannite are frequently twinned. It also forms as granular masses. The colour is brownish black, and the streak is brown. Hausmannite is opaque, except in very thin fragments when it is translucent. It has a submetallic lustre.
• **FORMATION** Forms in rocks that have undergone contact metamorphism. It also occurs in hydrothermal veins.
• **TESTS** It is soluble in concentrated hydrochloric acid.

uneven fracture

pyramidal crystals

TETRAGONAL

SG 4.84	Cleavage Good	Fracture Uneven

Group Oxides	Composition Oxides and hydroxides	Hardness Soft

WAD

Not strictly a mineral, wad is a mixture of several oxide and hydroxide minerals, especially of manganese. It usually contains pyrolusite and psilomelane. It has an amorphous appearance, and may be reniform, arborescent, encrusting, or massive in habit. Wad is often a dull black colour, though it may be lead-grey, bluish, or brownish black. The streak is dark brown or blackish. It is an opaque mineral, with a dull or earthy lustre.
• **FORMATION** Occurs in sedimentary environments with manganese minerals
• **TESTS** When heated in a closed test tube, water is given off.

massive habit

rock groundmass

dull lustre

SG 2.8–4.4	Cleavage None	Fracture Uneven

Group Hydroxides	Composition $(Ba,H_2O)Mn^{+4},Mn^{+3})_5O_{10}$	Hardness 5–6

ROMANECHITE

MASSIVE ROMANECHITE

In the past, psilomelane has been used as the name of an individual mineral. However, recent studies have found that the psilomelane is actually the amorphous species, romanechite. It forms in massive, botryoidal, reniform, stalactitic, and earthy habits. It is black to dark grey, and the streak is black, or brownish black, and shining. It is opaque, with a submetallic lustre.
• **FORMATION** Forms by the alteration of other minerals, especially manganese-rich silicates and carbonates. Romanechite is a common mineral, and forms in concretions, and where limestones have been replaced by other materials.
• **TESTS** It is soluble in hydrochloric acid, giving off chlorine gas. It gives off water if heated in a closed test tube.

massive habit

BOTRYOIDAL ROMANECHITE

botryoidal habit

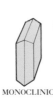

MONOCLINIC

opaque

submetallic lustre

SG 6.4	Cleavage Not determined	Fracture Uneven

Group Oxides	Composition Pyrochlore (Na,Ca,U)$_2$(Nb,Ta,Ti)$_2$O$_6$(OH,F)	Hardness 5–5½

PYROCHLORE-MICROLITE

This series of minerals forms as octahedral crystals, which are sometimes twinned. Other habits are as grains and irregular masses. Its colour is brown, reddish brown, or black. The streak is yellowish to brown. The series is translucent to opaque, and has a vitreous to resinous lustre.
• **FORMATION** Forms in pegmatites and carbonatites. Pyrochlore-Microlite is also found as an accessory mineral in nepheline syenites.
• **TESTS** Microlite's composition excludes uranium (U), niobium (Nb), and titanium (Ti). This series of minerals is infusible. It is soluble in hydrochloric acid, but only with great difficulty. A number of elements, such as thorium and uranium, can replace calcium and sodium in the chemical structure, when the mineral becomes radioactive.

quartz groundmass

PYROCHLORE

twinned pyrochlore crystals

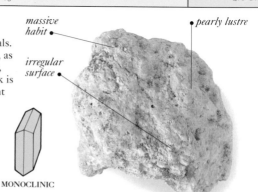

MICROLITE

vitreous lustre

twinned octahedra

CUBIC

uneven fracture on surfaces

SG 4.3–5.7	Cleavage Distinct	Fracture Subconchoidal to uneven

Group Hydroxides	Composition Al(OH)$_3$	Hardness 2½–3½

GIBBSITE

Forms tabular, pseudohexagonal crystals. Gibbsite also occurs in a massive habit, as coatings, and as crusts. It is white, grey, greenish, pinkish, or reddish; the streak is undetermined. Gibbsite is a transparent to translucent mineral, and it has a vitreous to pearly lustre.
• **FORMATION** Forms in hydro-thermal veins, and as an alteration product of aluminium minerals.
• **TESTS** Gibbsite smells of wet clay when you breathe over it.

massive habit

pearly lustre

irregular surface

MONOCLINIC

SG 2.4	Cleavage Perfect	Fracture Uneven

Group Oxides	Composition $SiO_2 \cdot nH_2O$		Hardness $5\frac{1}{2}$–$6\frac{1}{2}$

OPAL

iron nodule

The structure of opal is amorphous. It forms in a great variety of habits, including massive, botryoidal, reniform, stalactitic, globular, nodular, and concretionary. Precious opal is milky white, or black, with a brilliant interplay of colours, commonly red, blue, and yellow. The colours often change as a result of the warming of water in the mineral. Precious opals warmed in the hand, for example, will be particularly brilliant. Fire opal is orange or reddish, and may or may not have an interplay of colours. Common opal is grey, black, or green, and has no interplay of colours. The streak is white. Opal is transparent to opaque. Its lustre varies from vitreous to resinous, waxy or pearly, though vitreous is the most common lustre.

• **FORMATION** Forms at low temperatures from silica-rich water, especially around hot springs, but it can occur in almost any geological environment.

• **TESTS** Opal often fluoresces in ultra-violet light, and is insoluble in acids. When heated, it decomposes, and may turn into quartz as the water molecules are removed. When opal is exposed to air for any length of time, the mineral structure becomes fragile because of the loss of water and infilling with fractures.

nodule broken to reveal opal

PRECIOUS OPAL

concentric bands, representing the growth rings from a tree

WOOD OPAL

red colouring typical of fire opal

vitreous lustre on freshly broken surfaces

resinous lustre

FIRE OPAL

conchoidal fracture well displayed

SG 1.9–2.3	Cleavage None	Fracture Conchoidal

Group Hydroxides	Composition $Mg(OH)_2$		Hardness $2\frac{1}{2}$

BRUCITE

CRYSTALLINE BRUCITE

This mineral forms as broad, tabular crystals. It can be massive, foliated, fibrous (nemalite), and granular in habit. It is white, pale green, grey, bluish, and, when it contains manganese, yellow to brown in colour. There is a white streak. Brucite is transparent. It has a waxy, vitreous, or pearly lustre (the fibrous varieties are silky). Flexible, inelastic laminae are produced from the perfect cleavage when this mineral is carefully broken.

• **FORMATION** Forms in metamorphosed lime- stones, and in schists, and serpentinites.

• **TESTS** Brucite is soluble in hydrochloric acid, with no effervescence. It is also infusible.

• *tabular crystal*

• *fibrous habit*

TRIGONAL / HEXAGONAL

• *silky lustre*

NEMALITE

SG 2.38–2.40	Cleavage Perfect	Fracture Uneven

Group Hydroxides	Composition FeO(OH)		Hardness 5–5½

GOETHITE

This mineral sometimes occurs as vertically striated, prismatic crystals, but more frequently as massive, botryoidal, stalactitic, and earthy specimens. The colour is blackish brown, or reddish to yellowish brown. The streak is orange to brownish. Goethite is opaque. The lustre is adamantine on crystal faces, and otherwise dull.

• **FORMATION** Goethite forms by the oxidation of iron-rich deposits.

• **TESTS** Turns magnetic when heated.

striated goethite • *crystals*

groundmass • *of quartz*

ORTHORHOMBIC

SG 3.3–4.3	Cleavage Perfect	Fracture Uneven

Group Hydroxides	Composition FeO(OH).nH$_2$O	Hardness 5–5½

LIMONITE

Crystals are not formed by limonite. It is an amorphous material, and occurs in earthy masses, concretions, mammillary, and stalactitic forms, with a radiating fibrous structure. It often occurs as a pseudomorph after pyrite and other iron minerals. The colour is yellow, brownish yellow, brown, and blackish. There is a yellow-brown streak. It is translucent or semi-opaque, and has a vitreous, submetallic, silky, or dull lustre.

• **FORMATION** Forms as a secondary mineral in the oxidation zones of iron deposits. Limonite also occurs by precipitation in the sea and fresh water, and in bogs.

• **TESTS** This mineral gives off water when heated in a closed test tube. Dissolves very slowly in acid.

earthy mass

specimen has dull lustre

SG 2.7–4.3	Cleavage None	Fracture Uneven

Group Hydroxides	Composition MnO(OH)	Hardness 4

MANGANITE

This mineral forms as striated, prismatic crystals, which are often in bundles. Twinning is common. It also occurs in massive, fibrous, columnar, granular, concretionary, and stalactitic habits. It is dark grey to black. There is a reddish brown to black streak. Manganite is an opaque mineral, and it has a submetallic lustre.

• **FORMATION** Forms in low temperature hydrothermal veins, and also in shallow marine deposits, lakes, and bogs. Some manganite is deposited from meteoric water circulating underground. It is often partially altered to pyrolusite by fluids circulating in, and on, the earth's surface. Its own crystal form remains unchanged.

• **TESTS** Soluble in hydrochloric acid, and gives off chlorine.

opaque

prismatic, striated crystals

submetallic lustre

MONOCLINIC

SG 4.3	Cleavage Perfect	Fracture Uneven

Group Hydroxides	Composition $FeO(OH)$ and $Al_2O_32H_2O$	Hardness 1–3

BAUXITE

A mixture of several minerals, bauxite's composition includes hydrated aluminium oxide, gibbsite, boehmite, diaspore, and iron oxides. Strictly speaking, bauxite should be classified as a rock, but it is sometimes grouped with minerals. The varied composition means that its properties are also variable. The habit is generally massive, concretionary, oolitic, or pisolitic. The colour varies from white to yellowish, or red, and reddish brown. The streak is normally white. Bauxite has a dull or earthy lustre, and is opaque.
• **FORMATION** Forms by the weathering and decay of rocks that contain aluminium silicates. This is most likely to occur under tropical conditions, when heavy rains leach the silicates from the rock, leaving behind the aluminium minerals.
• **TESTS** Bauxite smells of wet clay if breathed on. It is infusible, and virtually insoluble.

pisolitic habit

rounded fragments in groundmass

SG 2.3–2.7	Cleavage None	Fracture Uneven

Group Hydroxides	Composition $AlO(OH)$	Hardness 6½–7

DIASPORE

This mineral forms as platy, acicular, or tabular crystals, as well as in massive, foliated, scaly, or stalactitic habits. It is frequently disseminated and granular. The colour may be white, colourless, greyish, yellowish, greenish, brown, purple, or pink. There is a white streak. Diaspore is a transparent to translucent mineral. The lustre is vitreous, but pearly on cleavages.
• **FORMATION** Forms in altered igneous rocks and in marbles. It occurs with many minerals, including magnetite, spinel, dolomite, chlorite, and corundum. Diaspore is also found in clay deposits, when it occurs with bauxite and aluminium-rich clay minerals.
• **TESTS** It is insoluble, and infusible.

vitreous lustre

emery groundmass

platy habit

translucent to transparent

ORTHORHOMBIC

SG 3.3–3.5	Cleavage Perfect	Fracture Conchoidal

Group Hydroxides	Composition $FeO(OH)$		Hardness 5

LEPIDOCROCITE

This mineral may form as flattened, platy crystals, but it more commonly occurs in massive or fibrous habits. The colour is deep red to reddish brown, and the streak is orange. Lepidocrocite is a transparent mineral, and it has a submetallic lustre.
• **FORMATION** Forms with minerals such as goethite, as a secondary mineral.
• **TESTS** It is strongly magnetic when heated. It dissolves slowly in hydrochloric acid, but much more quickly in nitric acid.

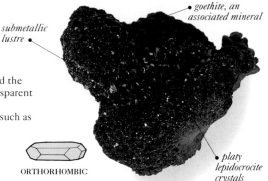

submetallic lustre

goethite, an associated mineral

platy lepidocrocite crystals

ORTHORHOMBIC

SG 3.9	Cleavage Perfect	Fracture Uneven

Group Oxides	Composition $WO_3.H_2O$		Hardness 1–2½

TUNGSTITE

Crystals are microscopic and platy, but rarely occur. Tungstite more commonly forms in massive, earthy, or powdery habits. The colour may be yellow, or yellowish green, and the streak is yellow. It is a transparent to translucent mineral, with an earthy or resinous lustre.
• **FORMATION** Forms in environments where primary tungsten minerals have been altered.
• **TESTS** Tungstite is soluble in alkaline solutions, but it is insoluble in acids.

resinous lustre

quartz groundmass

earthy tungstite

ORTHORHOMBIC

SG 5.5	Cleavage Perfect	Fracture Uneven

Group Hydroxides	Composition $Sb^{+3}Sb_2^{+5}O_6(OH)$		Hardness 4–5½

STIBICONITE

This mineral may be prismatic after the shape of the mineral it replaced. The usual habits are massive, compact, or botryoidal, though stibiconite also forms in crusts. The colour is white to pale yellowish; it may also be orange, brown, grey, or black, due to impurities. The streak is yellow-white. It is transparent to translucent, with a pearly to earthy lustre.
• **FORMATION** Forms by the alteration of stibnite.
• **TESTS** Gives off water when heated in a closed test tube.

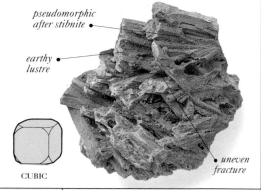

pseudomorphic after stibnite

earthy lustre

uneven fracture

CUBIC

SG 3.3–5.5	Cleavage Not determined	Fracture Uneven

CARBONATES, NITRATES, AND BORATES

CARBONATES ARE compounds in which one or more metallic or semi-metallic elements combine with the $(CO_3)^{-2}$ carbonate radical. Calcite, the commonest carbonate, forms when calcium combines with the carbonate radical. When barium substitutes for calcium, witherite is formed; when manganese substitutes, rhodochrosite is formed. Carbonates usually form well-developed rhombohedral crystals.

They tend to dissolve readily in hydrochloric acid, and are generally vividly coloured.

Nitrates are compounds in which one or more metallic elements combine with the nitrate $(NO_2)^{-1}$ radical (e.g. nitratine). Borates, also included in this section, are formed when metallic elements combine with the borate $(BO_3)^{-3}$ radical (e.g. ulexite, colemanite).

Group Carbonates	Composition $CaCO_3$		Hardness 3½–4

ARAGONITE

The prismatic and elongated crystals formed by aragonite are often twinned. If intergrown, such twins may produce pseudo-hexagonal forms. The habit can also be columnar, stalactitic, fibrous, radiating, and coral-like, when it is called flos ferri, meaning "flower of iron". Aragonite is white, colourless, grey, yellowish, green, blue, violet, reddish, or brown. There is a white streak. It is transparent to translucent, and has a vitreous lustre.
• **FORMATION** Widespread, forming in metamorphic and sedimentary rocks, in caves in limestone areas, in mineral veins, and around hot springs.
• **TESTS** It is soluble in cold, dilute hydrochloric acid, with effervescence, and is often fluorescent under ultra-violet light.

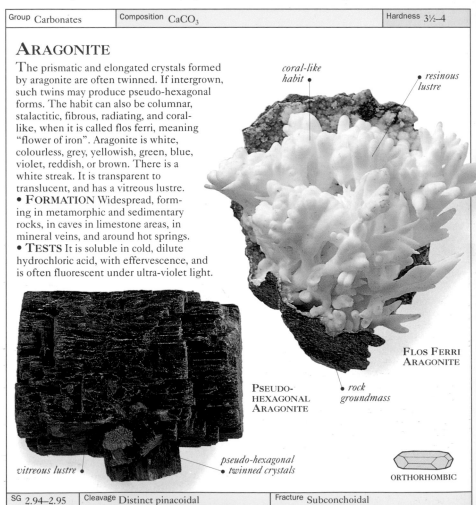

coral-like habit

resinous lustre

FLOS FERRI ARAGONITE

PSEUDO-HEXAGONAL ARAGONITE

rock groundmass

vitreous lustre

pseudo-hexagonal twinned crystals

ORTHORHOMBIC

SG 2.94–2.95	Cleavage Distinct pinacoidal		Fracture Subconchoidal

Group Carbonates	Composition $CaCO_3$		Hardness 3

CALCITE

Crystals are rhombohedral and scalenohedral, with combinations producing nail-head and dog-tooth forms. Iceland spar rhombs show double refraction. Twinning is common. Calcite can also form in massive, granular, fibrous, and stalactitic habits. It is white, colourless, grey, red, brown, green, and black. The streak is white to greyish. Calcite is transparent to translucent, with a vitreous to pearly or dull lustre.
• **FORMATION** Forms in many rocks. Calcite makes up the bulk of limestones and marbles.
• **TESTS** It effervesces with cold, dilute hydrochloric acid.

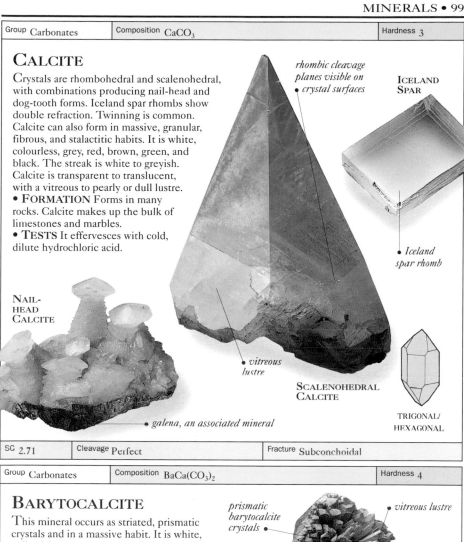

rhombic cleavage planes visible on • crystal surfaces

ICELAND SPAR

• *Iceland spar rhomb*

NAIL-HEAD CALCITE

• *vitreous lustre*

SCALENOHEDRAL CALCITE

• *galena, an associated mineral*

TRIGONAL/ HEXAGONAL

SG 2.71	Cleavage Perfect	Fracture Subconchoidal

Group Carbonates	Composition $BaCa(CO_3)_2$		Hardness 4

BARYTOCALCITE

This mineral occurs as striated, prismatic crystals and in a massive habit. It is white, yellowish, grey, or greenish. Barytocalcite is transparent to translucent, and has a vitreous or resinous lustre.
• **FORMATION** Forms in hydrothermal veins – faults or joints in the rock strata that have been invaded by hot, chemically active fluids. The veins may be derived from residual liquids, associated with granitic magmas, and brines trapped in buried marine sediments. Minerals are formed from the chemical elements carried in these fluids.
• **TESTS** This mineral effervesces with hydrochloric acid.

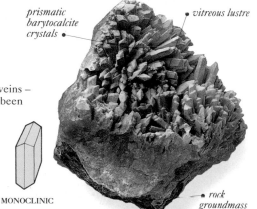

prismatic barytocalcite crystals •

• *vitreous lustre*

MONOCLINIC

• *rock groundmass*

SG 3.66–3.71	Cleavage Perfect	Fracture Subconchoidal to uneven

Group Carbonates	Composition MnCO₃	Hardness 3½–4

RHODOCHROSITE

This mineral sometimes forms as rhombohedral, scalenohedral, prismatic, or tabular crystals. More often, rhodochrosite occurs in massive, granular, stalactitic, globular, nodular, or botryoidal habits. The colour is typically pink to red, though it may also be brown, orange, or yellowish. The streak is white. Transparent to translucent, rhodochrosite has a vitreous to pearly lustre.
• **FORMATION** Forms in hydrothermal veins, and in altered manganese deposits.
• **TESTS** Rhodochrosite is soluble in warm hydrochloric acid, with effervescence.

RHODOCHROSITE CRYSTALS

• *rhombohedral crystals*

BANDED RHODOCHROSITE

• *nodular specimen, cut open to show concentric banding*

TRIGONAL / HEXAGONAL

SG 3.7	Cleavage Perfect rhombohedral	Fracture Uneven

Group Carbonates	Composition CaMg(CO₃)₂	Hardness 3½–4

DOLOMITE

The crystals are rhombohedral with curved faces, which become "saddle-shaped". Dolomite may also form in massive and granular habits. It is colourless, white, grey, pink, or brown; the streak is white. Ranging from transparent to translucent, it has a vitreous to pearly lustre.
• **FORMATION** Forms in hydrothermal veins, and in magnesian limestones.
• **TESTS** It dissolves slowly in cold, dilute hydrochloric acid. This is a good test for distinguishing it from calcite, which reacts vigorously, effervescing.

quartz groundmass •

curved crystal faces •

twinned dolomite crystals •

TRIGONAL / HEXAGONAL

SG 2.85	Cleavage Perfect rhombohedral	Fracture Subconchoidal

Group Carbonates	Composition $Ca(Fe,Mg,Mn)(CO_3)_2$	Hardness $3\frac{1}{2}-4$

ANKERITE

This mineral, which is part of a group with dolomite, forms rhombohedral crystals. Other habits in which it occurs are massive and granular. Ankerite is white, grey, yellowish brown, or brown in colour, and the streak is white. This is a translucent mineral, with a vitreous to pearly lustre.

• **FORMATION** Ankerite forms in mineral veins, sometimes with gold and sulphides.

• **TESTS** Ankerite is soluble when placed in hydrochloric acid.

twinned, rhombohedral crystals

pearly lustre

TRIGONAL /
HEXAGONAL

SG 2.97	Cleavage Perfect rhombohedral	Fracture Subconchoidal

Group Carbonates	Composition $ZnCO_3$	Hardness $4-4\frac{1}{2}$

SMITHSONITE

This mineral forms rhombohedral crystals, often with curved faces; sometimes it forms scalenohedral crystals. Smithsonite may also occur in massive, botryoidal, reniform, granular, and stalactitic habits. It can be white, grey, yellow, green, blue, pink, purple, or brown. The streak is white. This is a translucent mineral, and it has a vitreous or pearly lustre.

• **FORMATION**
Forms in parts of oxidized copper-zinc deposits. It is associated with malachite, azurite, pyromorphite, cerussite, and hemimorphite.

• **TESTS** It is soluble in hydrochloric acid.

small rounded masses indicate botryoidal habit

BLUE SMITHSONITE

pearly lustre

rock groundmass

botryoidal smithsonite

WHITE SMITHSONITE

TRIGONAL /
HEXAGONAL

SG 4.3–4.45	Cleavage Perfect rhombohedral	Fracture Subconchoidal to uneven

Group Carbonates	Composition $FeCO_3$	Hardness 4

SIDERITE

This mineral forms as rhombohedral, tabular, prismatic, and scalenohedral crystals, often with curved faces, and sometimes twinned. It also occurs in massive, granular, compact, botryoidal, and oolitic habits. Siderite is pale yellowish, grey, brown, greenish, reddish, or almost black in colour. The streak is white. It is a translucent mineral, and it has a vitreous, pearly, or silky lustre.

• FORMATION Forms in hydrothermal veins, as well as in sedimentary strata.

• TESTS Siderite becomes magnetic when heated, and it dissolves slowly in cold hydrochloric acid. When the acid is heated, the solution effervesces.

RHOMBOHEDRAL
SIDERITE

twinned crystals

weathered limestone groundmass

TRIGONAL /
HEXAGONAL

botryoidal siderite

pearly lustre

BOTRYOIDAL
SIDERITE

SG 3.96	Cleavage Perfect rhombohedral	Fracture Uneven

Group Carbonates	Composition $MgCO_3$	Hardness 3–4

MAGNESITE

This mineral forms as rhombohedral crystals and, rarely, as prismatic, tabular, or scalenohedral crystals. It also occurs in massive, lamellar, fibrous, and granular habits. It may be colourless, white, grey, yellowish, or brown; the streak is white. It varies from transparent to translucent, and has a vitreous or dull lustre.

• FORMATION Forms in hydrothermal veins, metamorphic rocks, and sediments.

• TESTS Magnesite is soluble in warm hydrochloric acid, with effervescence.

serpentine, an associated mineral

perfect rhombohedral cleavage

phlogopite, an associated mineral

uneven fracture

magnesite cleavage mass

TRIGONAL /
HEXAGONAL

SG 3.0–3.1	Cleavage Perfect rhombohedral	Fracture Conchoidal to uneven

Group Carbonates	Composition $BaCO_3$	Hardness 3–3½

WITHERITE

The crystals form as twinned prismatic, often pseudohexagonal, dipyramids. Witherite also occurs in massive, granular, fibrous, and columnar habits. It may be colourless, white, grey, yellow, green, or brown, with a white streak. Transparent to translucent, it has a vitreous to resinous lustre.
• **FORMATION** Forms in hydrothermal veins,with quartz, calcite, and barite.
• **TESTS** Witherite is soluble in dilute hydrochloric acid, with effervescence. Barium in the structure raises specific gravity. Powdered witherite colours a flame apple green.

twinned witherite crystals

galena, an associated mineral

translucent witherite crystals

striations on crystal face

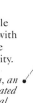

ORTHORHOMBIC

SG 4.29	Cleavage Distinct	Fracture Uneven

Group Carbonates	Composition $SrCO_3$	Hardness 3½

STRONTIANITE

This mineral forms in prismatic, often acicular, crystals. It also occurs in massive, granular, fibrous, and concretionary habits. It may be white, colourless, grey, yellowish, brownish, greenish, or reddish; the streak is consistently white. Strontianite is a transparent to translucent mineral, and has a vitreous to resinous lustre.
• **FORMATION** Forms in hydrothermal veins, and in hollows in limestone and marl. Strontianite also forms in sulphide-rich veins, associated with galena, sphalerite, and chalcopyrite; it is also associated with carbonates, such as calcite and dolomite, and with quartz.
• **TESTS** This mineral is soluble in dilute hydrochloric acid, with effervescence. Strontianite colours a flame crimson, if powdered before it is tested.

vitreous lustre

acicular crystal habit

translucent crystal face

twinned crystals

striations on crystal face

ORTHORHOMBIC

SG 3.78	Cleavage Perfect prismatic	Fracture Uneven

Group Carbonates	Composition $PbCO_3$	Hardness 3–3½

CERUSSITE

Crystals are often tabular, but can be acicular. Clusters of twinned crystals are common. Cerussite also occurs in massive, granular, compact, and stalactitic habits. It is often white or colourless, but can be grey, greenish, or blue in colour, as a result of inclusions, such as lead. The streak is white. Cerussite is transparent to translucent, and it has an adamantine, vitreous, or resinous lustre.
• FORMATION Forms in the altered parts of mineral veins, with lead, copper, and zinc.
• TESTS Soluble in acids, in particular dilute nitric acid, when it produces effervescence. Sometimes it fluoresces in ultra-violet light.

striations on crystal faces

ORTHORHOMBIC

twinned, tabular crystals

prismatic cleavage

vitreous lustre

SG 6.55	Cleavage Distinct prismatic	Fracture Conchoidal

Group Carbonates	Composition $Mg_2CO_3(OH)_2.3H_2O$	Hardness 2½

ARTINITE

This mineral forms as sprays of acicular crystals. It can also occur as fibrous aggregates, which frequently radiate, and as spherical masses. The colour and streak are white. It is a transparent mineral. The crystals have a vitreous lustre, and the fibrous aggregates are silky.
• FORMATION Artinite is found in ultrabasic igneous rocks that have been oxidized by a process called serpent-inization, which is similar to metamorphism, and which is brought about by fluids permeating the rocks.
• TESTS Artinite dissolves readily in dilute cold acids, with effervescence. It does not fuse, but gives off water and carbon dioxide when it is heated in a flame.

silky lustre on aggregates

serpentine, an associated mineral

small radiating artinite crystals

MONOCLINIC

SG 2.0	Cleavage Perfect	Fracture Uneven

Group Carbonates	Composition $Cu_2CO_3(OH)_2$	Hardness $3\frac{1}{2}$–4

MALACHITE

When they occur, crystals are acicular or prismatic, and often twinned. More usual habits are stalactitic, botryoidal masses with a fibrous, banded structure, and crusts. Malachite is a rich green, and has a pale green streak. It is translucent to opaque, and it has a vitreous to adamantine lustre on crystal faces; fibrous habits have a silky lustre.
• **FORMATION** Forms in the altered and oxidized regions of copper deposits, often with secondary minerals, including azurite.
• **TESTS** It is soluble in dilute hydrochloric acid, with effervescence.

cut and polished specimen, shows concentric internal banding •

BANDED
MALACHITE

• uneven fracture

BOTRYOIDAL
MALACHITE

MONOCLINIC

SG 4.0	Cleavage Perfect	Fracture Subconchoidal to uneven

Group Carbonates	Composition $Cu_3(CO_3)_2(OH)_2$	Hardness $3\frac{1}{2}$–4

AZURITE

This mineral forms as tabular and short, prismatic crystals, which may be twinned. It also occurs in massive, nodular, stalactitic, and earthy habits. It is usually a rich, deep azure-blue. The streak is a paler blue. Azurite varies from transparent to opaque, and it has a vitreous or dull lustre.
• **FORMATION** Forms in the oxidized regions of copper deposits.
• **TESTS** It is soluble in hydrochloric acid, with effervescence. It fuses easily, and turns black when heated.

twinned azurite crystals •

vitreous lustre •

limonite groundmass •

patches of green malachite around margins

MONOCLINIC

• short, tabular azurite crystals

SG 3.77–3.78	Cleavage Perfect	Fracture Conchoidal

Group Carbonates	Composition $(Zn,Cu)_5(CO_3)_2(OH)_6$	Hardness 1–2

AURICHALCITE

This mineral forms as acicular or slender, lath-shaped crystals. It also occurs as tufted aggregates and encrustations, and is occasionally granular, columnar, or lamellar in habit. The colour is pale green, greenish blue, or sky blue, and the streak is pale blue-green. It is a transparent mineral, and it has a silky or pearly lustre.

•**FORMATION** Forms in the altered and oxidized parts of copper and zinc veins with copper minerals, such as azurite and malachite.

•**TESTS** Aurichalcite is soluble in dilute hydrochloric acid, with effervescence. It colours a flame green as a result of its copper content, but it does not fuse.

silky lustre

small, tufted aurichalcite aggregates

radiating masses of acicular aurichalcite crystals

limonite groundmass

ORTHORHOMBIC

SG 3.96	Cleavage Perfect	Fracture Uneven

Group Carbonates	Composition $Pb_4(SO_4)(CO_3)_2(OH)_2$	Hardness 2½–3

LEADHILLITE

Crystals are pseudohexagonal, tabular, or prismatic; twinned crystals are common. Leadhillite can also occur in massive or granular habits. It is white, colourless, grey, yellowish, pale green, or pale blue. The streak is white. Leadhillite is transparent to translucent. The lustre is resinous to adamantine.

• **FORMATION** Leadhillite forms in the oxidized parts of lead-bearing veins. It occurs with minerals such as galena, cerussite, anglesite, and linarite.

• **TESTS** Leadhillite may sometimes fluoresce orange.

perfect cleavage

twinned, tabular crystals

resinous lustre

MONOCLINIC

oxidized groundmass

SG 6.55	Cleavage Perfect basal	Fracture Conchoidal

Group Carbonates	Composition $Zn_5(CO_3)_2(OH)_6$	Hardness 2–2½

HYDROZINCITE

pearly lustre •

This mineral rarely forms as crystals; when they occur, crystals are small, flattened or elongated and lath-shaped, often tapering to a sharp point. More usually, habits are massive, compact, botryoidal, encrusting, and stalactitic. The colour is usually white or pale grey, but may be yellow, pink, or brown. Hydrozincite has a white streak. It is a translucent mineral, with a pearly to silky, or sometimes a dull lustre.
• **FORMATION** Forms in the altered parts of zinc-bearing veins.
• **TESTS** It is soluble in hydrochloric acid. When heated, it changes into a yellowish mass of zincite. It sometimes fluoresces blue under ultra-violet light.

MONOCLINIC

botryoidal habit •

encrusting habit •

SG 4	Cleavage Perfect	Fracture Uneven

Group Carbonates	Composition $Na_3(CO_3)(HCO_3) \cdot 2H_2O$	Hardness 2½–3

TRONA

• *vitreous lustre*

This mineral forms as prismatic or tabular crystals. It can also occur in massive, fibrous, and columnar habits. The colour is greyish white, pale yellow, or pale brown. The streak is white. Trona is a transparent to translucent mineral. It has a glistening, vitreous lustre.
• **FORMATION** Occurs in evaporite deposits, with borax, glauberite, and other salts, and with evaporite minerals, such as halite, gypsum, sylvite, and dolomite. Trona also occurs as an efflorescence on the soil surface in arid regions.
• **TESTS** Trona is soluble in hydrochloric acid, with effervescence. It gives off water when it is heated in a closed test tube.

MONOCLINIC

massive habit •

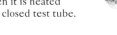

• *layered structure*

SG 2.1	Cleavage Perfect	Fracture Uneven

Group Nitrates	Composition NaNO₃		Hardness 1½–2

NITRATINE

Crystals, which rarely occur, are rhombohedral in form, and often twinned. Nitratine more commonly occurs in massive or granular habits, and in crusts. White or colourless, it is frequently discoloured by impurities, when it becomes grey, yellow, or brown. The streak is white. It is a transparent mineral, with a vitreous lustre.

• **FORMATION** Occurs in arid areas as an efflorescent deposit on the surface, associated with gypsum. Nitratine often covers large areas of land. In the deserts of northern Chile, large deposits occur over a region about 724 kilometres (450 miles) long, and from 16 to 80 kilometres (10 to 50 miles) wide.

• **TESTS** It is easily soluble in water. It will dissolve in surface waters when in crusts on the ground. If placed in a flame, it fuses very easily, and colours the flame bright yellow. It is deliquescent, which means it takes in atmospheric moisture.

sandy coating indicates arid nature of origin

massive habit

crust of granular crystals

TRIGONAL / HEXAGONAL

SG 2.27	Cleavage Perfect rhombohedral		Fracture Conchoidal

Group Borates	Composition Na₂B₄O₅(OH)₄.8H₂O		Hardness 2–2½

BORAX

This mineral forms short, prismatic crystals. The crystals are rarely twinned. It also occurs in a massive habit, and as crusts. Borax is white, colourless, grey, greenish, or bluish. The streak is white. This is a transparent to opaque mineral, which has a vitreous or earthy lustre.

• **FORMATION** Borax forms around hot springs, and in evaporite deposits.

• **TESTS** Borax is soluble in water. When placed near a flame, it fuses very easily, and colours the flame yellow. After a period of time, it will start to lose water, and will always turn white. A bitter-sweet taste is characteristic of borax.

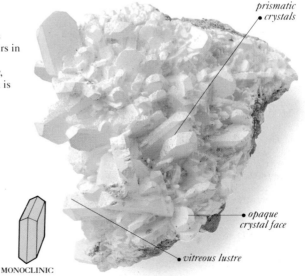

prismatic crystals

opaque crystal face

vitreous lustre

MONOCLINIC

SG 1.7	Cleavage Perfect		Fracture Conchoidal

Group Borates	Composition $Ca_2B_6O_{11}.5H_2O$	Hardness $4\frac{1}{2}$

COLEMANITE

The crystals are short and prismatic. Colemanite also occurs in massive and granular habits, and as rounded aggregates. The mineral may be white, yellow, or grey; the streak is white. It ranges from transparent to translucent. The lustre is vitreous.
- **FORMATION** Colemanite forms in evaporite deposits.
- **TESTS** Colemanite is soluble in hydrochloric acid. It fuses easily, breaks up, and colours a flame green.

prismatic crystals

translucent crystal

MONOCLINIC

SG 2.42	Cleavage Perfect		Fracture Uneven to conchoidal

Group Borates	Composition $NaCaB_5O_6(OH)_6.5H_2O$	Hardness $2\frac{1}{2}$

ULEXITE

Crystals are acicular, often in rounded aggregates. The habit may also be fibrous, or in tufted masses. Ulexite is white or colourless, and the streak is white. This mineral is transparent to translucent, and has a vitreous or silky lustre.
- **FORMATION** In evaporite basins.
- **TESTS** Ulexite is insoluble in cold water, but soluble in hot water. It fuses easily, and swells, and also colours a flame yellow.

silky lustre

crystals have translucent ends

mass of thin, fibrous crystals

TRICLINIC

SG 1.96	Cleavage Perfect		Fracture Uneven

Group Borates	Composition $Na_2B_4O_6(OH)_2.3H_2O$	Hardness $2\frac{1}{2}-3$

KERNITE

Crystals are short and prismatic, but rare. The habit is usually as cleaved masses with a fibrous structure. Kernite is colourless when fresh; otherwise it is white. The streak is white. This is a transparent to opaque mineral, and it has a vitreous, dull, or silky lustre.
- **FORMATION** Kernite forms in evaporite deposits, and in mineral veins.
- **TESTS** Soluble in cold water.

cleaved mass

transparent

vitreous lustre

MONOCLINIC

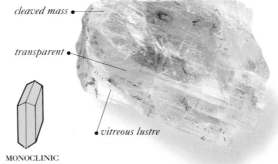

SG 1.9	Cleavage Perfect		Fracture Splintery

SULPHATES, CHROMATES,
MOLYBDATES AND TUNGSTATES

S ULPHATES ARE compounds in which one or more metallic elements combine with the sulphate $(SO_4)^{-2}$ radical. Gypsum, the most abundant sulphate, occurs in evaporite deposits. Barite typically occurs in hydrothermal veins. Most sulphates are soft, light in colour, and tend to have low densities. Chromates are compounds in which metallic elements combine with the chromate $(CrO_4)^{-2}$ radical. Chromates are small in number, rare, and brightly coloured (e.g. crocoite). Molybdates and tungstates form when metallic elements combine with molybdate $(MoO_4)^{-2}$, and tungstate $(WO_4)^{-2}$ radicals. These are often dense, brittle, and vividly coloured (e.g. wulfenite, lead molybdate, and scheelite, and calcium tungstate).

Group Sulphates	Composition $CaSO_4.2H_2O$		Hardness 2

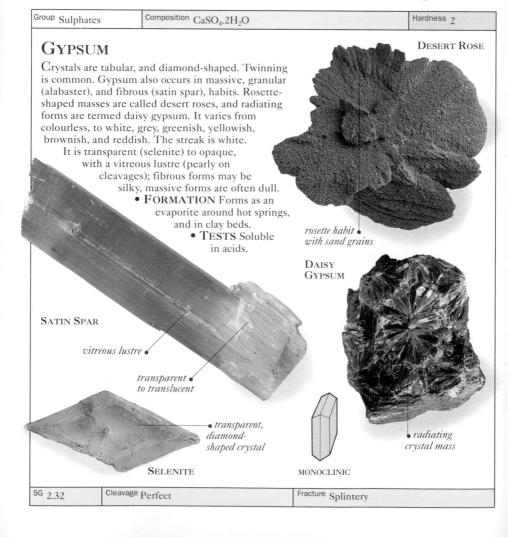

GYPSUM

Crystals are tabular, and diamond-shaped. Twinning is common. Gypsum also occurs in massive, granular (alabaster), and fibrous (satin spar), habits. Rosette-shaped masses are called desert roses, and radiating forms are termed daisy gypsum. It varies from colourless, to white, grey, greenish, yellowish, brownish, and reddish. The streak is white. It is transparent (selenite) to opaque, with a vitreous lustre (pearly on cleavages); fibrous forms may be silky, massive forms are often dull.
• **FORMATION** Forms as an evaporite around hot springs, and in clay beds.
• **TESTS** Soluble in acids.

DESERT ROSE

rosette habit •
with sand grains

DAISY GYPSUM

SATIN SPAR

vitreous lustre •

transparent
to translucent

• *transparent,*
diamond-
shaped crystal

• *radiating*
crystal mass

SELENITE

MONOCLINIC

SG 2.32	Cleavage Perfect		Fracture Splintery

Group Sulphates	Composition $SrSO_4$	Hardness 3–3½

CELESTINE

The crystals form as tabular or prismatic specimens. Other habits are massive, fibrous, granular, or nodular. Celestine is colourless, white, grey, blue, green, yellowish, orange, reddish, or brown. The streak is white. It is transparent to translucent, and has a vitreous lustre (pearly on cleavages).
• FORMATION Forms in hydrothermal veins with minerals such as calcite and quartz, as well as in many sedimentary rocks, like limestones. Also found in some evaporite deposits, and some basic igneous rocks.
• TESTS Sometimes fluoresces under ultra-violet light. It is insoluble in acids, but slightly soluble in water. When heated, this mineral fuses easily, giving a milk-white globule, and colouring the flame crimson.

prismatic celestine crystals •

• sulphur groundmass

ORTHORHOMBIC

SG 3.96–3.98	Cleavage Perfect	Fracture Uneven

Group Sulphates	Composition $CaSO_4$	Hardness 3–3½

ANHYDRITE

This mineral occurs as tabular or prismatic crystals, but usually forms in massive, granular, and fibrous habits. Anhydrite ranges from white, grey, or bluish, to pinkish, reddish, and brownish. A colourless form also occurs. There is a white streak. It is a transparent to translucent mineral, and it has a vitreous, pearly, or greasy lustre.
• FORMATION It is commonly found as an evaporite with other evaporites, such as dolomite, gypsum, halite, sylvite, and calcite – often in salt domes. Very rarely, it occurs as a hydrothermal vein mineral, with quartz and calcite.
• TESTS When heated, it fuses easily and colours the flame brick-red.

massive habit •

cleavage planes •

ORTHORHOMBIC

SG 2.98	Cleavage Perfect	Fracture Uneven to splintery

Group Sulphates	Composition $BaSO_4$	Hardness 3–3½

BARITE

This mineral forms tabular and prismatic crystals, which can be very large. It also occurs as small, sand-bearing, rose-shaped concretions called desert roses. Other habits are granular, lamellar, fibrous, cockscomb, earthy, or columnar. Barite can be colourless, white, grey, yellowish, brown, reddish, bluish, or greenish. The streak is white. Barite is a transparent to translucent mineral, with a vitreous, resinous, or pearly lustre.

• **FORMATION** Forms in hydrothermal veins with a number of other minerals, including quartz, calcite, fluorite, galena, pyrite, dolomite, chalcopyrite, and sphalerite. Barite also forms in clay nodules, in veins in sedimentary strata, and around hot springs.

• **TESTS** This mineral fuses with difficulty, colouring the flame yellowish green. It is insoluble in acids, and some varieties are fluorescent. Its high specific gravity is a useful aid to identification.

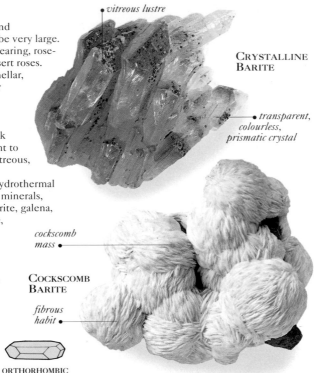

vitreous lustre

CRYSTALLINE BARITE

transparent, colourless, prismatic crystal

cockscomb mass

COCKSCOMB BARITE

fibrous habit

ORTHORHOMBIC

SG 4.5	Cleavage Perfect	Fracture Uneven

Group Sulphates	Composition $PbSO_4$	Hardness 2½–3

ANGLESITE

Crystals are tabular and prismatic. Other habits are massive, granular, nodular, and stalactitic. It can be colourless, white, grey, yellowish, pale green, or pale blue. The streak is colourless. This is a transparent to opaque mineral. It has a vitreous, adamantine, or resinous lustre.

• **FORMATION** Forms in the oxidized parts of lead veins.

• **TESTS** Often shows yellow fluorescence under ultra-violet light.

striated, prismatic anglesite crystal

transparent

vitreous lustre

galena, an associated mineral

ORTHORHOMBIC

SG 6.3–6.4	Cleavage Good basal	Fracture Conchoidal

Group Sulphates	Composition $CuSO_4.5H_2O$	Hardness $2\frac{1}{2}$

CHALCANTHITE

Short, prismatic, and thick, tabular crystals are formed by chalcanthite. Other habits exhibited are stalactitic, fibrous, massive, granular, compact, and encrusting. The colour is sky-blue to dark blue, greenish blue, or greenish, and the streak is colourless. This is a transparent to translucent mineral. It has a vitreous to resinous lustre.

• **FORMATION** Chalcanthite forms in oxidized parts of copper sulfide veins. This oxidization is usually brought about by waters circulating from above, which have their origin in rain (meteoritic). Hydrothermal fluids originating from deep underground, and rising under pressure, can also alter mineral veins. When water seeps through mine tunnels and shafts, chalcanthite crystallizes as crusts and stalactites on roofs and supports. It is found most frequently in areas of the world that have an arid climate.

• **TESTS** Chalcanthite is soluble in water. It gives off water when heated in a closed test tube. It has a distinctive, metallic taste, which helps to identify it, and it is poisonous.

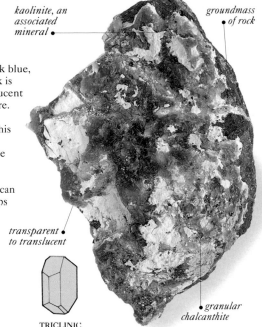

kaolinite, an associated mineral

groundmass of rock

transparent to translucent

granular chalcanthite

TRICLINIC

SG 2.28	Cleavage Imperfect	Fracture Conchoidal

Group Sulphates	Composition $MgSO_4.7H_2O$	Hardness $2–2\frac{1}{2}$

EPSOMITE

Crystals rarely occur. Epsomite is usually massive, in acicular crusts, or stalactitic. It is white, pinkish, colourless, or greenish, and the streak is white. This is a transparent to translucent mineral. It has a vitreous to silky lustre.

• **FORMATION** Forms on walls in mines, in limestone caverns, and on rock faces. Epsomite is also found in arid parts of the world, where it occurs in the oxidized parts of pyrite deposits.

• **TESTS** Epsomite is very soluble in water. It has a bitter, salty taste. Epsomite effloresces in dry air, and gives off water when it is heated in a test tube.

acicular masses and fibrous strands

silky to vitreous lustre

ORTHORHOMBIC

SG 1.68	Cleavage Perfect	Fracture Conchoidal

Group Sulphates	Composition $KAl_3(SO_4)2(OH)_6$	Hardness $3\frac{1}{2}$–4

ALUNITE

This mineral forms rhom-
bohedral, often pseudo-
cubic, crystals, but usually
occurs in massive, granular, and
compact habits. It may also be fibrous.
The colour is usually white, but may
be greyish, reddish, yellowish, or
brown with discoloration. The streak
is white. Alunite is transparent to
nearly opaque, with a vitreous or
pearly lustre.
• **FORMATION** In volcanic
vents and as a vein mineral.
• **TESTS** It gives off water when
heated in a closed test tube.

pearly lustre •

• *compact
habit*

TRIGONAL/
HEXAGONAL

SG 2.6–2.9	Cleavage Distinct basal	Fracture Conchoidal

Group Sulphates	Composition $KFe_3^{+2}(SO_4)_2(OH)_6$	Hardness $2\frac{1}{2}$–$3\frac{1}{2}$

JAROSITE

Very small, tabular or pseudo-cubic crystals are
formed by jarosite. Other habits are massive,
granular, fibrous, or earthy. The colour varies
from yellowish brown to brown. The streak
is pale yellow. This mineral is translucent.
Jarosite may have a vitreous or resinous
lustre on clean surfaces.
• **FORMATION** Forms in fissures
and layers, within iron-rich deposits.
Jarosite occurs as a result of
secondary alteration of iron-rich
minerals. This is brought about
by the circulation of water, and
other fluids, through the upper
parts of the earth's crust.
• **TESTS** Jarosite's
distinctive pseudo-cubic
crystals are a useful aid
to identification.

mass of jarosite
• *crystals*

• *goethite, an
associated
mineral*

• *vitreous lustre*

TRIGONAL/
HEXAGONAL

SG 2.90–3.26	Cleavage Distinct	Fracture Uneven

Group Sulphates	Composition $Na_2Ca(SO_4)_2$	Hardness $2\frac{1}{2}$–3

GLAUBERITE

This mineral forms tabular, prismatic, or dipyramidal crystals. It may be colourless, grey, or yellowish, with a white streak. Glauberite is a transparent to translucent mineral. It has a vitreous lustre, which changes to pearly on cleavage surfaces.

• **FORMATION** Glauberite forms in evaporite deposits. These deposits are formed when areas of saline water, salt lakes, or marine lagoons cut off from the main part of an ocean, dry out.

• **TESTS** This mineral is partially soluble in water, and soluble in hydrochloric acid.

MONOCLINIC

composite crystal

vitreous lustre

transparent to translucent

SG 2.8	Cleavage Perfect	Fracture Conchoidal

Group Sulphates	Composition Na_2SO_4	Hardness $2\frac{1}{2}$–3

THENARDITE

Crystals are tabular, dipyramidal, or prismatic, and commonly twinned. Thenardite also forms as crusts. It may be colourless, greyish white, yellowish, brownish, or reddish. Thenardite is a transparent to translucent mineral. It has a vitreous or resinous lustre.

• **FORMATION** Forms in the deposits of salt lakes, as well as occurring on the soil surface in arid areas. When it occurs in salt lakes, thenardite may be associated with other evaporites, such as gypsum, halite, sylvite, and glauberite. Thenardite may also be found on the surface of recently erupted, and cooled, lava flows. It can occur around fumaroles, where it forms as a crust-like deposit.

• **TESTS** This mineral is highly soluble when placed in cold water. In common with several other evaporites, such as halite and sylvite, thenardite has a salty taste.

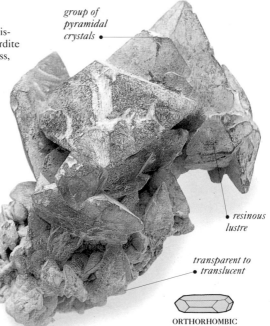

group of pyramidal crystals

resinous lustre

transparent to translucent

ORTHORHOMBIC

SG 2.66	Cleavage Perfect	Fracture Uneven

Group Sulphates	Composition $K_2MgCa_2(SO_4)_4.2H_2O$	Hardness $3\frac{1}{2}$

POLYHALITE

This mineral rarely forms crystals; when they occur, crystals are small, highly modified, elongated, or tabular. Usually, the habit is as fibrous or foliated masses. Polyhalite is frequently flesh-pink to brick-red, as a result of iron oxide inclusions. When pure, it is colourless, white, or grey. It has a white streak. This is a transparent to translucent mineral; the lustre is resinous or silky.
• **FORMATION** Forms in evaporite sequences of rocks, with minerals such as halite, gypsum, sylvite, carnallite, and anhydrite. Forms rarely from volcanic activity.
• **TESTS** Tastes salty, but more bitter than halite.

transparent to translucent •

• fibrous habit

TRICLINIC

SG 2.78	Cleavage Perfect	Fracture Uneven

Group Sulphates	Composition $PbCu(SO_4)(OH)_2$	Hardness $2\frac{1}{2}$

LINARITE

The thin, tabular, or prismatic crystals formed by linarite are often randomly orientated in aggregates. Twinned crystals are common. As well as in these habits, linarite forms in crusts. Its colour is deep blue, and it has a pale blue streak. This is a translucent to transparent mineral. Its lustre is vitreous to subadamantine.
• **FORMATION** Forms in the oxidized parts of lead and copper veins that have been altered by circulating fluids, mainly water, where it is associated with many other secondary minerals, such as brochantite, anglesite, and chalcanthite.
• **TESTS** Linarite produces a white coating, and no effervescence, when placed in dilute hydrochloric acid. However, it is soluble in dilute nitric acid. When placed in a flame it fuses. With continued heating it crackles, turning black.

• prismatic linarite crystals

• rock groundmass

MONOCLINIC

SG 5.3	Cleavage Perfect	Fracture Conchoidal

Group Sulphates	Composition $Fe^{+2}Fe_4^{+3}(SO_4)_6(OH)_2.2OH_2O$	Hardness 2½–3

COPIAPITE

The usual habits of this mineral are as tabular crystals, crusts, and scaly aggregates, or masses. Copiapite is yellow, golden-yellow, or orange-yellow, though it may be greenish yellow to olive-green. It is transparent to translucent, and has a pearly lustre.
• **FORMATION** Forms when sulphides, such as iron pyrite, are oxidized.
• **TESTS** Soluble in water, producing a yellowish colour. It fuses at quite low temperatures.

scaly aggregates of crystals •

pearly • *lustre*

TRICLINIC

SG 2.08–2.17	Cleavage Perfect	Fracture Uneven

Group Sulphates	Composition $Cu_4Al_2(SO_4)(OH)_{12}.2H_2O$	Hardness 3

CYANOTRICHITE

This mineral forms minute, acicular crystals in tufted aggregates. Other habits are as coatings, or fibrous veinlets. It is pale to dark blue, and has a pale blue streak. Cyanotrichite is a translucent mineral, and has a silky lustre.
• **FORMATION** Forms in the oxidized zone of ore veins, especially those of copper.
• **TESTS** Soluble in acids. Fuses in a flame.

radiating acicular crystals •

rock • *groundmass*

ORTHORHOMBIC

SG 2.74–2.95	Cleavage None	Fracture Uneven

Group Sulphates	Composition $Cu_4SO_4(OH)_6$	Hardness 3½–4

BROCHANTITE

The usual habits are as stout prismatic, acicular, or tabular crystals, aggregates, and drusy crusts. Twinning is common. It is emerald-green to blackish green; the streak is pale green. Brochantite is transparent to translucent. Its lustre is vitreous.
• **FORMATION** Forms in oxidation zone of copper deposits.
• **TESTS** This mineral is soluble in hydrochloric and nitric acids.

mass of acicular brochantite crystals •

MONOCLINIC

azurite, an associated mineral •

SG 3.97	Cleavage Perfect	Fracture Conchoidal to uneven

Group Chromates	Composition PbCrO₄		Hardness 2½–3

CROCOITE

Slender, prismatic crystals are formed by crocoite, usually in aggregates. This mineral also occurs in a massive habit. The colour is orange-red, often bright, and sometimes orange, red, or yellow. The streak is orange-yellow. Crocoite is a translucent mineral. It has an adamantine to vitreous lustre.

• **FORMATION** Forms in the altered and oxidized parts of veins and deposits containing chromium and lead. Crocoite is a secondary mineral, resulting from the alteration of other lead minerals by hydrothermal fluids. It occurs with a variety of other minerals, including wulfenite, cerussite, pyromorphite, and vanadinite.

• **TESTS** Crocoite fuses fairly easily in a flame, and is soluble in strong acids. The first extraction of chromium was carried out from this mineral.

prismatic crystal

some striations on crystal face

MONOCLINIC

SG 6.0	Cleavage Distinct prismatic	Fracture Conchoidal to uneven

Group Molybdates	Composition PbMoO₄		Hardness 2½–3

WULFENITE

This mineral forms square-shaped, tabular crystals, and also prismatic crystals. Other habits are massive and granular. Wulfenite is typically coloured orange, or yellow, but may be brown, grey, or greenish brown. The colours often appear brilliant. The streak is white. This is a transparent to translucent mineral. It has a resinous to adamantine lustre.

• **FORMATION** Forms in the parts of ore veins that have been altered by circulating fluids, mainly water. Wulfenite can occur with a great variety of other minerals, including cerussite, limonite, vanadinite, galena, pyromorphite, and malachite, as well as mimetite.

• **TESTS** Wulfenite fuses easily. It is soluble in hydrochloric acid when heated; but it dissolves more slowly in cold acid.

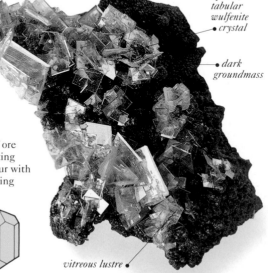

square, tabular wulfenite crystal

dark groundmass

vitreous lustre

TETRAGONAL

SG 6.5–7.0	Cleavage Distinct pyramidal	Fracture Subconchoidal

Group Tungstates	Composition $(Fe,Mn)WO_4$	Hardness 4–4½

WOLFRAMITE

An intermediate member in the ferberite-hübnerite series of minerals. The prismatic or tabular crystals formed by wolframite are often twinned. The mineral also occurs in a massive habit. It is brownish black in colour, with a reddish brown to brownish black streak. This is a translucent to opaque mineral, with a submetallic lustre.
• **FORMATION** Forms in quartz veins of granitic pegmatites, often associated with minerals such as cassiterite and arsenopyrite.
• **TESTS** Wolframite fuses slowly. The brownish colour is due to the presence of ferberite, while hübnerite contributes its reddish brown colouring.

prismatic crystal

tabular crystal with striated face

MONOCLINIC

SG 7.1–7.5	Cleavage Perfect	Fracture Uneven

Group Tungstates	Composition $CaWO_4$	Hardness 4½–5

SCHEELITE

Pseudo-octahedral or dipyramidal crystals are formed by scheelite. The crystals are commonly twinned. Other habits are massive, granular, or columnar. Scheelite is white, colourless, grey, pale yellow, orange-yellow, brownish green, reddish, or purple. The streak is white. It is a transparent to translucent mineral, with a vitreous to adamantine lustre.
• **FORMATION** Forms in hydrothermal veins, in contact metamorphic rocks, and in pegmatites. It also occurs in placer deposits, and is frequently found with wolframite. It is an important ore of tungsten.
• **TESTS** This mineral gives a bright, bluish white fluorescence under shortwave ultra-violet light. It is also soluble in acids, and fusible, but only with difficulty.

magnetite groundmass

bipyramidal scheelite crystals

TETRAGONAL

SG 5.9–6.1	Cleavage Distinct	Fracture Subconchoidal to uneven

PHOSPHATES, ARSENATES, AND VANADATES

PHOSPHATES, arsenates, and vanadates are all compounds in which metallic elements combine with phosphate $(PO_4)^{-8}$; arsenate $(ASO_4)^{-8}$, $(ASO_3)^{-1}$; or vanadate $(VO_4)^{-3}$, $(VO_3)^{-1}$ radicals. Although several hundred phosphate, arsenate, and vanadate species are recognized, they are not abundant. Some phosphates, such as arsenic, are primary; however most members of the overall group form from the oxidation of primary sulphides. Their properties are variable, but generally they tend to be soft, brittle, colourful, and well-crystallized. Phosphates include the radioactive minerals, torbernite and autunite, lead-rich pyromorphite, bright blue lazulite, and turquoise,

which gives its name to a shade of blue. The hardness of phosphates is particularly variable, ranging from 1½ in vivianite to 5–6 in turquoise.

———— • ————

Many of the arsenates are highly sought-after by collectors, particularly the well-crystallized and brightly coloured species, such as adamite, erythrite, mimetite, and bayldonite. Arsenates tend to have a specific gravity of 3–5, apart from mimetite which, because it contains lead, has a specific gravity of 7.1–7.3. These minerals are usually found to be of low hardness. Vanadinite is probably the best known and commonest of the vanadates, and occurs as beautiful red or orange hexagonal crystals.

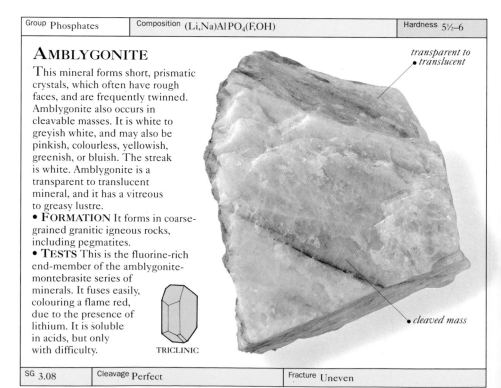

Group Phosphates		Composition $(Li,Na)AlPO_4(F,OH)$		Hardness 5½–6

AMBLYGONITE

This mineral forms short, prismatic crystals, which often have rough faces, and are frequently twinned. Amblygonite also occurs in cleavable masses. It is white to greyish white, and may also be pinkish, colourless, yellowish, greenish, or bluish. The streak is white. Amblygonite is a transparent to translucent mineral, and it has a vitreous to greasy lustre.

• **FORMATION** It forms in coarse-grained granitic igneous rocks, including pegmatites.

• **TESTS** This is the fluorine-rich end-member of the amblygonite-montebrasite series of minerals. It fuses easily, colouring a flame red, due to the presence of lithium. It is soluble in acids, but only with difficulty.

transparent to translucent

TRICLINIC

cleaved mass

SG 3.08	Cleavage Perfect		Fracture Uneven

Group Phosphates	Composition $(Mg,Fe)Al_2(PO_4)_2(OH)_2$	Hardness $5\frac{1}{2}$–6

LAZULITE

Pseudo-dipyramidal crystals are usually formed by lazulite, but tabular crystals also form. The crystals can be quite large, and are frequently twinned. Other habits in which this mineral commonly forms are massive, granular, and compact. Its colour is blue, but ranges from a rich azure to light blue, or bluish green. The streak is white. Lazulite is a translucent to opaque mineral, with a vitreous to dull lustre.
• **FORMATION** Lazulite forms in a variety of environments, including quartz veins, granitic pegmatites, and metamorphic rocks, such as metaquartzite. Pegmatic lazulite typically occurs with andalusite and rutile. Metamorphic associates include quartz, garnet, kyanite, muscovite, pyrophyllite, sillimanite, and corundum.
• **TESTS** This mineral gives off water when heated in a closed test tube.

pyramidal lazulite crystal

quartz groundmass

vitreous lustre on crystal face

MONOCLINIC

twinned lazulite crystals

SG 3.1	Cleavage Indistinct to good prismatic	Fracture Uneven to splintery

Group Phosphates	Composition $Pb_5(PO_4)_3Cl$	Hardness $3\frac{1}{2}$–4

PYROMORPHITE

This mineral usually forms short, hexagonal prisms, which are often barrel-shaped. It also occurs in globular, reniform, granular, earthy, botryoidal, and fibrous habits. It can be green, orange, grey, brown, or yellow in colour. The streak is white. Pyromorphite is a transparent to translucent mineral. It has a resinous to adamantine lustre.
• **FORMATION** Forms in the oxidation zone of lead veins, as a secondary mineral.
• **TESTS** Pyromorphite is soluble in certain acids.

limonite groundmass

aggregates of prismatic, hexagonal pyromorphite crystals

TRIGONAL / HEXAGONAL

SG 6.5–7.1	Cleavage Very poor prismatic	Fracture Uneven to subconchoidal

Group Phosphates	Composition $Fe_3(PO_4)_2.8H_2O$	Hardness 1½–2

VIVIANITE

Elongated, prismatic, or tabular crystals are usually formed. It also occurs in massive, bladed, or fibrous habits. It is colourless when fresh. The mineral's streak is colourless to bluish white. It is transparent to translucent, and it has a vitreous or pearly lustre.
• **FORMATION** Forms in the oxidation zone of iron and manganese-rich deposits.
• **TESTS** Soluble in hydrochloric acid, and fuses easily.

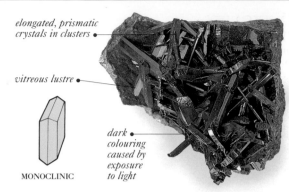

elongated, prismatic crystals in clusters

vitreous lustre

dark colouring caused by exposure to light

MONOCLINIC

SG 2.68	Cleavage Perfect	Fracture Uneven

Group Phosphates	Composition $Cu(UO_2)_2(PO_4)_2.8–12H_2O$	Hardness 2–2½

TORBERNITE

This mineral forms as tabular crystals. Other habits are as scaly or lamellar aggregates. It is green in colour, and the streak is pale green. Torbernite is a transparent to translucent mineral, and it has a vitreous to pearly lustre.
• **FORMATION** A secondary uranium mineral derived from the alteration of uraninite.
• **TESTS** It is radioactive. It is also chemically unstable, and often becomes metatorbernite.

vitreous lustre

tabular torbernite crystals

iron-rich groundmass

TETRAGONAL

SG 3.22	Cleavage Perfect basal	Fracture Uneven

Group Phosphates	Composition $Ca(UO_2)_2(PO_4)_2.10–12H_2O$	Hardness 2–2½

AUTUNITE

This mineral forms as tabular crystals, which are sometimes twinned. It also occurs as crusts, aggregates, and grains. The colour is yellow to green. The streak is yellow. It is transparent to translucent. The lustre is vitreous to pearly.
• **FORMATION** Forms by the alteration of primary uranium minerals.
• **TESTS** Autunite is a radioactive mineral.

vitreous lustre

translucent

tabular, twinned crystal aggregate

perfect basal cleavage

TETRAGONAL

SG 3.05–3.2	Cleavage Perfect basal	Fracture Uneven

Group Phosphates	Composition YPO_4	Hardness 4–5

XENOTIME

This mineral forms as prismatic and pyramidal crystals. It may also occur as equant crystals. Rough crystals occur in aggregates, and rosette-shaped crystal groups sometimes form. Twinned crystals are rare. The colour is yellowish brown to reddish brown, or grey, pale yellow, greenish, or reddish. The streak is pale brown, or can be yellowish brown. It is translucent to opaque, and it has a vitreous to resinous lustre.

• **FORMATION** Forms in pegmatites, and also in many other acid igneous rocks, but in very small quantities. In addition, xenotime forms in metamorphic rocks, and in alpine veins. It has been found in sediments as a detrital mineral.

• **TESTS** It is very similar to zircon, but zircon is much harder.

TETRAGONAL

aggregate of rough crystals

pyramidal crystal

SG 4.4–5.1	Cleavage Perfect prismatic	Fracture Uneven

Group Phosphates	Composition $(Ce,La,Nd,Th)PO_4$	Hardness 5–5½

MONAZITE

This forms a series of monazite – (Ce), monazite – (Lu), and monazite – (Nd). The crystals are tabular or prismatic crystals, and are usually small and twinned. Crystal faces are often rough, or striated. The habit can also be as granular masses. Monazite is brown, reddish brown, yellowish brown, pink, yellow, greenish, or nearly white in colour. The streak is white. This is a transparent to translucent mineral, and it has a resinous, waxy, or vitreous lustre.

• **FORMATION** Forms in pegmatites, in metamorphic rocks, and in veins. It is common in placer deposits, including river and beach sands. Very large monazite crystals, weighing several kilograms have been found in pegmatites.

• **TESTS** Monazite is a mildly radioactive mineral.

MONOCLINIC

uneven fracture

prismatic crystal

vitreous lustre

SG 4.6–5.4	Cleavage Distinct	Fracture Conchoidal to uneven

Group Phosphates	Composition $CuAl_6(PO_4)_4(OH)_8.4H_2O$	Hardness 5–6

TURQUOISE

This mineral rarely forms crystals, but when they occur, it is as small, short, prismatic specimens. The more common habits are massive, granular, cryptocrystalline, stalactitic, and concretionary; it also forms in crusts, and veinlets. Turquoise is bright blue to pale blue, greenish blue, green, and grey. It has a white or pale green streak. The crystals are transparent, and have a vitreous lustre; massive forms are opaque, with a waxy or dull lustre.

• **FORMATION** Forms in igneous and sedimentary, aluminium-rich rocks that have been much altered, often by surface water.

• **TESTS** Turquoise is soluble in hydrochloric acid that has been heated.

crust of turquoise

TRICLINIC

rock groundmass

SG 2.6-2.8	Cleavage Good	Fracture Conchoidal

Group Phosphates	Composition $Al_3(PO_4)_2(OH,F)_3.5H_2O$	Hardness 3½–4

WAVELLITE

This mineral occurs occasionally as minute, prismatic crystals. It also forms as acicular, radiating aggregates, which are often spherical. Additionally, it forms crusts. The colour is white to greenish white, and green; also yellowish green to yellow, and yellowish brown. There is a white streak. Wavellite is a transparent to translucent mineral, and has a vitreous, resinous or pearly lustre.

• **FORMATION** Forms on rock fracture and joint surfaces as a secondary mineral.

• **TESTS** This mineral dissolves in most acids, and is infusible. It gives off water when heated in a closed test tube.

radiating acicular wavellite crystals

rock groundmass

ORTHORHOMBIC

SG 2.36	Cleavage Perfect	Fracture Subconchoidal to uneven

Group Phosphates	Composition $Al(PO_4).2H_2O$	Hardness $3\frac{1}{2}-4\frac{1}{2}$

VARISCITE

Pseudo-octahedral crystals are only rarely formed. Commonly, it occurs in massive and concretionary habits, and as crusts, or veins. The colour is green. Variscite is a transparent to translucent mineral. It has a vitreous to waxy or dull lustre.
• **FORMATION** Forms where water rich in phosphates has altered aluminium-rich rocks.
• **TESTS** Soluble only if heated before placed in acid. It is infusible.

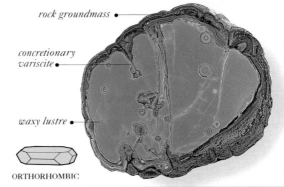

rock groundmass •

concretionary variscite •

waxy lustre •

ORTHORHOMBIC

SG 2.6–2.9	Cleavage Perfect	Fracture Conchoidal or uneven to splintery

Group Phosphates	Composition $Ca_5(PO_4)_3(F,Cl,OH)$	Hardness 5

APATITE

This is a closely related mineral group, that forms as prismatic or tabular crystals, and in massive, compact, and granular habits. Apatite is usually green in colour, but may be white, colourless, yellow, bluish, reddish, brown, grey, or purple. It has a white streak. Apatite is transparent to translucent, and has a vitreous to subresinous lustre.
• **FORMATION** Forms in igneous rocks, and in metamorphosed limestones.
• **TESTS** Soluble in hydrochloric acid.

calcite • *groundmass*

prismatic apatite • *crystals*

TRIGONAL / HEXAGONAL

SG 3.1–3.2	Cleavage Poor	Fracture Conchoidal to uneven

Group Phosphates	Composition $CaBe(PO_4)(F,OH)$	Hardness 5–5½

HERDERITE

This mineral occurs as prismatic or tabular crystals, which are often pseudo-orthorhombic. It also forms in fibrous aggregates. Herderite is colourless, pale yellow, or greenish white. It is transparent to translucent, and has a vitreous lustre.
• **FORMATION** Herderite forms in granitic pegmatites.
• **TESTS** This mineral is soluble in most acids. Some specimens fluoresce under ultra-violet light.

vitreous lustre •

prismatic crystal •

MONOCLINIC

SG 2.95–3.01	Cleavage Poor	Fracture Subconchoidal

Group Arsenates	Composition $Zn_2AsO_4(OH)$	Hardness 3½

ADAMITE

Forms as elongated, tabular, or equant crystals, which may be twinned. It can also occur in a habit of spheroidal masses. It is usually bright yellow-green in colour. The streak is white. Adamite is a transparent to translucent mineral. It has a vitreous lustre.
• **FORMATION** Forms in the oxidized parts of ore veins. Adamite is associated with many other minerals, such as calcite, limonite, and malachite, as well as azurite, smithsonite, and hemimorphite.
• **TESTS** This mineral is soluble in dilute acids. Adamite is also sometimes fluorescent in ultra-violet light, and is fusible when tested with a flame.

spheroidal adamite masses •

CRYSTALLINE ADAMITE

• crust of limonite

limonite groundmass •

SPHEROIDAL ADAMITE

• uneven fracture

• twinned, tabular adamite crystals

ORTHORHOMBIC

SG 4.3–4.4	Cleavage Good	Fracture Subconchoidal to uneven

Group Arsenates	Composition $Ni_3(AsO_4)_2 \cdot 8H_2O$	Hardness 1½–2½

ANNABERGITE

This mineral forms prismatic, striated crystals. Other habits are as crusts, and earthy or powdery masses. Annabergite is white, grey, pale green, or yellow-green. The streak is paler than the colour. It is a transparent to translucent mineral, and it has a vitreous or pearly lustre.
• **FORMATION** Forms in the altered parts of nickel veins.
• **TESTS** Gives off water when heated in a closed test tube.

MONOCLINIC

crusty coating of annabergite on rock surface •

• pearly lustre

SG 3.07	Cleavage Perfect	Fracture Uneven

Group Arsenates	Composition $Cu_3(AsO_4)(OH)_3$	Hardness 2½–3

CLINOCLASE

The crystals form as elongated or tabular shapes, and may have a rhombohedral appearance, in which case they are described as pseudo-rhombohedral. Crystals occur either isolated, or as rosettes. This mineral is dark greenish blue to greenish black in colour, and has a bluish green streak. Clinoclase is transparent to translucent. It has a vitreous lustre on crystal faces, which becomes pearly on the cleavage surfaces.

• **FORMATION** Forms as a secondary mineral in the oxidation zone of copper sulphide deposits, both on and beneath the earth's surface. Clinoclase is frequently associated with olivenite, a member of the same mineral group.

• **TESTS** Clinoclase is soluble in acids, and produces a garlic smell when heated.

broken clinoclase rosette, with internal, radiating structure

MONOCLINIC

uneven fracture

olivenite, an associated mineral

vitreous lustre

SG 4.33	Cleavage Perfect	Fracture Uneven

Group Arsenates	Composition $Co_3(AsO_4)_2.8H_2O$	Hardness 1½–2½

ERYTHRITE

The prismatic to acicular crystals formed by this mineral are often striated, or in bladed aggregates. Erythrite also occurs in a habit of earthy masses. In colour, it is deep purple to pale pink. The streak is just a shade paler than the colour. This mineral ranges from transparent to translucent, and it has an adamantine to vitreous or pearly lustre.

• **FORMATION** Forms in the parts of cobalt veins that have been altered by circulating fluids, and where oxidation has occurred.

• **TESTS** Soluble in hydrochloric acid.

bladed aggregates of crystals in striated acicular habit

vitreous lustre

MONOCLINIC

SG 3.18	Cleavage Perfect	Fracture Uneven

Group Arsenates	Composition $Pb_5(AsO_4)_3Cl$	Hardness $3\frac{1}{2}$–4

MIMETITE

This mineral forms acicular to slender prismatic crystals; sometimes, these crystals can be barrel-shaped, in which case they are called campylite crystals. Other habits include botryoidal, reniform, and granular. Mimetite ranges in colour from yellow, orange, and brown, to white, colourless, and greenish. It has a white streak. This is a transparent to translucent mineral, and it has a vitreous to resinous lustre.

• **FORMATION** Forms in the oxidation zone of lead deposits that have been altered by circulating hydrothermal fluids. It is often found with pyromorphite, vanadinite, galena, anglesite, hemimorphite, and arsenopyrite.

• **TESTS** Soluble in hydrochloric acid. It will fuse easily if put in a flame, when a very strong smell, which is reminiscent of garlic, is produced.

prismatic crystal •

translucent •

PRISMATIC MIMETITE

• romanechite, and associated groundmass

• barrel-shaped campylite crystals

MONOCLINIC

CAMPYLITE

SG 7.0-7.3	Cleavage None	Fracture Subconchoidal to uneven

Group Arsenates	Composition $Cu_2(AsO_4)(OH)$	Hardness 3

OLIVENITE

Prismatic, acicular, or tabular crystals are formed by olivenite. Other habits are as globular or reniform masses. The colour is olive-green, brown, yellowish, grey, or white. Olivenite has an olive-green streak. Its name derives from this colour connection. It is a translucent to opaque mineral, and the lustre is vitreous to silky.

• **FORMATION** Forms in the oxidation zone of copper sulphide deposits. Olivenite occurs with the minerals malachite, azurite, calcite, goethite, and dioptase, as well as scorodite.

• **TESTS** It is soluble in acids, and produces a garlic smell when heated.

quartz groundmass •

globular masses of acicular olivenite crystals •

ORTHORHOMBIC

SG 4.4	Cleavage Indistinct	Fracture Uneven to conchoidal

Group Arsenates	Composition $FeAsO_4.2H_2O$	Hardness 3½–4

SCORODITE

The crystals formed by scorodite are pyramidal, prismatic, and tabular. Scorodite also occurs in massive and earthy habits. It is pale green, greyish green, bluish green, blue, brownish, colourless, yellowish, or violet. The streak is white. This is a transparent to translucent mineral. Its lustre is vitreous to resinous, or dull.
• **FORMATION** Forms in the oxidation zone of arsenic deposits.
• **TESTS** This mineral is soluble in hydrochloric, as well as nitric acids. When heated, a smell that is reminiscent of garlic is produced. If heated in a closed test tube, water is given off.

pyramidal scorodite crystal

rock groundmass

ORTHORHOMBIC

vitreous lustre

SG 3.28	Cleavage Imperfect	Fracture Subconchoidal

Group Arsenates	Composition $(Pb, Cu)_3(AsO_4)_2(OH)_2$	Hardness 4½

BAYLDONITE

Usually forms in a massive habit, but also in granular, and powdery, habits. The latter habits may occur on rock surfaces, and it is difficult to detect any crystal form unless a high magnification is used. This mineral also occurs as crusts, and rounded concretions, which may have a fibrous, thread-like, internal structure. The colour is often bright grass-green, but can be yellowish, or dark green. No streak has been determined. Light hardly passes through crystalline specimens, so bayldonite is described as subtranslucent. The lustre is resinous, and the surface is almost sticky in appearance.
• **FORMATION** This mineral forms in the oxidation zone of copper-bearing deposits. Balydonite is associated with many minerals, including olivenite, azurite, malachite, and mimetite.
• **TESTS** Balydonite will give off water when it is heated in a closed test tube.

crust of bayldonite on quartz groundmass

resinous lustre

MONOCLINIC

SG 5.6–5.7	Cleavage None	Fracture Uneven

Group Vanadates	Composition $K_2(UO_2)_2V_2O_8.3H_2O$	Hardness 2

CARNOTITE

Crystals are very small and platy. Carnotite also forms as powdery, microcrystalline masses, or crusts. It is bright yellow, or greenish yellow. The streak is yellow. It is semi-opaque. The crystals have a pearly lustre, but the masses are dull.
• **FORMATION** Forms as a secondary mineral, deposited from groundwaters passing through uranium deposits.
• **TESTS** Carnotite is radioactive, and dissolves in acids.

rock groundmass

crust of carnotite

MONOCLINIC

SG 4.75	Cleavage Perfect basal	Fracture Uneven

Group Vanadates	Composition $Ca(UO_2)_2V_2O_8.5-8H_2O$	Hardness 2

TYUYAMUNITE

This mineral forms as very small scales and laths. Other habits are massive, compact, and microcrystalline. The colour is greenish yellow to yellow, and the streak is yellow. Tyuyamunite is translucent to opaque, and has a waxy, pearly, adamantine, or dull lustre.
• **FORMATION** Tyuyamunite forms as a secondary alteration product of primary uranium minerals.
• **TESTS** It is a radioactive mineral.

scaly habit

dull lustre

tyuyamunite coating on rock surface

ORTHORHOMBIC

SG 3.3–3.6	Cleavage Perfect basal	Fracture Uneven

Group Vanadates	Composition $Cu_3V_2O_7(OH)_2.2H_2O$	Hardness 3½

VOLBORTHITE

This mineral forms as encrusting scales, often with triangular or hexagonal outlines. Lamellar twinning is common. It also occurs as rosette-like, or honeycomb, aggregates. The colour is green, yellow, or brown, and the streak is undetermined. It is translucent, with a vitreous to pearly lustre.
• **FORMATION** An alteration product of other vanadium minerals.
• **TESTS** It is soluble in acids.

rock groundmass

crusty coating of volborthite

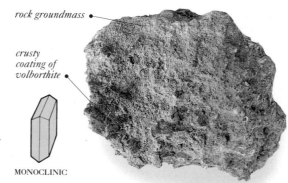

MONOCLINIC

SG 3.42	Cleavage Perfect basal	Fracture Uneven

Group Vanadates	Composition $Pb_5(VO_4)_3Cl$	Hardness 3

VANADINITE

The prismatic crystals formed by vanadinite are sometimes hollow. The colour ranges from bright red and orange-red, to brownish red, brown, or yellow. The streak may be white or yellowish. Vanadinite is a transparent to translucent mineral, and it has a resinous to subadamantine lustre.
• **FORMATION** Forms in the oxidation zone of lead deposits.
• **TESTS** Vanadinite gives a number of characteristic results when tested with acids or heat. It fuses easily in a flame, and is soluble in nitric acid. If the resulting liquid is left to evaporate, a red residue will remain, distinguishing it from other related minerals which will leave a white deposit.

rock groundmass

prismatic vanadinite crystals

TRIGONAL/ HEXAGONAL

subadamantine lustre

SG 6.88	Cleavage None	Fracture Conchoidal to uneven

Group Vanadates	Composition $Pb(Zn,Cu)(VO_4)(OH)$	Hardness 3–3½

DESCLOIZITE

This mineral forms as pyramidal, tabular, or prismatic crystals. The crystals often have rough or uneven faces. It also occurs as crusts, plumose aggregates, and botryoidal masses. The colour is orange-red to reddish brown, or blackish brown, and the streak is yellowish orange to reddish brown. Descloizite is a transparent to translucent mineral, and it has a vitreous to greasy lustre.
• **FORMATION** Forms as a secondary mineral in the parts of ore veins and deposits which have been altered by oxidation.
• **TESTS** It is soluble in hydro-chloric and nitric acids. Descloizite also fuses easily in a flame.

plumose mass of crystals

translucent

ORTHORHOMBIC

vitreous to greasy lustre

SG 6.24–6.26	Cleavage None	Fracture Uneven to conchoidal

SILICATES

SILICATES ARE compounds in which metallic elements combine with either single or linked Si-O tetrahedra $(SiO_4)^{-4}$. Structurally, silicates are divided into six classes: Neosilicates have isolated $(SiO_4)^{-4}$ tetrahedra linked by a non-silicon cation; Sorosilicates feature two tetrahedra joined and sharing one common oxygen ion; Cyclosilicates have tetrahedra joined into rings; Inosilicates have tetrahedra joined into either single or double-chains; Phyllosilicates have sheet-like structures formed by the sharing of three oxygen ions by each adjacent tetrahedron; Tectosilicates are "framework" silicates in which every silicon atom shares all four of its oxygen ions with neighbouring silicon atoms.

———— • ————

Silicates are the largest and most abundant class of minerals, while primary silicates are the main constituents of igneous and metamorphic rocks. Silicates tend to be hard, transparent to translucent, and of average density.

Group Silicates	Composition Fe_2SiO_4 - Mg_2SiO_4	Hardness 6½–7

OLIVINE

This series of minerals forms as thick, tabular crystals, frequently with wedge-shaped terminations. Other habits are massive, compact, and granular. The colour is green, greenish yellow, yellowish brown, brown, and white, and the streak is colourless. These are transparent to translucent minerals, and they have a vitreous lustre. The gem variety of forsteritic olivine is called peridot.

• **FORMATION** An end-member of the olivine series of minerals, forsterite forms in basic and ultrabasic igneous rocks, and is also found in marbles. It is rich in magnesium. Fayalite, the other end-member, is rich in iron, and forms in acid igneous rocks, which have cooled rapidly.

• **TESTS** Olivine is soluble in hydro-chloric acid, with gelatinization.

transparent

striated crystal •

PERIDOT

vitreous lustre

tabular forsterite crystals •

• *altered limestone groundmass*

FORSTERITE

ORTHORHOMBIC

SG 3.27–4.32	Cleavage Imperfect	Fracture Conchoidal

Group Silicates	Composition $Mg_3Al_2(SiO_4)_3$	Hardness $7-7\frac{1}{2}$

PYROPE GARNET

The crystals are dodecahedral or trapezohedral.
Pyrope usually occurs as rounded grains. The
colour ranges from pinkish or purplish red, to
crimson, and nearly black. The streak is white
in colour. The mineral is transparent to
translucent, and it has a vitreous lustre.
• **FORMATION** Pyrope forms in a
variety of ultrabasic igneous rocks,
including peridotite. It also occurs in
associated serpentinites.
• **TESTS** Fuses fairly easily, and is
virtually insoluble in acids.

conchoidal fracture

rounded grains

CUBIC

SG $3.5-3.8$	Cleavage None	Fracture Conchoidal

Group Silicates	Composition $Ca_3Al_2(SiO_4)_3$	Hardness $6\frac{1}{2}-7$

GROSSULAR GARNET

This mineral forms as dodecahedral
or trapezohedral crystals. Other habits
are massive, compact, or granular.
The colour varies greatly, and may be
green, yellowish green, yellow, brown,
red, orange, reddish brown, white, pink,
grey, or black. It has a white streak. Grossular is transparent to nearly opaque, and
has a vitreous or resinous lustre.
• **FORMATION** Forms in a variety
of metamorphic rocks, though it
most commonly occurs in marble.
• **TESTS** Insoluble in acids.

twinning

CUBIC

striated crystal

SG $3.4-3.6$	Cleavage None	Fracture Uneven to conchoidal

Group Silicates	Composition $Fe_3Al_2(SiO_4)_3$	Hardness $7-7\frac{1}{2}$

ALMANDINE GARNET

The crystals are dodecahedral,
rhombdodecahedral, or trapezohedral.
Almandine also forms in massive, granular, and
compact habits. Its colour may be deep red to
reddish brown, and brownish black. There is
a white streak. It is transparent to translucent, with a vitreous or resinous lustre.
• **FORMATION** This
mineral forms in regio-
nally metamorphosed
rocks, such as schist.
• **TESTS** It is insoluble
in acids. It fuses fairly easily.

rhombdodecahedral almandine crystals

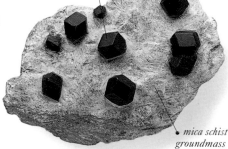

CUBIC

mica schist groundmass

SG $4.1-4.3$	Cleavage None	Fracture Uneven to conchoidal

Group Silicates	Composition $(Mg,Fe)_7(SiO_4)_3(F,OH)_2$	Hardness 6

HUMITE

Small, stubby crystals with a varied, often highly modified, habit are formed by this mineral. The colour is white, yellow, dark orange, or brown. Humite is transparent to translucent, and it has a vitreous lustre on fresh crystal surfaces.
• **FORMATION** Forms in contact metamorphosed limestones, and in some mineral veins. It occurs with numerous minerals, including calcite, graphite, spinel, diopside, idocrase, garnet, and other types of minerals typical of metamorphosed limestones. The humite group consists of humite, clinohumite, norbergite, and chondrodite.
• **TESTS** No further tests are required to identify it.

yellowish brown humite crystals

sanidine, an associated mineral

mica

ORTHORHOMBIC

rock groundmass

SG 3.24	Cleavage Poor	Fracture Uneven

Group Silicates	Composition $(Mg,Fe)_5(SiO_4)_2(F,OH)_2$	Hardness 6–6½

CHONDRODITE

This mineral is a member of the humite group. It forms as varied, usually highly modified, crystals, in which lamellar twinning is common. The habit may also be massive. The colour is yellow, red, or brown. Chondrodite is a transparent to translucent mineral, and it has a vitreous lustre.
• **FORMATION** Forms in limestones which have been altered by contact metamorphism. It sometimes occurs in the rare, calcite-rich group of igneous rocks called carbonatites.
• **TESTS** It is soluble in hot hydrochloric acid, and produces a precipitate that takes on a gelatinous appearance as the solution cools down. It is also infusible.

twinned chondrodite crystals

MONOCLINIC

rock groundmass

crystals with magnetite, an associated mineral

SG 3.16–3.26	Cleavage Poor	Fracture Uneven

Group Silicates	Composition $Al_2SiO_4(F,OH)_2$	Hardness 8

TOPAZ

This mineral occurs as well-formed prismatic crystals, which can be of great size, and may weigh over 100 kilogrammes (220 lb). Topaz can also form in massive, granular, and columnar habits. The colour of this mineral is very variable: it may be white, colourless, grey, yellow, orange, brown, bluish, greenish, purple, or pink. The streak is colourless. Topaz is transparent to translucent, and has a vitreous lustre.

• **FORMATION** Forms most commonly in pegmatites. Topaz can also form in veins and cavities in granitic rocks. Topaz occurs with a variety of minerals, including quartz.

• **TESTS** Insoluble in acids; infusible when flame heated.

prismatic topaz crystal

crystals in pegmatite groundmass

ORTHORHOMBIC

SG 3.49–3.57	Cleavage Perfect	Fracture Subconchoidal to uneven

Group Silicates	Composition Zn_2SiO_4	Hardness 5½

WILLEMITE

Hexagonal prismatic crystals, which are frequently terminated by rhombohedra, are formed by this mineral. It may also occur in massive, fibrous, compact, and granular habits. Willemite may be white, colourless, grey, green, yellow, brown, or reddish. The streak is colourless. Willemite is transparent to translucent, and it has a vitreous or resinous lustre.

• **FORMATION** Forms in the oxidized zone of zinc ore deposits, in veins, by secondary alteration, and in metamorphosed limestone rocks.

• **TESTS** It can be very phosphorescent. It is soluble in hydrochloric acid. Also exhibits bright-green fluorescence under ultra-violet light.

vitreous to resinous lustre

franklinite, an associated mineral

prismatic willemite crystals

rock groundmass

TRIGONAL / HEXAGONAL

SG 3.89–4.19	Cleavage Basal	Fracture Uneven

Group Silicates	Composition $(Fe,Mg,Zn)_2Al_9(Si,Al)_4O_{22}(OH)_2$	Hardness $7-7\frac{1}{2}$

STAUROLITE

This mineral forms short, prismatic crystals, which are often in the form of cruciform twins. The colour is dark brown, reddish brown, yellowish brown, or brownish black. The streak is colourless to greyish. Staurolite is translucent to nearly opaque, and has a vitreous to resinous lustre.

• **FORMATION** Forms deep in the earth's crust, in regionally metamorphosed rocks, such as gneisses and mica schists, that have been formed by extremes of temperature and pressure. It is associated with metamorphic minerals such as kyanite, muscovite, garnet, and quartz.

• **TESTS** Some varieties have manganese traces, in which case they will fuse.

twinned staurolite crystals

mica schist groundmass

MONOCLINIC

vitreous lustre

prismatic staurolite crystal

uneven to subconchoidal fracture

SG $3.65-3.83$	Cleavage Distinct	Fracture Uneven to subconchoidal

Group Silicates	Composition $(Fe,Mg,Mn)_2Al_4Si_2O_{10}(OH)_4$	Hardness $6\frac{1}{2}$

CHLORITOID

Crystals are rare. When they occur, they are tabular or pseudohexagonal, and commonly twinned. Chloritoid usually forms in foliated or massive habits, or as scales or plates. It is dark grey, or greenish to greenish black in colour. No streak has been determined. This is a translucent mineral. It has a pearly lustre on cleavage surfaces.

• **FORMATION** Forms in rocks, such as schist and phyllite, which have been regionally metamorphosed. Chloritoid also forms in pegmatites. Associated minerals are muscovite, chlorite, garnet, staurolite (above), as well as kyanite.

• **TESTS** Chloritoid is soluble in concentrated sulphuric acid, but not in hydrochloric acid. It fuses, but only with some difficulty.

foliated chloritoid

dark grey chloritoid crystals in pegmatite groundmass

pearly lustre on cleavage surfaces

TRICLINIC / MONOCLINIC

SG 3.6	Cleavage Perfect	Fracture Uneven

Group Silicates	Composition $ZrSiO_4$	Hardness $7\frac{1}{2}$

ZIRCON

This mineral forms as prismatic crystals with bipyramidal terminations, and also as radiating fibrous aggregates. Twinned crystals are common. Other habits include irregular grains. Zircon is colourless, red, brown, yellow, green, or grey. Zircon is a transparent to opaque mineral, and has a vitreous, adamantine, or greasy lustre.

• **FORMATION** Forms in igneous rocks, such as syenite, and in certain metamorphic rocks. Zircon also occurs in many detrital sedimentary rocks, where it is a product of weathering and erosion of primary, zircon-bearing rocks.

• **TESTS** Zircon is often a radioactive mineral, because it can contain small amounts of uranium and thorium.

zircon crystals set in syenite • groundmass

prismatic • zircon

TETRAGONAL

• vitreous lustre

SG 4.6–4.7	Cleavage Imperfect	Fracture Uneven to conchoidal

Group Silicates	Composition Al_2SiO_5	Hardness $6\frac{1}{2}$–$7\frac{1}{2}$

ANDALUSITE

This mineral forms prismatic crystals, with an almost square cross-section. (Chiastolite is a variety of andalusite with a cruciform cross-section.) Andalusite also occurs in massive, fibrous, or columnar habits. The colour is pink, reddish, brownish, whitish, greyish, or greenish, and the streak is colourless. This is a transparent to nearly opaque mineral. Its lustre is vitreous.

• **FORMATION** Forms in granites, and pegmatites, and in many metamorphosed rocks. It occurs with kyanite, cordierite, sillimanite, and corundum.

• **TESTS** This mineral is insoluble in any fluids, and infusible when heated with a flame.

prismatic andalusite crystal •

quartz groundmass •

• uneven fracture

ORTHORHOMBIC

distinct cleavage •

SG 3.13–3.16	Cleavage Distinct prismatic	Fracture Uneven to subconchoidal

Group Silicates	Composition Al_2SiO_5	Hardness $6\frac{1}{2}$–$7\frac{1}{2}$

SILLIMANITE

Long prismatic crystals, with an almost square cross-section, are formed by this mineral. It can occur in fibrous masses. Sillimanite may be white, colourless, grey, yellowish, brownish, greenish, or bluish. The streak is colourless. It is a transparent to translucent mineral, and it has a vitreous to silky lustre.

• **FORMATION** Sillimanite forms in metamorphic rocks, and also in some igneous rocks.

• **TESTS** This mineral is infusible, and insoluble in acids.

vitreous lustre •

• *rock groundmass*

ORTHORHOMBIC

elongated • *prismatic sillimanite crystals*

SG 3.23–3.27	Cleavage Perfect	Fracture Uneven

Group Silicates	Composition Al_2SiO_5	Hardness $5\frac{1}{2}$–7

KYANITE

Trimorphous with sillimanite and andalusite, kyanite forms elongated, flattened, and bladed crystals which are often twisted or bent. It also occurs in massive and fibrous habits. The colour is blue, white, grey, green, yellow, pink, or almost black, and often varies in a single crystal. There is a colourless streak. It is a transparent to translucent mineral, and it has a vitreous lustre, which becomes pearly on cleavage surfaces.

• **FORMATION** Kyanite forms in many metamorphic rocks, especially schists and gneisses. Its presence in schists allows geologists to estimate the temperature and pressure conditions in which they formed.

• **TESTS** Its hardness is 6–7 across cleavage planes, but only 4–5 along cleavage planes.

staurolite, an associated mineral •

rock groundmass •

elongated • *kyanite crystals*

TRICLINIC

vitreous lustre •

SG 3.53–3.67	Cleavage Perfect	Fracture Uneven

Group Silicates	Composition $CaTiSiO_5$	Hardness 5–5½

SPHENE

The crystals formed by sphene are wedge-shaped or prismatic, and commonly twinned. This mineral also occurs in massive, lamellar, and compact habits. The colour may be brown, yellow, green, grey, red, or black, and often varies within a single crystal. A colourless form also occurs. The streak is white. It is a transparent to nearly opaque mineral, and it has an adamantine to resinous lustre.

• **FORMATION** Sphene occurs in many igneous rocks as an accessory mineral.

• **TESTS** It is soluble in sulphuric acid.

MONOCLINIC

wedge-shaped crystals •

twinned crystals •

• *adamantine lustre*

SG 3.45–3.55	Cleavage Distinct	Fracture Conchoidal

Group Silicates	Composition $Al_7(BO_3)(SiO_4)_3O_3$	Hardness 8½

DUMORTIERITE

On the rare occasions that dumortierite forms crystals, they are prismatic. The usual habits are massive, fibrous, radiating, and columnar. The colour may be blue, violet, pink, or brown, and the streak is white. Dumortierite is a transparent to translucent mineral, and it has a vitreous to dull lustre.

• **FORMATION** This mineral forms in coarse-grained, acid igneous rocks, including pegmatites. Rocks rich in aluminium often contain dumortierite, especially when they have been altered by contact metamorphism. The exceptionally coarse-grained pegmatites are formed by very slow cooling of magmatic fluids in a chemically-rich environment, at some depth in the earth's crust.

• **TESTS** It does not dissolve in any acids, and it is infusible if placed in a flame.

ORTHORHOMBIC

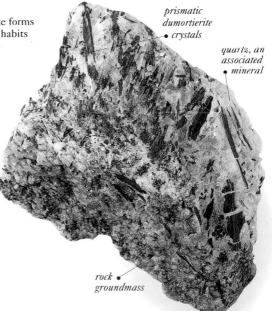

prismatic dumortierite • *crystals*

quartz, an associated • *mineral*

rock • *groundmass*

SG 3.41	Cleavage Good	Fracture Uneven

Group Silicates	Composition BeAlSiO$_4$(OH)	Hardness 7½

EUCLASE

This mineral forms as prismatic crystals. It may be colourless, whitish, pale green, blue, or pale blue. The streak is white. Euclase is transparent to translucent, and it has a vitreous lustre on crystal surfaces.
• **FORMATION** Forms in granite pegmatites. It can also occur in alluvial placer sediments.
• **TESTS** This mineral is insoluble in acids, and fuses with some difficulty.

MONOCLINIC

prismatic crystals

perfect cleavage

striated crystal

SG 3.05–3.10	Cleavage Perfect	Fracture Conchoidal

Group Silicates	Composition K$_2$Ca$_4$Al$_2$Be$_4$Si$_{24}$O$_{60}$H$_2$O	Hardness 5½–6

MILARITE

This mineral forms as prismatic crystals. It is colourless, brownish, pale green, or yellowish green, with a white streak. It is transparent to translucent, with a vitreous lustre.
• **FORMATION** Milarite forms in alpine veins and pegmatites.
• **TESTS** Gives off water when heated in a closed test tube.

TRIGONAL/ HEXAGONAL

rock groundmass

prismatic milarite crystal

SG 2.46–2.61	Cleavage None	Fracture Conchoidal to uneven

Group Silicates	Composition Na$_4$ (Ca,Ce)$_2$(Fe^{+2}Mn^{+2}Y)ZrSi$_8$O$_{22}$ (OH, Cl)$_2$	Hardness 5–5½

EUDIALYTE

Crystals are tabular, rhombohedral, or prismatic. Eudialyte is yellowish brown, to brownish red, red, or pink in colour, and the streak is colourless. It is a translucent mineral, and has a vitreous to dull lustre.
• **FORMATION** Forms in coarse-grained acid and intermediate igneous rocks.
• **TESTS** This mineral is easily dissolved in acids.

TRIGONAL/ HEXAGONAL

eudialyte crystals

arfvedsonite, an associated mineral

uneven fracture

SG 2.74–2.98	Cleavage Indistinct	Fracture Uneven

Group Silicates	Composition CaBSiO₄(OH)	Hardness 5–5½

DATOLITE

This mineral forms as short prismatic, very variable, crystals, and also as granular or compact masses. It is colourless, white, pale yellow, pale green, or tinted pink, reddish, or brown by impurities. The streak is colourless. Datolite is a transparent to translucent mineral, with a vitreous lustre.
• **FORMATION** This mineral forms in veins and cavities in basaltic igneous rocks. It also occurs with calcite, quartz, and some zeolite minerals.
• **TESTS** It is soluble in acids, and turns a flame green.

short prismatic crystals

uneven fracture

vitreous lustre

MONOCLINIC

SG 2.8–3.0	Cleavage None	Fracture Uneven to conchoidal

Group Silicates	Composition Y₂FeBe₂,Si₂O₁₀	Hardness 6½–7

GADOLINITE

Crystals are prismatic, but rarely form. Gadolinite usually occurs in massive and compact habits. The colour varies considerably from black to greenish black, brown, and sometimes light green, with a greenish grey streak. It is a translucent to transparent mineral, with a vitreous to greasy lustre.
• **FORMATION** Forms in coarse-grained intermediate igneous rocks. Gadolinite can also occur in acid igneous rocks, and in pegmatites formed by the slow cooling of intruded magma. This mineral can occur with other minerals, including allanite and fluorite, and has been discovered in schists, and other regionally metamorphosed rocks.
• **TESTS** Gadolinite is a radioactive mineral, which dissolves in acids, leaving a gelatinous precipitate. Although gadolinite is not fusible when heated, it will, however, become flaky and turn brown in colour.

greasy lustre

massive habit

prismatic crystal

MONOCLINIC

SG 4.0–4.65	Cleavage None	Fracture Conchoidal

Group Silicates	Composition $Ca_2(Al,Fe)_3(SiO_4)_3(OH)$	Hardness 6–7

EPIDOTE

Occurring as prismatic crystals, which are often striated, epidote also forms thick, tabular and acicular crystals. Other habits are massive, granular, and fibrous. The colour is yellowish green to green, brownish green to greenish black, or black. There is a colourless or greyish streak. Epidote is a transparent to nearly opaque mineral, and it has a vitreous lustre.
• **FORMATION** Forms in metamorphic and igneous rocks.
• **TESTS** It is insoluble, and fuses fairly easily.

striated prismatic crystals

vitreous lustre

translucent

MONOCLINIC

SG 3.35–3.50	Cleavage Perfect	Fracture Uneven

Group Silicates	Composition $Ca_2Al_3(SiO_4)_3(OH)$	Hardness 6½–7

ZOISITE

This mineral occurs as prismatic crystals, which often have deep, vertical striations. It also forms in massive, compact, and columnar habits. The colour may be white, grey, green, greenish brown, pink (thulite), colourless, blue, or purple (tanzanite). There is a colourless streak. It is a transparent to translucent mineral. The lustre is vitreous.
• **FORMATION** Zoisite forms in many rocks, including metamorphosed sediments and granites.
• **TESTS** Insoluble in acids.

THULITE

massive habit

pegmatite groundmass

prismatic zoisite crystals

ZOISITE

deep striations running vertically on crystal faces

ORTHORHOMBIC

SG 3.55	Cleavage Perfect	Fracture Uneven to conchoidal

Group Silicates	Composition $Ca_2Al_3(SiO_4)_3(OH)$	Hardness 6½

CLINOZOISITE

Crystals are prismatic, and often deeply striated. The mineral also forms as acicular crystals, and in massive, granular, or fibrous habits. It may be grey, yellow, pale green, pink, or colourless. The streak is colourless or greyish. It is a transparent to translucent mineral and has a vitreous lustre.
• **FORMATION** Forms in contact metamorphosed limestones, and regionally metamorphosed rocks.
• **TESTS** Insoluble in acids.

mass of radiating acicular crystals

vitreous lustre

MONOCLINIC

SG 3.21–3.38	Cleavage Perfect	Fracture Uneven

Group Silicates	Composition $Ca_2Al(Si,Al)O_7$	Hardness 5–6

GEHLENITE

A member of the melilite group, gehlenite occurs as short, prismatic crystals, and also in massive and granular habits. Gehlenite can be greyish green, brown, yellow, or colourless. The streak is undetermined. It is transparent to translucent, with a vitreous to resinous lustre.
• **FORMATION** Gehlenite forms in basaltic lavas and contact metamorphosed limestones.
• **TESTS** Soluble in strong acids.

massive habit

short prismatic gehlenite crystals

calcite, an associated mineral

uneven fracture   TETRAGONAL

SG 3.04	Cleavage Distinct	Fracture Uneven to conchoidal

Group Silicates	Composition $Ca_2MgSi_2O_7$	Hardness 5–6

AKERMANITE

This mineral forms prismatic crystals, which may be twinned. It can occur in massive and granular habits. Akermanite varies from colourless to greyish, brown, and green. It is transparent to translucent, with a vitreous to resinous lustre.
• **FORMATION** Forms in thermally metamorphosed impure limestones.
• **TESTS** It is soluble in strong acids, with gelatization.

prismatic crystal

TETRAGONAL

SG 2.94	Cleavage Distinct	Fracture Uneven to conchoidal

Group Silicates	Composition $Zn_4Si_2O_7(OH)_2.H_2O$	Hardness $4\frac{1}{2}$–5

HEMIMORPHITE

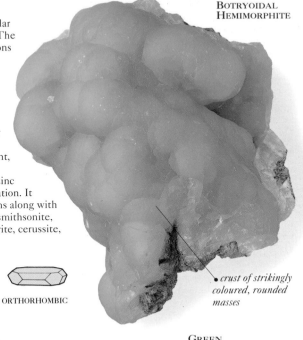

This mineral forms as thin, tabular crystals, with vertical striations. The crystals have different terminations at each end, which are termed hemimorphic. Hemimorphite also occurs in massive, compact, granular, botryoidal, stalactitic, fibrous, and encrusting habits. The colour is white, colourless, blue, greenish, grey, yellowish or brown, and the streak is colourless. It is transparent to translucent, with a vitreous or silky lustre.

• **FORMATION** Forms where zinc veins have been altered by oxidation. It commonly occurs in mineral veins along with many other minerals, including smithsonite, galena, calcite, anglesite, sphalerite, cerussite, and aurichalcite.

• **TESTS** It gives off water when heated in a closed tube. It is soluble in acids with gelatinization, and fuses only with great difficulty.

ORTHORHOMBIC

• *crust of strikingly coloured, rounded masses*

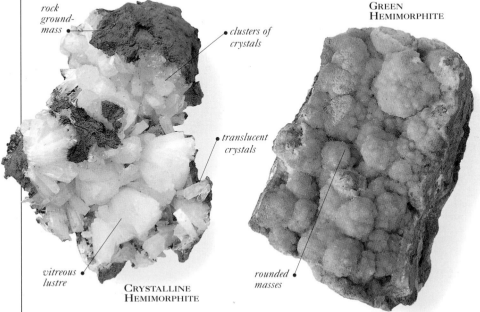

rock ground-mass •

• *clusters of crystals*

GREEN
HEMIMORPHITE

• *translucent crystals*

vitreous lustre •

CRYSTALLINE
HEMIMORPHITE

rounded masses •

SG 3.4–3.5	Cleavage Perfect	Fracture Uneven to conchoidal

Group Silicates	Composition $Ca_{10}Mg_2Al_4(SiO_4)_5(Si_2O_7)_2(OH)_4$	Hardness 6–7

VESUVIANITE

Also known as idocrase, this mineral forms short prismatic and pyramidal crystals. It can occur in massive, granular, columnar, and compact habits. Idocrase is green, brown, white, yellow, red, or purple. A blue variety is called cyprine, and californite is white or yellow. It is transparent to translucent and the lustre is vitreous to resinous. A semi-precious gemstone when transparent, vesuvianite was discovered at Mount Vesuvius, Italy.

• **FORMATION** Vesuvianite forms in impure limestones that have been altered by contact metamorphism. It also occurs in some igneous rocks, including nepheline syenite. It is found with many minerals, including diopside, epidote, garnets, calcite, phlogopite, and wollastonite.

TETRAGONAL

• **TESTS** This mineral is virtually insoluble in acids.

prismatic crystals

vitreous lustre on crystal faces

IDOCRASE

columnar crystals

resinous lustre

thulite, an associated mineral

CYPRINE

massive habit

resinous lustre

CALIFORNITE

SG 3.33–3.45	Cleavage Indistinct	Fracture Uneven to conchoidal

Group Silicates	Composition $Be_3Al_2Si_6O_{18}$	Hardness 7–8

BERYL

This mineral occurs as prismatic crystals, which are sometimes terminated with small pyramids. The crystals are often striated parallel to their length, and may be of vast size; specimens up to 5.5 m (18feet) long have been recorded. It also forms in massive, compact, and columnar habits. The colour varies greatly, and gives rise to named varieties. It may be colourless, white, green (emerald), yellow (heliodor), pink (morganite), red, and blue (aqua-marine). The streak is white. Beryl is transparent to translucent, with a vitreous lustre.

• **FORMATION** Forms in pegmatites and granites and in some regionally metamorphosed rocks.

• **TESTS** It fuses with difficulty, rounding the edges of small fragments.

transparent

prismatic crystal

rock groundmass

BERYL

rock groundmass

perfect prismatic crystal

HELIODOR

transparent

vitreous lustre

EMERALD

transparent to translucent

MORGANITE

vitreous lustre

AQUAMARINE

TRIGONAL/ HEXAGONAL

SG 2.6–2.9	Cleavage Indistinct	Fracture Uneven to conchoidal

Group Silicates	Composition $Na(Mg,Fe,Li,Mn,Al)_3Al_6(BO_3)_3Si_6.O_{18}(OH,F)_4$	Hardness 7–7½

TOURMALINE

The prismatic crystals formed by this group are often vertically striated. These crystals may be rounded triangular in cross-section. It also forms in massive and compact habits. Seven distinct species make up the tourmaline group: elbaite (multi-hued), schorl (black), buergerite and dravite (brown), rubellite (pink), chromdravite (green), and uvite (black, brown, yellow-green). Crystals are often pink at one end and green at the other, and may be of considerable size. There is a colourless streak. Tourmaline is transparent to opaque, and has a vitreous lustre.

• **FORMATION** Forms in granites and pegmatites, as well as in some metamorphic rocks. Tourmaline may be found with a wide range of minerals, including beryl, zircon, quartz, and feldspar.

• **TESTS** This group is insoluble in acids. The darker minerals tend to fuse with more difficulty than the red and green varieties.

vertically striated crystal

RUBELLITE

vitreous lustre

ELBAITE

feldspar groundmass

prismatic crystal

transparent bi-coloured crystal

TOURMALINE

vitreous lustre

quartz, an associated mineral

schorl crystal

SCHORL

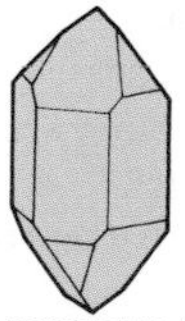

TRIGONAL/ HEXAGONAL

SG 3.0–3.2	Cleavage Very indistinct	Fracture Uneven to conchoidal

Group Silicates	Composition $CaFe^{+2}_2Fe^{+3}(SiO_4)_2(OH)$	Hardness $5\frac{1}{2}$–6

ILVAITE

The crystals of this mineral are thick and prismatic, and diamond-shaped in cross-section. The crystal faces may be striated vertically. Ilvaite also occurs in massive, columnar, and compact habits. It is a very dark coloured mineral, often black to greyish brown, or brownish black in colour. The streak is black, often with greenish or brownish tints. This is an opaque mineral, with a dull, submetallic lustre, which sometimes appears glossy.

• **FORMATION** Forms in rocks which have been intruded by magma, or come into contact with lava, and as a result have been altered by contact metamorphism. It also occurs, less commonly, in the igneous rock, syenite.

• **TESTS** When placed in hydrochloric acid, ilvaite is soluble, with gelatinization. It fuses easily in a flame.

prismatic crystals

vertical striations

submetallic lustre

diamond-shaped crystal cross-sections

ORTHORHOMBIC

SG 3.8–4.1	Cleavage Distinct	Fracture Uneven

Group Silicates	Composition $CuSiO_2(OH)_2$	Hardness 5

DIOPTASE

This mineral forms prismatic crystals, often with rhombohedral terminations. It may also occur as crystalline aggregates, or in a massive habit. The colour is a striking emerald to deep bluish green, and the streak is pale greenish blue. Dioptase is transparent to translucent. It has a vitreous lustre.

• **FORMATION** Occurs where copper veins have been altered by oxidation, and in hollows and cavities in the surrounding rocks. Dioptase is usually associated with limonite, chrysocolla, and cerussite, as well as wulfenite.

• **TESTS** Soluble in hydrochloric acid, nitric acid, and ammonia. Infusible.

prismatic crystals

perfect rhombohedral cleavage

rhombohedral terminations

TRIGONAL / HEXAGONAL

aggregate of crystals

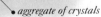

SG 3.28–3.35	Cleavage Perfect	Fracture Uneven to conchoidal

Group Silicates	Composition $Mg_2Al_4Si_5O_{18}$	Hardness 7–7½

CORDIERITE

Crystals are short and prismatic, and twinning is common. Other habits are massive and granular. It is blue, but can be greenish, yellowish, grey, or brown, and is often strongly pleochroic. The streak is colourless. Cordierite is transparent to translucent, with a vitreous lustre.
• **FORMATION** Cordierite forms in igneous and contact metamorphic rocks.
• **TESTS** Fusible on thin edges in flames.

distinct cleavage

rock groundmass

ORTHORHOMBIC

prismatic cordierite crystal

transparent to translucent

SG 2.53–2.78	Cleavage Distinct	Fracture Conchoidal

Group Silicates	Composition $Ca_2(Fe^{+2},Mn^{+2})Al_2BSi_4O_{15}(OH)$	Hardness 6–7

AXINITE

Crystals are tabular and wedge-shaped. Other habits are massive and lamellar. Axinite is reddish brown, yellow, colourless, blue, violet, or grey, and has a colourless streak. It is transparent to translucent, and it has a vitreous lustre.
• **FORMATION** Forms in calcareous rocks altered by contact metamorphism.
• **TESTS** Axinite fuses easily.

tabular, wedge-shaped crystals

vitreous lustre

TRICLINIC

transparent to translucent

SG 3.2–3.4	Cleavage Good	Fracture Uneven to conchoidal

Group Silicates	Composition $BaTiSi_3O_9$	Hardness 6–6½

BENITOITE

The crystals are pyramidal or tabular. Benitoite is blue, purple, pink, white, or colourless, and often vari-coloured. The streak is colourless. It is a transparent to translucent mineral, with a vitreous lustre.
• **FORMATION** Forms in serpentinites and also in schists.
• **TESTS** It fluoresces blue under shortwave ultra-violet light.

rock groundmass

pyramidal benitoite crystals

vitreous lustre

TRIGONAL / HEXAGONAL

natrolite, an associated mineral

SG 3.64–3.68	Cleavage Indistinct	Fracture Conchoidal to uneven

Group Silicates	Composition $Mg_2Si_2O_6$	Hardness 5–6

ENSTATITE

A member of the pyroxene group, enstatite forms rarely as prismatic crystals, and usually in massive, fibrous, or lamellar habits. It may be colourless, green, brown, or yellowish, and has a colourless or grey streak. Enstatite is a transparent to nearly opaque mineral, and it has a vitreous or pearly lustre.
• FORMATION Commonly forms in basic and ultrabasic igneous rocks, such as gabbro, dolerite, norite, and peridotite.
• TESTS Insoluble, and almost infusible.

small prismatic crystals

ORTHORHOMBIC

SG 3.2–3.4	Cleavage Good	Fracture Uneven

Group Silicates	Composition $(Mg,Fe)_2Si_2O_6$	Hardness 5–6

HYPERSTHENE

A pyroxene, hypersthene forms rarely as prismatic crystals, and usually in massive or lamellar habits. The colour is brownish green or black. The streak is brownish grey. It is a translucent to opaque mineral, and has a submetallic lustre.
• FORMATION Hypersthene forms both in ultrabasic and basic igneous rocks.
• TESTS It is fusible, and may display schillerization.

cleaved fragment

submetallic lustre

ORTHORHOMBIC

uneven fracture

SG 3.4–3.8	Cleavage Good	Fracture Uneven

Group Silicates	Composition $CaMgSi_2O_6$	Hardness 5½–6½

DIOPSIDE

A pyroxene, diopside forms short prismatic crystals, which are often twinned. Other habits are massive, lamellar, granular, and columnar. It is colourless, white, grey, green, greenish black, yellowish brown, or reddish brown, and has a white to grey streak. It is transparent to nearly opaque, with a vitreous lustre.
• FORMATION Diopside forms in many metamorphic rocks, and in basic igneous rocks.
• TESTS It is insoluble in acids.

prismatic diopside crystal in groundmass

vitreous lustre

MONOCLINIC

SG 3.22–3.38	Cleavage Good	Fracture Uneven

Group Silicates	Composition $CaFeSi_2O_6$	Hardness 6

HEDENBERGITE

Crystals are short prismatic, and commonly twinned. More usual habits are massive, bladed, or lamellar. The colour varies from brownish green, greyish green, or dark green, to greyish black, or black. There is a white or grey streak. It is translucent to nearly opaque, with a vitreous to resinous or dull lustre.
• FORMATION In marbles, and in a variety of igneous rocks.
• TESTS This pyroxene is insoluble, and fuses fairly easily.

mass of bladed crystals

vitreous lustre

MONOCLINIC

SG 3.50–3.56	Cleavage Good	Fracture Uneven to conchoidal

Group Silicates	Composition $(Ca,Na)(Mg,Fe,Al,Ti)(Si,Al)_2O_6$	Hardness 5½–6

AUGITE

A pyroxene, augite occurs as short prismatic crystals, which are often twinned. It also forms in massive, compact, and granular habits. The colour is brown, greenish, or black. There is a greyish green streak. It is translucent to nearly opaque, with a vitreous to dull lustre.
• FORMATION Forms in many basic and ultrabasic igneous rocks, and in high grade metamorphic rocks.
• TESTS Usually insoluble in acids.

prismatic augite crystal

vitreous lustre

rock groundmass

uneven fracture

MONOCLINIC

SG 3.23–3.52	Cleavage Good	Fracture Uneven to conchoidal

Group Silicates	Composition $NaFeSi_2O_6$	Hardness 6

AEGIRINE

A member of the pyroxene group, aegirine forms long, vertically striated, prismatic crystals, which are often twinned. It also occurs as fibrous aggregates. The colour is dark green, greenish black, black, or reddish brown. There is a pale yellowish grey streak. It is translucent to opaque, with a vitreous to resinous lustre.
• FORMATION Forms in intermediate igneous rocks and in metamorphic rocks.
• TESTS Fuses easily.

long, prismatic aegirine crystal

vertical striations

MONOCLINIC

SG 3.55–3.60	Cleavage Good	Fracture Uneven

Group Silicates	Composition $LiAlSi_2O_6$	Hardness $6\frac{1}{2}-7\frac{1}{2}$

SPODUMENE

This mineral forms as prismatic crystals, which are often flattened, twinned, and vertically striated. They may be of great size. It also occurs as cleavable masses. The colour varies greatly. It may be colourless, white, grey, yellowish, greenish, emerald green (hiddenite), pink, or lilac (kunzite). The streak is white. Spodumene is transparent to translucent. This pyroxene has a vitreous lustre.

• **FORMATION** Forms in granitic pegmatites. It is found with other pegmatite minerals, including feldspar, muscovite, biotite and lepidolite mica, quartz, columbite-tantalite, beryl, tourmaline, and topaz. It is metastable, and is often found partially or totally altered to clay or mica.

• **TESTS** Spodumene is an insoluble mineral. It fuses, colouring the flame red due to the presence of lithium.

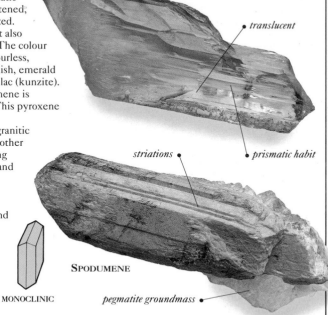

KUNZITE

translucent

striations • prismatic habit

SPODUMENE

MONOCLINIC

pegmatite groundmass •

SG 3.0–3.2	Cleavage Perfect	Fracture Uneven

Group Silicates	Composition $Na(Al,Fe)Si_2O_6$	Hardness 6–7

JADEITE

It is rare for jadeite to form crystals. When it does, the crystals are small, prismatic, and elongated. They are usually striated, and often twinned. It mostly occurs in massive or granular habits. The colour is typically green, but can be white, grey, mauve, and, when stained by iron oxides, brown, or yellow. The streak is colourless. Jadeite is an important orna-mental gem, and is translucent, with a vitreous to greasy lustre.

• **FORMATION** Forms in serpentinized ultrabasic igneous rocks, and in some schists. It has also been found as small veins and lens-shaped inclusions in chert and greywacke.

• **TESTS** Jadeite is insoluble.

massive habit •

• greasy lustre

MONOCLINIC

SG 3.24	Cleavage Good	Fracture Splintery

Group Silicates	Composition $Ca_2(Mg,Fe)_4Al(Si_7Al)O_{22}(OH,F)_2$	Hardness 5–6

HORNBLENDE

This amphibole forms prismatic crystals, often hexagonal in cross-section, and frequently twinned. It also occurs in massive, compact, granular, columnar, bladed, and fibrous habits. It is green, greenish brown, or black. The streak is white or grey. It is translucent to opaque. The lustre is vitreous. There is an angle of 60° or 120° between cleavage planes.
• **FORMATION** In igneous rocks, and also found in the metamorphic rock, amphibolite.
• **TESTS** Insoluble. Fuses with difficulty.

• *prismatic hornblende crystals*

• *twinned crystals*

MONOCLINIC

SG 3.28–3.41	Cleavage Perfect	Fracture Uneven

Group Silicates	Composition $(Mg,Fe)_7Si_8O_{22}(OH)_2$	Hardness 5½–6

ANTHOPHYLLITE

This amphibole forms prismatic crystals, but it is rare for it to do so. It occurs in massive, fibrous, or lamellar habits. The colour is white to grey, greenish, brownish green, and brown. There is a colourless or grey streak. This mineral is transparent to almost opaque. It has a vitreous lustre.
•**FORMATION** Forms in crystalline schists and gneisses.
• **TESTS** Insoluble, but fuses with difficulty.

ORTHORHOMBIC

• *mass of fibrous, radiating crystals*

• *vitreous lustre*

• *radiating aggregate*

SG 2.85–3.57	Cleavage Perfect	Fracture Uneven

Group Silicates	Composition $(Fe,Mg)_7Si_8O_{22}(OH)_2$	Hardness 5–6

GRUNERITE

An end member of the cummingtonite–grunerite amphibole series, grunerite forms as fibrous or lamellar crystals, which are often in radiating aggregates. They are very commonly twinned. It is grey, dark green, or brown. Grunerite is translucent to nearly opaque, and has a silky lustre.
• **FORMATION** In rocks which have undergone contact metamorphism
• **TESTS** It is insoluble.

• *opaque*

• *fibrous habit*

MONOCLINIC

silky lustre •

SG 3.44–3.60	Cleavage Good	Fracture Uneven

Group Silicates	Composition $Na_2(Mg,Fe)_3Al_2Si_8O_{22}(OH)_2$	Hardness 6

GLAUCOPHANE

A member of the amphibole group, it forms as slender, prismatic crystals. Other habits are massive, fibrous, and granular. It is grey, blue, bluish black, or lavender-blue. The streak is a greyish blue. Glaucophane is a translucent mineral, and has a vitreous to dull or pearly lustre.
• **FORMATION** Forms in metamorphic rocks, chiefly those subjected to low temperature and high pressure conditions.
• **TESTS** It is insoluble in acids, and fuses readily to a green-coloured glass.

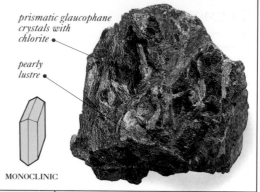

prismatic glaucophane crystals with chlorite

pearly lustre

MONOCLINIC

SG 3.08–3.15	Cleavage Perfect	Fracture Uneven to conchoidal

Group Silicates	Composition $Na_3(Fe^{+2},Mg)_4Fe^{+3}Si_8O_{22}(OH)_2$	Hardness 5

RIEBECKITE

Long, prismatic crystals with parallel striations occur in this mineral. It may also be massive, fibrous, and asbestiform (crocidolite). The colour is dark blue to black. No streak has been determined. Riebeckite is translucent, and it has a vitreous or silky lustre.
• **FORMATION** Forms in many igneous rocks, and in schists.
• **TESTS** Fuses easily.

group of prismatic crystals

vitreous lustre

MONOCLINIC

SG 3.32–3.38	Cleavage Perfect	Fracture Uneven

Group Silicates	Composition $Ca_2(Mg,Fe)_5Si_8O_{22}(OH)_2$	Hardness 5–6

ACTINOLITE

The crystals form as long, bladed specimens, commonly twinned. Actinolite may be in lamellar and columnar aggregates, often radiating, and in massive, fibrous, or granular habits. The colour is light to blackish green. The streak is white. Actinolite is transparent to nearly opaque, and has a vitreous lustre. A compact variety is called nephrite, a form of jade.
• **FORMATION** Forms in schists and amphibolites, commonly from the metamorphism of basic igneous rocks.
• **TESTS** Insoluble in hydrochloric acid.

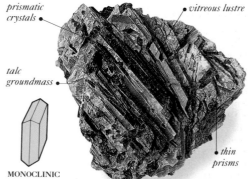

prismatic crystals

vitreous lustre

talc groundmass

thin prisms

MONOCLINIC

SG 3.0–3.44	Cleavage Good	Fracture Uneven to subconchoidal

Group Silicates	Composition $Ca_2(Mg,Fe)_5Si_8O_{22}(OH)_2$	Hardness 5–6

TREMOLITE

This mineral occurs as long, bladed crystals, which are often twinned. It also forms as columnar, fibrous, or plumose aggregates, often radiating, and in massive or granular habits. It is colourless, white, grey, green, pink, or brown. The streak is white. Tremolite is transparent to translucent; it has a vitreous lustre. It forms a series with actinolite.

• **FORMATION** Forms in contact metamorphosed dolomites, and in serpentinites.

• **TESTS** Insoluble in acids.

plumose aggregate of tremolite crystals

MONOCLINIC

vitreous to silky lustre

SG 2.9–3.2	Cleavage Good	Fracture Uneven to subconchoidal

Group Silicates	Composition $Na_3(Fe,Mg)_4FeSi_8O_{22}(OH)_2$	Hardness 5–6

ARFVEDSONITE

This mineral occurs as prismatic and tabular crystals, frequently in aggregates. It is often twinned. The colour is greenish black to black. The streak is dark, bluish grey. Arfvedsonite is almost opaque, and has a vitreous lustre.

• **FORMATION** Forms in igneous rocks, especially syenite. Also found in some regionally metamorphosed rocks, including schists.

• **TESTS** Insoluble in acids. Fuses easily, producing magnetic black glass.

cleaved arfvedsonite crystal fragments

MONOCLINIC

rock groundmass

SG 3.37–3.50	Cleavage Perfect	Fracture Uneven

Group Silicates	Composition $Na_2Ca(Mg,Fe)_5Si_8O_{22}(OH)_2$	Hardness 5–6

RICHTERITE

The crystal forms of this mineral are long and prismatic. The colour is brown, yellow, brownish red, or pale to dark green. There is a pale yellow streak. Richterite is transparent to translucent, and it has a vitreous lustre on fresh surfaces.

• **FORMATION** Forms in extrusive alkali-rich igneous rocks, and in contact metamorphosed limestones.

• **TESTS** This mineral is almost insoluble when placed in acids, but fuses easily when heated in a flame.

prismatic richterite crystals

vitreous lustre

quartz groundmass

MONOCLINIC

SG 2.97–3.13	Cleavage Perfect	Fracture Uneven

Group Silicates	Composition $(Mn^{+2},Fe^{+2},Mg,Ca)SiO_3$	Hardness 5½–6½

RHODONITE

This mineral occurs as tabular crystals, often with rounded edges, and also in massive, compact, and granular habits. The colour is pink to rose-red, and can be brownish red. It often has black veins of manganese-rich alteration products. The streak is white. It is a transparent to translucent mineral. Rhodonite has a vitreous lustre on crystal faces, which becomes pearly on cleavage surfaces.

• **FORMATION** This mineral forms in metamorphic rocks rich in manganese, and metasomatically altered sediments. These rocks include skarns and marbles, especially those which were originally impure limestones.

• **TESTS** Rhodonite fuses fairly easily. This process produces a glassy substance which may be coloured.

vitreous lustre

uneven fracture

massive habit

transparent to translucent

TRICLINIC

SG 3.57–3.76	Cleavage Perfect		Fracture Conchoidal to uneven

Group Silicates	Composition $NaCa_2Si_3O_8(OH)$	Hardness 4½–5

PECTOLITE

This mineral occurs as aggregates of needle-like (acicular) crystals, which usually form globular masses. It may also form as tabular crystals. Pectolite is white, greyish, or colourless. The streak is white. It is translucent, with a vitreous or silky lustre on clean surfaces.

• **FORMATION** Pectolite forms in cavities in basaltic lava, often with zeolite minerals, such as heulandite, phillipsite, analcine, chabazite, and natrolite. These cavities are usually vesicles where gas bubbles existed in the lava. When the vesicles are infilled, they are referred to as amygdales and the rock texture is called amygdaloidal.

• **TESTS** This mineral gelatinizes with hydrochloric acid. If heated in a closed test tube, water is given off.

translucent

acicular habit

radiating aggregates of crystals

silky lustre

TRICLINIC

SG 2.74–2.88	Cleavage Perfect		Fracture Uneven

Group Silicates	Composition $CaSiO_3$	Hardness 4½–5

WOLLASTONITE

Crystals are tabular, and frequently twinned. Wollastonite also forms in massive, fibrous, granular, and compact habits. The colour is white to greyish, and sometimes very pale green, or colourless. There is a white streak. This is a transparent to translucent mineral, and it has a vitreous to pearly lustre on fresh faces.

• **FORMATION** Forms by the metamorphism of impure limestones. When this occurs, wollastonite may be associated with brucite and epidote. These minerals often produce the brightly coloured veins in marble. Wollastonite also occurs in some igneous rocks, and in regionally metamorphosed slates, phyllites, and schists.

• **TESTS** It is soluble in acids, producing a separation of the silica in its composition. This mineral also fuses fairly easily.

transparent to translucent

twinned crystals

splintery fracture

fibrous habit

TRICLINIC

SG 2.87–3.09	Cleavage Perfect	Fracture Splintery

Group Silicates	Composition $KNa_2Li(Fe^{2+},Mn^{2+})_2Ti_2Si_8O_{24}$	Hardness 5–6

NEPTUNITE

This mineral occurs as prismatic crystals, with a square cross-section. The colour is black, though there may be some deep reddish brown internal reflections. The streak is reddish brown in colour. Neptunite is an almost opaque mineral, and has a vitreous lustre.

• **FORMATION** Forms as an accessory mineral in intermediate, plutonic, igneous rocks, such as nepheline syenite, and in pegmatites of similar, broad chemical composition. It also forms in serpentinites, where it is associated with the minerals benitoite, natrolite, and joaquinite.

• **TESTS** When placed in hydrochloric acid, neptunite is insoluble. In a flame, it is infusible.

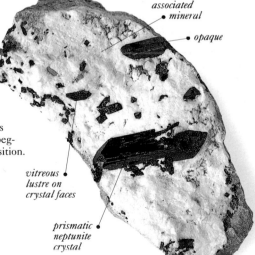

natrolite, an associated mineral

opaque

vitreous lustre on crystal faces

prismatic neptunite crystal

MONOCLINIC

SG 3.19–3.23	Cleavage Perfect	Fracture Conchoidal

Group Silicates	Composition $(Mg,Fe)_3Si_2O_5(OH)_4$	Hardness $2\frac{1}{2}–3\frac{1}{2}$

ANTIGORITE

Crystals are minute and flaky, or lath-shaped. Antigorite also occurs in massive, fibrous, or foliated habits. It is white, yellow, green, or brown. The streak is white. It is translucent to opaque, with a resinous or pearly lustre.
• **FORMATION** This mineral forms in serpentinites, derived from ultrabasic, igneous rocks.
• **TESTS** Antigorite fuses with difficulty.

MONOCLINIC

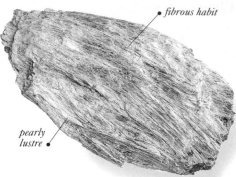

fibrous habit

pearly lustre

SG 2.61	Cleavage Perfect basal	Fracture Conchoidal or splintery

Group Silicates	Composition $Mg_3Si_2O_5(OH)_4$	Hardness $2\frac{1}{2}$

CHRYSOTILE

This mineral forms in massive and fibrous habits. The fibrous variety of chrysotile (a variety of asbestos) separates into flexible fibers. The colour is white, grey, green, yellow, or brown. It is translucent, with a silky to greasy lustre.
• **FORMATION** Forms in serpentinites, by the alteration of ultrabasic rocks.

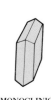

MONOCLINIC

mass of thin fibres

broken and bent fibres

silky or greasy lustre

SG 2.53	Cleavage None	Fracture Uneven

Group Silicates	Composition $Mg_3Si_4O_{10}(OH)_2$	Hardness 1

TALC

Thin tabular crystals are formed by talc. It can also occur in massive, compact, foliated, and fibrous habits. The colour is pale to dark green, grey, brownish, or white. There is a white streak. Talc is translucent, with a dull to pearly or greasy lustre.
• **FORMATION** Forms by the alteration of ultrabasic igneous rocks and dolomites.
• **TESTS** It is easily scratched, and feels greasy.

CUBIC

pearly or greasy lustre

massive habit

SG 2.58–2.83	Cleavage Perfect	Fracture Uneven

Group Silicates	Composition $(Cu,Al)_2H_2Si_2O_5(OH)_4 \cdot nH_2O$	Hardness 2–4

CHRYSOCOLLA

This mineral forms as acicular, microscopic crystals, in radiating groups, or in close-packed aggregates. It also occurs in massive, earthy, cryptocrystalline, and botryoidal habits. The colour is green, blue, and blue-green. Chrysocolla can also be brown to black when impurities are present. The streak is white. This mineral is translucent to nearly opaque, and it has a vitreous to earthy lustre.
• **FORMATION** Chrysocolla forms in the altered parts of copper deposits. It occurs with azurite, malachite, and cuprite. It is also an important mineral for ore prospectors, as its presence may suggest that copper deposits are nearby.
• **TESTS** It decomposes in hydrochloric acid.

massive habit

vitreous lustre

opaque

MONOCLINIC

SG 2.0–2.4	Cleavage None	Fracture Uneven to conchoidal

Group Silicates	Composition Be_2SiO_4	Hardness 7½–8

PHENAKITE

This mineral forms as prismatic or rhombohedral crystals which are often twinned. It also occurs in granular and acicular habits, and as radiating, fibrous spherulites. It may be colourless, yellow, pink, or brown, with a white streak. Phenakite is a transparent mineral, and has a vitreous lustre.
• **FORMATION** Forms in hydrothermal veins, and in granitic igneous rocks. These rocks include pegmatites and greisens (altered granites). It can also occur in some schists. In this occurrence, phenakite is associated with beryl, chrysoberyl, topaz, quartz, and apatite.
• **TESTS** Phenakite is insoluble in acids, and infusible.

rhombohedral crystal

twinned crystals

TRIGONAL/
HEXAGONAL

SG 2.93–3.00	Cleavage Distinct	Fracture Conchoidal

Group Silicates	Composition $KAl_2(Si_3Al)O_{10}(OH,F)_2$	Hardness 2½–4

MUSCOVITE

Tabular, pseudo-hexagonal crystals, are formed by muscovite, and twinning is common. Other habits are lamellar, and cryptocrystalline. Muscovite also forms as scaly and compact masses, and disseminated flakes. It varies from colourless to white or grey, and it may be tinged with yellow, green, brown, red, or violet. The streak is colourless. It is a transparent to translucent mineral, with a vitreous to pearly lustre.
• **FORMATION** Forms in igneous rocks, especially those of acid composition like granite, and in metamorphic rocks such as schist and gneiss. There is a particular schist, called mica schist, which can be extremely rich in muscovite.
• **TESTS** This mineral is insoluble in acids.

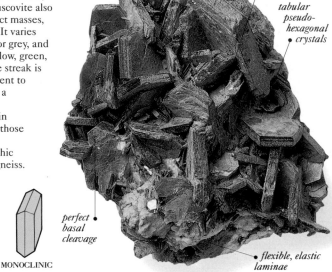

pearly lustre

tabular pseudo-hexagonal crystals

perfect basal cleavage

MONOCLINIC

flexible, elastic laminae

SG 2.77–2.88	Cleavage Perfect basal	Fracture Uneven

Group Silicates	Composition $K(Li,Al)_3 (Si, Al)_4O_{10}(F,OH)_2$	Hardness 2½–3

LEPIDOLITE

This mineral occurs as tabular, pseudo-hexagonal crystals, and as scaly aggregates, and cleavable masses. The colour is pink, purple, greyish, and white, though it can be colourless. The streak is also colourless. Lepidolite is a transparent to translucent mineral, with a pearly lustre.
• **FORMATION** Forms in acid igneous rocks, such as granite and pegmatite. This mineral is often associated with tourmaline, amblygonite, and spodumene. Lepidolite can be found in mineral veins that are rich in tin.
• **TESTS** It colours a flame red, and is insoluble in acids.

pegmatitic groundmass

tabular lepidolite crystal

MONOCLINIC

vitreous lustre

SG 2.8–3.3	Cleavage Perfect basal	Fracture Uneven

Group Silicates	Composition $K(Mg,Fe^{+2})_3(Al,Fe^{+3})Si_3O_{10}(OH,F)_2$	Hardness $2\frac{1}{2}$–3

BIOTITE

The tabular or short prismatic crystals formed by biotite often have a pseudo-hexagonal outline. The colour varies from black, or dark brown, to reddish brown, green, and, very rarely, white. The streak is colourless. It is transparent to nearly opaque, with a splendent or vitreous lustre.
• **FORMATION** Forms in both igneous and metamorphic rocks.
• **TESTS** Biotite is soluble in concentrated sulphuric acid.

splendent lustre on crystal faces

tabular crystal

MONOCLINIC

SG 2.7–3.4	Cleavage Perfect basal	Fracture Uneven

Group Silicates	Composition $KMg_3Si_3AlO_{10}(OH,F)_2$	Hardness 2–$2\frac{1}{2}$

PHLOGOPITE

This mineral forms as prismatic and pseudo-hexagonal crystals which are often tapered and sometimes twinned. It also occurs as plates and scales. Phlogopite may be colourless, yellowish-brown, brownish-red, greenish, or white. There is a colourless streak. It is transparent to translucent, with a pearly lustre.
• **FORMATION** In ultrabasic igneous and metamorphic rocks.
• **TESTS** This mineral is soluble in concentrated sulphuric acid.

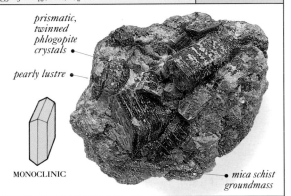

prismatic, twinned phlogopite crystals

pearly lustre

mica schist groundmass

MONOCLINIC

SG 2.76–2.90	Cleavage Perfect basal	Fracture Uneven

Group Silicates	Composition $(K,Na)(Fe,Al,Mg)_2(Si,Al)_4O_{10}(OH)_2$	Hardness 2

GLAUCONITE

Minute, lath-shaped crystals are formed by glauconite. It also occurs as rounded, granular aggregates. Usually, it is a dull green colour, but can also be yellowish green, or bluish green. Glauconite is a translucent to opaque mineral, with a dull or glistening lustre.
• **FORMATION** This mineral forms in marine sedimentary strata.
• **TESTS** Glauconite gives off water when it is heated.

aggregate of small indistinct grains

dull lustre

MONOCLINIC

SG 2.4–2.95	Cleavage Perfect basal	Fracture Uneven

Group Silicates	Composition $(Mg,Fe,Al)_3 (Al,Si)_4O_{10}(OH)_2.4H_2O$	Hardness 1½

VERMICULITE

Vermiculite is the name given to a group of minerals. A typical example forms platy, tabular crystals, with a pseudo-hexagonal outline in the monoclinic system. The colour varies from greenish, to golden yellow or brown. The streak is pale yellow. It is a translucent mineral, with a vitreous lustre.
• **FORMATION** From the alteration of biotite and phlogopite.
• **TESTS** When heated, it can expand into a twisted, worm-like shape.

pseudo-hexagonal outline

flat tabular habit

SG 2.3	Cleavage Perfect	Fracture Uneven

Group Silicates	Composition $(Fe^{+2},Mg,Fe^{3+})_5Al(Si_3Al)O_{10}(OH,O)_8$	Hardness 2–2½

CLINOCHLORE

Crystals are tabular with a hexagonal cross-section. Clinochlore also occurs in massive, foliated, scaly, granular, or earthy habits. It may be white to yellowish, or colourless, as well as green. The streak is colourless to greenish white. It is transparent to opaque, with a pearly lustre.
• **FORMATION** Forms in many metamorphic rocks, especially schists.
• **TESTS** Soluble in strong acids.

pearly lustre

tabular crystals

MONOCLINIC

SG 2.63–2.98	Cleavage Perfect	Fracture Uneven

Group Silicates	Composition $(Mg,Fe)_3Fe_3(Al,Si_3)O_{10}(OH)_8$	Hardness 3

CHAMOSITE

Occurring in compact, massive habits, chamosite may also be oolitic. The colour ranges from greenish to black. There is a white or pale green streak. Chamosite is a translucent mineral, with a vitreous or earthy lustre.
• **FORMATION** This mineral forms in various sedimentary rocks, such as ironstones and clays, where it occurs with siderite (iron carbonate).
• **TESTS** Gives off water when heated.

massive habit

MONOCLINIC

earthy lustre

SG 3–3.4	Cleavage Not determined	Fracture Uneven

Group Silicates	Composition $Al_2Si_2O_5(OH)_4$	Hardness 2–2½

KAOLINITE

This group of minerals, which includes kaolinite, nacrite, and halloysite, forms very small pseudo-hexagonal platelets or scales. It may also occur in massive, compact habits, and in earthy or clayey masses. Kaolinite varies from white and colourless, to yellowish, brownish, reddish, or bluish. There is a white streak. The kaolinite group is transparent to translucent, with a pearly to dull or earthy lustre.

• **FORMATION** Forms by the alteration of feldspars and other aluminium-rich silicate minerals. This can be brought about by weathering, especially in humid regions, or, on a much larger scale, by hydrothermal fluids rising from depth through rocks. When this occurs, granite is reduced to an unconsolidated mass of quartz and mica sand, with white, kaolinite clay.

• **TESTS** These minerals are plastic when moist, and lose water when heated in a closed tube. Special optical tests are needed to tell kaolinite minerals apart.

• *dull lustre*

KAOLINITE

• *powdery habit on mass of altered granite*

TRICLINIC

NACRITE

HALLOYSITE

• *pearly lustre*

• *friable*

• *nacrite crystal aggregate*

• *massive habit*

SG 2.6–2.63	Cleavage Perfect basal	Fracture Uneven

Group Silicates	Composition $Ca_2Al_2Si_3O_{10}(OH)_2$	Hardness 6–6½

PREHNITE

This mineral can form prismatic, tabular, or pyramidal crystals, but usually occurs in botryoidal, reniform, stalactitic, granular, or compact habits. It is usually green in colour, but may be white, colourless, yellow, or grey. It has a colourless streak. Prehnite is transparent to translucent, with a vitreous to pearly lustre.
• **FORMATION** Forms in hollows in basaltic lavas.
• **TESTS** This mineral gives off water when it is heated.

massive calcite

prehnite crystals

ORTHORHOMBIC

SG 2.90–2.95	Cleavage Distinct	Fracture Uneven

Group Silicates	Composition $(Ni,Mg)_6Si_4O_{10}(OH)_8$	Hardness 2–4

GARNIERITE

The crystals formed by garnierite are usually lamellar. It can occur as microcrystalline crusts, and in a massive habit. The brilliant green colour is characteristic, though it may also be white. The streak is light green. It is a transparent to opaque mineral, and the lustre can be greasy, waxy, or earthy.
• **FORMATION** Forms when nickel sulphides are altered by fluids in igneous rocks.
• **TESTS** It is infusible.

massive habit

waxy lustre

MONOCLINIC

SG 2.3–2.5	Cleavage None	Fracture Splintery

Group Silicates	Composition $Mg_4Si_6O_{15}(OH)_2.6H_2O$	Hardness 2–2½

SEPIOLITE

This mineral occurs in massive, fibrous, compact, earthy, and nodular (Meershaum) habits. The colour may be white, reddish, yellowish, greyish, or bluish green. The streak is whitish. Sepiolite is an opaque mineral, and it has a dull lustre.
• **FORMATION** Forms by the alteration of minerals in serpentinite.
• **TESTS** Sepiolite often occurs as dry, porous masses which can float on water.

massive habit

dull lustre

ORTHORHOMBIC

SG 2	Cleavage Not determined	Fracture Uneven

Group Silicates	Composition $KCa_4Si_8O_{20}(F,OH).8H_2O$	Hardness 4 ½–5

APOPHYLLITE

Crystals formed by apophyllite are pseudo-cubic, pyramidal, tabular, or prismatic. This mineral also forms in massive, lamellar, or granular habits. Apophyllite may be white, colourless, yellow, pink, or green. There is a white streak. This mineral is transparent to translucent, and has a vitreous to pearly lustre on fresh surfaces.

• FORMATION Apophyllite forms in hydrothermal veins, and in vesicular cavities, formed in basaltic lavas when they were rich in gas. Minerals associated with apophyllite include zeolites, gyrolite, calcite, quartz, stilbite, analcime, prehnite, and scolecite.

• TESTS It colours a flame violet. It is soluble when placed in hydrochloric acid. It also gives off water if heated in a closed test tube.

TETRAGONAL

vitreous lustre •

pseudo-cubic • *crystals*

transparent • *to translucent*

SG 2.3–2.5	Cleavage Perfect	Fracture Uneven

Group Silicates	Composition $NaCa_{16}(Si_{23}Al)O_{60}(OH)_5.15H_2O$	Hardness 3–4

GYROLITE

This mineral occurs as radiating lamellar crystals, spherules, or concretions. Gyrolite may be white or colourless. It is transparent to translucent, and it has a vitreous lustre.

• FORMATION Forms by the alteration of calcium silicate minerals. As a secondary mineral, gyrolite is associated with apophyllite, and occurs in hollows and cavities in rocks, especially basalts. Gyrolite spherules up to 5cm (2in), and clusters up to 30cm (12in) have been found.

• TESTS This mineral gives off water when heated in a closed test tube.

TRIGONAL/ HEXAGONAL

basalt ground- • *mass*

perfect • *cleavage*

radiating lamellar gyrolite crystals •

SG 2.34–2.45	Cleavage Perfect	Fracture Uneven

Group Silicates	Composition $Al_2Si_4O_{10}(OH)_2$	Hardness 1–2

PYROPHYLLITE

This mineral forms as tabular, elongated crystals, which are often distorted. It usually occurs as foliated, fibrous, radiating, and lamellar masses. It is white, grey, bluish, yellowish, greenish, and greenish brown, with a white streak. It is transparent to translucent. The lustre is pearly on fresh crystal surfaces, but this can become dull.
• **FORMATION** Forms in crystalline schists with talc, andalusite, sillimanite, and lazulite. It is also found in hydrothermal veins with minerals such as mica and quartz.
• **TESTS** Pyrophyllite has a greasy feel, similar to talc. It flakes when heated, and is insoluble in most liquids.

radiating mass of pyrophyllite crystals •

• *quartz, an associated mineral*

MONOCLINIC

SG 2.65–2.90	Cleavage Perfect	Fracture Uneven

Group Silicates	Composition $(K,Na)_3(Fe,Mn)_7Ti_2Si_8O_{24}(O,OH)_7$	Hardness 3

ASTROPHYLLITE

This mineral forms bladed crystals, often in stellate groups. The colour is bronze-yellow to golden yellow, and the streak is pale greenish brown. Astrophyllite is translucent in thin laminae, and the lustre is submetallic to pearly.
• **FORMATION** This mineral forms in cavities in igneous rocks, especially in syenite, which is a coarse-grained rock of intermediate composition. It also occurs in other plutonic rocks. Astrophyllite is·associated with minerals such as quartz, feldspar, zircon, riebeckite, sphene, mica, and acmite.
• **TESTS** When placed in acids, it is found to be slightly soluble. In a flame, astrophyllite fuses to a dark glassy substance which is slightly magnetic. When astrophyllite cleaves, thin laminae are produced, which break very easily.

radiating stellate groups of crystals •

perfect cleavage into thin brittle laminae •

• *submetallic lustre*

TRICLINIC

SG 3.3–3.4	Cleavage Perfect	Fracture Uneven

Group Silicates	Composition $(Na,K) AlSi_3O_8$	Hardness $6-6\frac{1}{2}$

ANORTHOCLASE

Belonging to the alkali feldspar series, this mineral forms as short prismatic or tabular crystals, with common twinning. It may occur as massive, lamellar, granular, or cryptocrystalline specimens. It is yellowish, colourless, reddish, white, grey, or greenish. It has a white streak, and is transparent to translucent, with a vitreous lustre.
• **FORMATION** Forms mainly in volcanic igneous rocks.
• **TESTS** It is insoluble in acids.

TRICLINIC

vitreous lustre

a single prismatic crystal

SG 2.56–2.62	Cleavage Perfect	Fracture Uneven

Group Silicates	Composition $KAlSi_3O_8$	Hardness $6-6\frac{1}{2}$

MICROCLINE

This mineral is an alkali feldspar and forms tabular or, more frequently, short prismatic crystals, which are very commonly twinned. It also occurs in a massive habit. The colour may be grey, white, yellowish, reddish, or pink. There is also a green-coloured form of microcline, which is usually known as amazonstone. The streak is white. This is a transparent to translucent mineral, with a lustre that is vitreous, or pearly on cleavage surfaces.
• **FORMATION** Commonly forms in igneous rocks, especially granites, pegmatites, and syenites. It also occurs in certain metamorphic rocks, particularly schists. In addition, microcline can be found in hydrothermal veins and areas of contact metamorphism. It is often associated with quartz and albite when it forms in pegmatites.
• **TESTS** It is insoluble in acids, except hydrofluoric acid, which should be used with care. It is infusible in a flame.

AMAZONSTONE

vitreous lustre

short prismatic microcline crystals

rock groundmass

TRICLINIC

MICROCLINE

SG 2.55–2.63	Cleavage Perfect	Fracture Uneven

Group Silicates	Composition $KAlSi_3O_8$	Hardness 6

SANIDINE

In the alkali feldspar group, this mineral occurs as prismatic or tabular crystals, which are often twinned. Sanidine is whitish or colourless. There is a white streak. It is a translucent mineral, with a vitreous lustre on crystal faces.
• **FORMATION** Forms in a variety of volcanic rocks, including trachyte and rhyolite. Sanidine can also be found in several varieties of contact metamorphosed rocks.
• **TESTS** Sanidine is insoluble in most acids, but will dissolve completely when placed in hydrofluoric acid. Great care, however, should be taken when using this acid.

• *prismatic sanidine crystal*

trachyte lava • *groundmass*

MONOCLINIC

SG 2.56–2.62	Cleavage Perfect	Fracture Conchoidal to uneven

Group Silicates	Composition $NaAlSi_3O_8$	Hardness 6–6½

ALBITE

The lower temperature, sodium-rich, end-member of the plagioclase feldspar series, albite forms tabular, often platy, crystals which are very commonly twinned. It may also be massive, granular, or lamellar in habit. The laminae are frequently curved. Albite is usually white, or colourless, but it may be bluish, grey, greenish, or reddish. There is a white streak. It is transparent to translucent, with a vitreous to pearly lustre.
• **FORMATION** This mineral occurs as an essential component of many igneous rocks, including granite, pegmatite, rhyolite, andesite, and syenite. Albite also occurs in some meta-morphic rocks, such as schists and gneisses, and in sedimentary rocks. Additionally, it may form in hydro-thermal veins. In some situations, it forms as the result of the alteration of other feldspars by albitization.
• **TESTS** It fuses with difficulty, colouring the flame yellow.

mass of twinned tabular crystals •

vitreous to pearly • *lustre*

crystal face •

TRICLINIC

SG 2.60–2.63	Cleavage Distinct	Fracture Uneven

Group Silicates	Composition $(Na,Ca)Al_{1-2}Si_{3-2}O_8$	Hardness $6-6\frac{1}{2}$

LABRADORITE

A member of the plagioclase feldspar
series, labradorite rarely forms crystals;
when crystals do occur, they are tabular,
and often twinned. Other habits are massive,
granular, or compact. Labradorite is blue, grey,
white, or colourless, and frequently exhibits a
rich play of colours on cleavage surfaces. The
streak is white. It is a translucent mineral,
with a vitreous lustre.
• **FORMATION** This mineral is an
important constituent of certain igneous
and metamorphic rocks. These include
basalt, gabbro, diorite, andesite, norite,
and amphibolite. Labradorite is common
in intermediate and basic rocks, but rare
in granitic rocks.
• **TESTS** The
schillerization, or play
of colours on broken
surfaces, is very
characteristic of
labradorite. It is also
soluble in acid, when
powdered.

uneven fracture •

TRICLINIC

vitreous lustre •

• *schillerization*

SG 2.69–2.72	Cleavage Perfect	Fracture Uneven to conchoidal

Group Silicates	Composition $CaAl_2Si_2O_8$	Hardness $6-6\frac{1}{2}$

ANORTHITE

*anorthite with
associated augite* •

The higher-temperature end member of the
plagioclase feldspar series, anorthite forms
short prismatic crystals, which are often
twinned. Other habits are lamellar or massive. Anorthite is grey, white, pink, or
colourless, and it has a white streak. It is
a transparent to translucent mineral, and
has a vitreous lustre.
• **FORMATION** Forms in many igneous
rocks, especially those of basic composition, formed at high temperatures. These
rocks include basalt, gabbro, dolerite, and
peridotite. This calcium-rich plagioclase
feldspar grades into sodium-
rich albite, which is formed
in lower temperature rocks.
Anorthite also forms in some
metamorphic rocks.
• **TESTS** It is soluble
in hydrochloric acid.

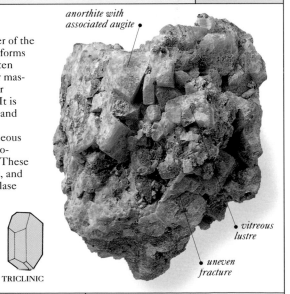

• *vitreous
lustre*

• *uneven
fracture*

TRICLINIC

SG 2.74–2.76	Cleavage Perfect	Fracture Conchoidal to uneven

Group Silicates	Composition $(Na,Ca)Al_{1-2}Si_{3-2}O_8$	Hardness 6–6½

ANDESINE

A member of the plagioclase feldspar series, andesine sometimes forms as tabular crystals, which are frequently twinned. Usually it occurs in massive, compact, or granular habits. This mineral is grey, white, or colourless, and the streak is white. Andesine is transparent to translucent, with a vitreous lustre on fresh crystal faces.

• **FORMATION** Commonly forms in intermediate igneous rocks, and in many metamorphic rocks. These include andesite lava and amphibolite. This member of the plagioclase feldspar series is almost intermediate between calcium-rich anorthite and sodium-rich albite.

• **TESTS** Sodium colours a flame yellow, whereas calcium will turn it brick-red. Both these colours will appear, according to temperature.

TRICLINIC

tabular andesine crystals set into igneous rock groundmass

vitreous lustre

uneven fracture

SG 2.66–2.68	Cleavage Perfect		Fracture Uneven to conchoidal

Group Silicates	Composition $(Na,Ca)Al_{1-2}Si_{3-2}O_8$	Hardness 6–6½

OLIGOCLASE

A member of the plagioclase feldspar series, oligoclase forms as tabular crystals, which are commonly twinned. More usual habits are massive, granular, or compact. It can be grey, white, greenish, yellowish, brown, reddish, or colourless, and there is a white streak. Oligoclase is transparent to translucent, and has a vitreous lustre.

• **FORMATION** This mineral forms in many igneous and metamorphic rocks. The igneous rocks are plutonic and volcanic, and include acid granite and pegmatite, intermediate syenite, trachyte and andesite, and basic basalt. In metamorphic situations, oligoclase is formed in high grade, regionally metamorphosed gneiss and schist.

• **TESTS** This mineral may show brilliant reflections from inclusions.

doubly terminated oligoclase crystal on quartz

vitreous lustre on crystal faces

TRICLINIC

SG 2.63–2.67	Cleavage Perfect		Fracture Uneven to conchoidal

Group Silicates	Composition $KAlSi_3O_8$	Hardness $6-6\frac{1}{2}$

ORTHOCLASE

An important rock-forming mineral, orthoclase
feldspar forms as prismatic or tabular crystals,
which are often twinned. Other habits are
massive, lamellar, and granular. It is white,
reddish, colourless, yellow, grey, or green,
and has a white streak. Orthoclase is a
transparent to translucent mineral,
with a vitreous to pearly lustre.
• **FORMATION** Forms in many
igneous and metamorphic rocks.
The igneous rocks include granite,
pegmatite, rhyolite, trachyte, and
syenite; metamorphic examples include
gneisses and schists.
This mineral can
also occur in some
sedimentary rocks.
• **TESTS** Ortho-
clase is insoluble
in acids, and is
almost infusible.

MONOCLINIC

*prismatic
orthoclase
crystals*

*quartz, an
associated
mineral*

SG 2.55–2.63	Cleavage Perfect	Fracture Uneven to conchoidal

Group Silicates	Composition $(Na,Ca)\,Al_{1-2}\,Si_{3-2}O_8$	Hardness $6-6\frac{1}{2}$

BYTOWNITE

A member of the plagioclase feldspar series,
bytownite forms as tabular crystals which are
commonly twinned. More frequently, it occurs
in massive, compact, and granular habits. It
is white, grey, brownish, or colourless, and
has a white streak. It is transparent to
translucent, and there is a vitreous lustre.
• **FORMATION** Forms as an essential
component of many igneous rocks,
such as dolerite, basalt, gabbro,
norite, and anorthosite. It is also
found in some metamorphic rocks,
including gneiss and schist, formed
by regional metamorphism.
• **TESTS** In common
with other members of
the plagioclase feldspar
series, bytownite shows
multiple twinning. This
helps distinguish it from
orthoclase, which has
simple twinning.

vitreous lustre

*perfect
cleavage*

uneven fracture

TRICLINIC

SG 2.72–2.74	Cleavage Perfect	Fracture Uneven to conchoidal

Group Silicates	Composition $(Na,Ca)_{4-8}Al_6Si_6(O,S)_{24}(SO_4Cl)_{1-2}$	Hardness 5½–6

HAUYNE

The dodecahedral or octahedral crystals formed by hauyne are frequently twinned. It also occurs as rounded grains. The colour ranges from blue to white, green, yellow, or red. The streak is bluish or white. Hauyne is a transparent to translucent mineral, and it has a vitreous or greasy lustre.
• FORMATION Hauyne forms in silica-poor lavas.
• TESTS Soluble in acids with gelatinization.

hauyne blue crystals
feldspar ground-mass

CUBIC

SG 2.44–2.50	Cleavage Indistinct	Fracture Uneven to conchoidal

Group Silicates	Composition $(Na,Ca)_{7-8}(Al,Si)_{12}O_{24}[(SO_4), Cl_2(OH)_2]$	Hardness 5–5½

LAZURITE

Crystals are dodecahedral, octahedral, or cubic, but rare. The usual habits are massive or compact. The colour is a deep blue, azure blue, violet blue, or greenish blue, and there is a bright blue streak. Lazurite is a translucent mineral, and it has a dull lustre.
• FORMATION Forms in limestones that have been metamorphosed by heat.
• TESTS It is soluble in hydrochloric acid, giving off a "bad eggs" smell.

dull lustre
cubic habit on calcite groundmass

CUBIC

SG 2.4–2.5	Cleavage Imperfect	Fracture Uneven

Group Silicates	Composition $Na_8Al_6Si_6O_{24}Cl_2$	Hardness 5½–6

SODALITE

This mineral occurs as dodecahedral crystals, commonly twinned. It can also form in massive, or granular habits, with a concentric internal structure. Sodalite ranges from light to dark blue, though it can be white, colourless, yellowish, greenish, or reddish. The streak is colourless. It is a transparent to translucent mineral, with a vitreous to greasy lustre.
• FORMATION Forms in certain igneous rocks, including syenites.
• TESTS Soluble in hydrochloric and nitric acids, with gelatinization.

massive habit

CUBIC

SG 2.14–2.40	Cleavage Poor	Fracture Uneven to conchoidal

Group Silicates	Composition $KAlSi_2O_6$	Hardness 5½–6

LEUCITE

This mineral forms as trapezohedral crystals, which may have striated faces. Twinning is common. It can also occur in massive or granular habits, and as disseminated grains. Leucite can be white, grey, or colourless, and there is a colourless streak. It is a transparent to translucent mineral, with a vitreous lustre.

• FORMATION Forms in lavas of basic composition, especially those rich in potassium, including basalts and phonolites. This mineral also alters very readily, and so is rarely found in lava of great geological age.

• TESTS It is soluble in hydrochloric acid. If heated above 625° C, leucite's crystal structure changes from tetragonal to cubic symmetry.

trapezohedral leucite crystal
vitreous lustre
groundmass of tuff

TETRAGONAL

SG 2.5	Cleavage Very poor	Fracture Conchoidal

Group Silicates	Composition $(Na,K)AlSiO_4$	Hardness 5½–6

NEPHELINE

This mineral commonly forms as prismatic hexagonal crystals, which are frequently twinned. It may also occur as compact, massive, or granular specimens. Nepheline varies from white, colourless, and grey, to yellowish, dark green, and brownish red. There is a white streak. It is a transparent to translucent mineral, and it has a vitreous to greasy lustre.

• FORMATION Forms in many silica-poor alkaline igneous rocks, particularly those of intermediate composition. It is found in syenites (nepheline syenite), and pegmatites, and occasionally in schists and gneisses.

• TESTS It gelatinizes when placed in hydrochloric acid. Nepheline also colours a flame yellow, indicating the presence of sodium in its chemical structure.

rock ground-mass
transparent to translucent
vitreous lustre
cavity with filling of hexagonal nepheline prisms

TRIGONAL/
HEXAGONAL

SG 2.5–2.7	Cleavage Indistinct	Fracture Conchoidal

Group Silicates	Composition $Na_8Al_6Si_6O_{24}(SO_4)$		Hardness 5½–6

NOSEAN

vitreous lustre •

This mineral forms as dodecahedral crystals, but is usually massive or granular in habit. It varies greatly, ranging from grey, bluish, and brown, to colourless, and white. Nosean has a colourless streak. It is a transparent to translucent mineral, and it has a vitreous lustre on fresh surfaces.

• **FORMATION** Forms in silica-poor lavas. These include the intermediate rock, phonolite, in which this sodalite-group mineral often occurs as larger crystals set into the rock groundmass, producing a porphyritic rock texture. Occasionally, nosean has also been recorded in volcanic bombs.

• **TESTS** This mineral gelatinizes when placed in contact with acid.

CUBIC

sanidine, an associated mineral •

well-formed nosean crystals •

SG 2.3–2.4	Cleavage Indistinct	Fracture Uneven to conchoidal

Group Silicates	Composition $Na_6Ca_2Al_6Si_6O_{24}(CO_3)_2$		Hardness 5–6

CANCRINITE

vitreous lustre •

Prismatic crystals are formed by cancrinite but they are rare. The usual habit is massive. It is white, yellow, orange, pink, reddish, or bluish, and has a colourless streak. It is transparent to translucent, and there is a vitreous, pearly, or greasy lustre.

• **FORMATION** Forms in a number of igneous rocks. These include alkali-rich rocks, where it can occur as a primary mineral or as an alteration product of nepheline. It is often associated with sodalite in syenites. Cancrinite has also been found in high-grade, regionally metamorphosed rocks, including gneisses.

• **TESTS** Cancrinite dissolves in hydrochloric acid, with effervescence, leaving behind a siliceous gel.

TRIGONAL/ HEXAGONAL

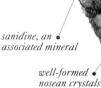

nepheline syenite groundmass •

SG 2.42–2.51	Cleavage Perfect	Fracture Uneven

Group Silicates	Composition $(Na,Ca,K)_4Al_3(Al,Si)_3Si_6O_{24}(Cl,F,OH,CO_3,SO_4)$	Hardness 5½–6

SCAPOLITE

Calcium-rich meionite, and sodium-rich marialite form a series of minerals with the group name scapolite. The group occurs as prismatic crystals, and also in granular and massive habits. Scapolite varies, and may be colourless, white, grey, bluish, greenish, yellowish, brownish, pink, or violet. There is a colourless streak. It is transparent to translucent, with a vitreous to pearly or resinous lustre.
• **FORMATION** This group forms in igneous rocks that have been altered from their original basic composition, and in metamorphic rocks, such as high-grade schists and gneisses.
• **TESTS** Soluble in hydrochloric acid.

• *prismatic scapolite crystals*

distinct • *cleavage*

rock • *groundmass*

uneven fracture •

vitreous • *lustre on crystal faces*

TETRAGONAL

SG 2.50–2.78	Cleavage Distinct	Fracture Uneven to conchoidal

Group Silicates	Composition $LiAlSi_4O_{10}$	Hardness 6–6½

PETALITE

This mineral forms, rarely, as small crystals, which are commonly twinned. More often, petalite forms as large, cleavable masses. It may be white, grey, pinkish, yellow, or colourless, and there is a white streak. Petalite is transparent to translucent, with a vitreous to pearly lustre.
• **FORMATION** Forms in very coarse-grained, acid igneous rocks. It is associated with a number of other minerals, including quartz, and lepidolite, spodumene, and other lithium-rich minerals.
• **TESTS** Petalite colours a flame crimson-red, and is insoluble.

vitreous lustre •

• *transparent to translucent*

• *perfect cleavage*

MONOCLINIC

SG 2.3–2.5	Cleavage Perfect	Fracture Subconchoidal

Group Silicates	Composition $NaAlSi_2O_6.H_2O$	Hardness 5–5½

ANALCIME

A zeolite mineral that occurs as well-formed trapezohedra, icositetrahedra, and modified cubes, analcime also forms in massive, granular, and compact habits. It may be white, colourless, grey, pink, yellowish, or greenish, with a white streak. Analcime is a transparent to translucent mineral, with a vitreous lustre.

• **FORMATION** Occurs in basaltic igneous rocks, and may be formed by the alteration of sodalite and nepheline. Analcime is also found in some detrital sediments, with other zeolites and calcite.

• **TESTS** When heated, it fuses and colours the flame yellow. This mineral is soluble in acids. It will yield water when heated in a closed test tube.

icositetrahedral crystal in cavity in groundmass •

vitreous lustre •

CUBIC

SG 2.22–2.29	Cleavage Very poor	Fracture Subconchoidal

Group Silicates	Composition $CaAl_2Si_4O_{12}.6H_2O$	Hardness 4–5

CHABAZITE

A member of the zeolite group of minerals, chabazite occurs as pseudo-cubic, rhombohedral crystals, which are often twinned. It may be white, yellowish, pinkish, reddish, greenish, or colourless, with a colourless streak. It is a transparent to translucent mineral, and the lustre is vitreous.

• **FORMATION** Forms in cavities in basaltic lavas, and in some limestones. It is associated with many other zeolites, such as harmotome, phillipsite, heulandite, and scolecite, and with quartz and calcite. It can occur in certain metamorphic rocks, such as schists, and forms around hot springs in the crust of minerals deposited from the hot fluids.

• **TESTS** Chabazite gives off water when heated in a closed test tube.

vitreous • *lustre*

• *basalt groundmass*

rhombohedral chabazite crystal •

uneven fracture •

TRIGONAL/ HEXAGONAL

SG 2.05–2.16	Cleavage Indistinct	Fracture Uneven

Group Silicates	Composition $(Ba,K)_{1-2}(Si,Al)_8O_{16}.6H_2O$	Hardness $4\frac{1}{2}$

HARMOTOME

This mineral is a zeolite, which occurs as twinned pseudo-tetragonal or pseudo-orthorhombic crystals, and as radiating aggregates. The colour may be white, grey, pink, yellow, brown, or colourless. It has a white streak. It is transparent to translucent, with a vitreous lustre.
- **FORMATION** Forms in vesicles in basalts.
- **TESTS** It is fusible, and soluble in hydrochloric acid.

MONOCLINIC

well formed crystal on rock groundmass •

vitreous lustre •

SG 2.41–2.50	Cleavage Distinct	Fracture Uneven to subconchoidal

Group Silicates	Composition $(Na,Ca)_{2-3}Al_3(Al,Si)_2Si_{13}O_{36}.12H_2O$	Hardness $3\frac{1}{2}$–4

HEULANDITE

A zeolite which occurs as tabular, trapezoidal crystals, heulandite also forms in massive and granular habits. It can be white, grey, yellow, pink, red, orange, colourless, and brown, and the streak is colourless. It is transparent to translucent, with a vitreous to pearly lustre.
- **FORMATION** In vesicles in basalts.
- **TESTS** Heulandite is fusible, and soluble in hydrochloric acid.

MONOCLINIC

rock groundmass •

foliated heulandite crystals •

SG 2.1–2.2	Cleavage Perfect	Fracture Uneven

Group Silicates	Composition $CaAl_2Si_4O_{12}.4H_2O$	Hardness 3–4

LAUMONTITE

This zeolite mineral forms as prismatic crystals, and also occurs in massive, fibrous, columnar, and radiating habits. It is white, grey, brownish, pink, or yellowish. The streak is colourless. It has a vitreous to pearly lustre, and is transparent to opaque.
- **FORMATION** Forms in igneous Basaltic cavities.
- **TESTS** Soluble in hydrochloric acid, with gelatinization.

MONOCLINIC

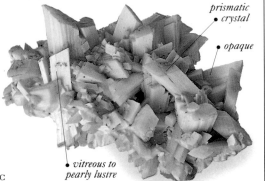

prismatic • crystal

• opaque

• vitreous to pearly lustre

SG 2.2–2.4	Cleavage Perfect	Fracture Uneven

Group Silicates	Composition $Na_2Al_2Si_3O_{10}.2H_2O$	Hardness 5–5½

NATROLITE

This zeolite mineral forms as slender or acicular, prismatic crystals, which are vertically striated. It may also be fibrous, radiating, massive, compact, or granular in habit. The colour is white, grey, yellowish, reddish, or colourless, and there is a white streak. It is transparent to translucent, with a vitreous to pearly lustre.
• **FORMATION** Forms in vesicles in basalts.
• **TESTS** Natrolite gelatinizes with acid.

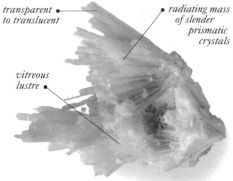

transparent to translucent

radiating mass of slender prismatic crystals

vitreous lustre

ORTHORHOMBIC

SG 2.20–2.26	Cleavage Perfect	Fracture Uneven

Group Silicates	Composition $Na_2Ca_2Al_6Si_9O_{30}.8H_2O$	Hardness 5

MESOLITE

This zeolite mineral occurs as fibrous or acicular crystals, which form tufts or compact masses. It is always twinned. The mineral is white, or colourless. It is transparent, and has a vitreous or silky lustre.
• **FORMATION** Forms in vesicles in basaltic lavas.
• **TESTS** It gelatinizes with acid. This mineral gives off water when heated in a closed test tube.

tufts of acicular crystals

transparent

vitreous lustre

silky lustre

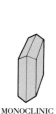

MONOCLINIC

SG 2.2–2.3	Cleavage Perfect	Fracture Uneven

Group Silicates	Composition $(K,Na,Ca)_{1-2}(Si,Al)_8O_{16}.6H_2O$	Hardness 4–4½

PHILLIPSITE

A zeolite which occurs as twinned crystals, phillipsite is white, colourless, reddish, or yellowish in colour. It is a transparent to translucent mineral, with a vitreous lustre.
• **FORMATION** This mineral occurs in vesicular cavities in basalts, in some deep marine deposits and around hot springs.
• **TESTS** Phillipsite is soluble in acids. It has two distinct cleavages.

twinned crystals

vitreous lustre

MONOCLINIC

SG 2.2	Cleavage Distinct	Fracture Uneven

Group Silicates	Composition $CaAl_2Si_3O_{10}.3H_2O$	Hardness 5

SCOLECITE

This zeolite mineral forms as vertically striated, thin, prismatic crystals. Scolecite may also occur as radiating fibrous masses. The colour may be white, yellowish, or colourless. It is a transparent to translucent mineral, and it has a vitreous to silky lustre.
• **FORMATION** Forms in vesicles in basalts.
• **TESTS** When heated, scolecite curls into worm-like shapes, and fuses.

MONOCLINIC

thin, radiating prismatic crystals

vitreous lustre

SG 2.27	Cleavage Perfect	Fracture Uneven

Group Silicates	Composition $NaCa_2Al_5Si_{13}O_{36}.14H_2O$	Hardness 3½–4

STILBITE

A zeolite occurring as rhombic crystals, stilbite exhibits cruciform penetration twinning. Other habits are bladed, globular, and radiating masses. The colour is white, grey, yellowish, pink, reddish, orange, or brown, and the streak is colourless. Stilbite is a transparent to translucent mineral, and it has a vitreous or pearly lustre.
• **FORMATION** In cavities in basalts and other lavas.
• **TESTS** It is soluble in hydrochloric acid.

MONOCLINIC

sheaf-like aggregates of stilbite crystals on quartz

vitreous lustre

SG 2.09–2.20	Cleavage Perfect	Fracture Uneven

Group Silicates	Composition $NaCa_2Al_5Si_5O_{20}.6H_2O$	Hardness 5–5½

THOMSONITE

This zeolite mineral forms as acicular, prismatic crystals, but more often as lamellar or radiating aggregates. The colour is white, colourless, yellowish, pink, or greenish. It has a colourless streak. This mineral is transparent to translucent, and has a vitreous to pearly lustre.
• **FORMATION** Thomsonite forms in cavities in lavas.
• **TESTS** It is soluble in hydrochloric acid, with gelatinization.

ORTHORHOMBIC

radiating prisms

vitreous lustre

basalt groundmass

SG 2.25–2.40	Cleavage Perfect	Fracture Uneven to subconchoidal

ROCKS

IGNEOUS ROCKS

I GNEOUS ROCKS form by the crystallization of once molten material. This molten rock is called magma and then lava once it reaches the surface. It is essentially a silicate melt and may contain, as well as silicon and oxygen, other elements, particularly aluminium, iron, calcium, sodium, potassium, and magnesium. These combine, as the magma or lava crystallizes, to form silicate minerals, which in combination make up igneous rocks.

Group Igneous	Origin Intrusive	Grain size Coarse	Crystal shape Anhedral, Euhedral

PINK GRANITE

The commonest intrusive rock, granite is acid. It has a total silica content greater than 65 per cent, and a minimum quartz content of 20 per cent. K-feldspars (orthoclase, microcline) are normally dominant over plagioclase (Na-rich) feldspar and often pink. Mica occurs as dark biotite or as silvery muscovite. Hornblende may be present.
• **TEXTURE** Granite is a coarse-grained rock, with crystals larger than 5mm (³⁄₁₆in) in diameter.
• **ORIGIN** Forms at considerable depth in the Earth's crust.

biotite mica

grey quartz crystals

pink orthoclase feldspar

Classification Acid	Occurrence Pluton	Colour Light

Group Igneous	Origin Intrusive	Grain size Coarse	Crystal shape Anhedral, Euhedral

WHITE GRANITE

A high silica content – over 65 per cent total silica, and not less than 20 per cent quartz – classifies white granite as an acid rock. K-feldspars (orthoclase and microcline) are dominant, and are white in colour. Usually, there is some albitic plagioclase. Dark biotite mica and hornblende give the rock a mottled appearance. Light, glittery muscovite is also common.
• **TEXTURE** A coarse-grained rock, with euhedral crystals of feldspar and mica and, usually, anhedral quartz.
• **ORIGIN** In plutonic environments.

white orthoclase feldspar

biotite mica

light grey quartz

Classification Acid	Occurrence Pluton	Colour Light

| Group Igneous | Origin Intrusive | Grain size Coarse | Crystal shape Anhedral, Euhedral |

PORPHYRITIC GRANITE

A granitic rock with more than 65 per cent silica, and a minimum of 20 per cent quartz. Pink orthoclase feldspar, and white microcline, or albitic feldspar are present. Biotite mica crystals and quartz are visible. Hornblende may add to the speckled appearance.
• TEXTURE Granite may be granular or porphyritic. The phenocrysts are usually of feldspar and may be up to 6cm (2½in) long.
• ORIGIN Forms by magma cooling in two stages at some depth in the Earth's crust.

biotite mica crystals

quartz crystals

light phenocrysts of orthoclase feldspar

| Classification Acid | Occurrence Pluton | Colour Light |

| Group Igneous | Origin Intrusive | Grain size Coarse | Crystal shape Anhedral, Euhedral |

GRAPHIC GRANITE

An acid igneous rock, this granite contains 20 per cent quartz, and over 65 per cent total silica. It is made up of K-feldspars (orthoclase and microcline) albitic plagioclase, grey quartz, and some dark biotite mica.
• TEXTURE Coarse-grained, with a graphic texture.
• ORIGIN Forms due to the simultaneous crystallization of quartz and K-feldspars.

pink colouring of orthoclase feldspar

grey quartz

| Classification Acid | Occurrence Pluton | Colour Light |

| Group Igneous | Origin Intrusive | Grain size Coarse | Crystal shape Anhedral, Euhedral |

HORNBLENDE GRANITE

This granitic rock is made up of more than 20 per cent quartz and over 65 per cent silica. K-feldspars (orthoclase and microcline) are more abundant than plagioclase feldspar. Hornblende occurs as small masses, and as prismatic crystals. Mica is also present in the rock.
• TEXTURE Coarse-grained, with equal-sized crystals, giving an even texture.
• ORIGIN Forms at various depths in the Earth's crust.

dark hornblende crystals

pale orthoclase feldspar

| Classification Acid | Occurrence Pluton | Colour Medium |

Group Igneous	Origin Intrusive	Grain size Coarse	Crystal shape Anhedral, Euhedral

ADAMELLITE

An acid rock, adamellite has more than 65 per cent total silica and over 20 per cent quartz. It contains a large quantity of feldspar – equally divided between K-feldspars (orthoclase and microcline) and plagioclase. Biotite mica gives adamellite a speckled appearance. Small grey grains of quartz occur in the matrix.

• **TEXTURE** This is a coarse-grained rock with generally equigranular grains (grains of the same size), though it can be porphyritic. The crystals are large enough to be seen with the naked eye. Most of the crystals in adamellite are euhedral, though some of the quartz is anhedral.

• **ORIGIN** Crystallizes in magmas associated with large plutons.

grey quartz *feldspar crystals over 5mm (⅕in) in diameter*

dark biotite mica

light feldspar

Classification Acid	Occurrence Pluton	Colour Light

Group Igneous	Origin Intrusive	Grain size Medium	Crystal shape Anhedral, Euhedral

WHITE MICROGRANITE

An acid rock with more than 65 per cent total silica and over 20 per cent quartz. It contains more K-feldspars (orthoclase and microcline) than plagioclase feldspar. There may be dark biotite and/or light muscovite mica. Patches of biotite may give microgranite a darker colour.

• **TEXTURE** Medium-grained, with crystals 5–0.5mm (³⁄₁₆–¹⁄₆₄in) in diameter. This makes mineral identification difficult. The grains are generally equigranular, but many of the crystals are anhedral, or sometimes porphyritic, because of more rapid cooling.

• **ORIGIN** In the outer margins of pegmatites. Also forms as minor intrusions, such as sills and dykes, from the crystallization of magma at moderate depth.

light orthoclase feldspar

grey quartz

biotite mica gives speckled appearance

Classification Acid	Occurrence Dyke, Sill	Colour Light, Medium

Group Igneous	Origin Intrusive	Grain size Medium	Crystal shape Anhedral, Euhedral

PINK MICROGRANITE

pink orthoclase

An acid rock with more than 65 per cent total silica and over 20 per cent quartz. If the predominant feldspar is pink orthoclase, this will influence the colour of the rock. When biotite mica is present in microgranite, it will appear as dark specks. The grey grains of quartz in the groundmass are often anhedral.
• TEXTURE Medium-grained, with crystals 5–0.5mm (³⁄₁₆–¹⁄₆₄in) in diameter. The crystals are generally of similar size.
• ORIGIN Usually forms in dykes and sills, from the solidifying of magma.

dark biotite mica crystals

Classification Acid	Occurrence Dyke, Sill	Colour Light, Medium

Group Igneous	Origin Intrusive	Grain size Medium	Crystal shape Anhedral, Euhedral

PORPHYRITIC MICROGRANITE

phenocrysts of feldspar

This acid rock contains over 65 per cent total silica and more than 20 per cent quartz. As with other granites, there is more K-feldspar (orthoclase and micro-cline) than plagioclase feldspar in porphyritic microgranite. This specimen has light-coloured feldspar phenocrysts set into a matrix which also contains dark biotite mica.
• TEXTURE This is a medium-grained rock, with crystals 5–0.5mm (³⁄₁₆–¹⁄₆₄in) in diameter. A porphyritic texture is common; the phenocrysts usually have good crystal shape, and may be aligned due to flow. These phenocrysts are usually of feldspar and are often euhedral. The porphyritic texture may indicate crystallization of the parent magma.
• ORIGIN Porphyritic microgranite forms in minor intrusions, such as sills and dykes.

medium-grained matrix

Classification Acid	Occurrence Dyke, Sill	Colour Medium

Group	Igneous/Met.	Origin	C'try Rock	Grain size	Fine	Crystal shape	Anhedral, Euhedral

XENOLITH

Xenolith is a term applied to rock fragments that are foreign to the body of igneous rock in which they occur. They are usually engulfed by magma, and partly altered. In some cases, a xenolith may be completely digested and loses its identity. This specimen is a dark mass of lava within pink granite. The granite's feldspar, mica, and quartz contrast noticeably with the dark xenolith.
• TEXTURE Xenolith is a medium- to fine-grained rock, with crystals of 0.5mm (⅟₆₄in) in diameter. The granite is coarse-grained, with crystals of 5mm (³⁄₁₆in) and over.
• ORIGIN Xenoliths occur in many igneous rocks and environments.

granite around margins

coarse grains

xenolith •

Classification	Acid to basic	Occurrence	Pluton, Volcano	Colour	Dark

Group	Igneous	Origin	Intrusive	Grain size	Medium	Crystal shape	Anhedral, Euhedral

QUARTZ PORPHYRY

An acid rock, with more than 65 per cent total silica, and over 10 per cent quartz. It contains phenocrysts of quartz and alkali feldspar (usually orthoclase) in a microcrystalline matrix. In quartz porphyry, orthoclase feldspar exceeds plagioclase feldspar. Some patches of hornblende are also visible in this specimen.
• TEXTURE This is a medium-grained rock, but with some larger crystals (phenocrysts) of various essential minerals, surrounded by smaller mineral grains. These smaller grains in the matrix are of similiar size. A porphyritic rock, quartz porphyry may have formed in two stages during the cooling of magma.
• ORIGIN Quartz porphyry forms in minor intrusive structures, such as sills and dykes, from the intrusion and cooling of magma. It does not usually form at great depth.

• phenocrysts in matrix

Classification	Acid	Occurrence	Dyke, Sill	Colour	Light, Medium

Group	Igneous	Origin	Intrusive	Grain size	Very coarse	Crystal shape	Euhedral

FELDSPAR PEGMATITE

This acid rock has the same mineral composition as granite. It contains a high proportion of feldspar (which is usually pink or white), greyish quartz, and dark mica or amphibole. The total silica content is well over 65 per cent.

- **TEXTURE** Due to slow cooling, pegmatites are very coarse-grained: some have crystals many metres long. In this specimen, the mass of white feldspar is over 10cm (4in) long. The minerals can be easily identified without a magnifying glass.
- **ORIGIN** Forms in plutonic environments, often in dykes and veins. Pegmatites tend to be concentrated at the margins of granite intrusions.

white feldspar crystals

large crystals

amphibole crystals

Classification	Acid	Occurrence	Pluton, Dyke, Sill	Colour	Light

Group	Igneous	Origin	Magma	Grain size	Very coarse	Crystal shape	Euhedral

MICA PEGMATITE

This is an acid rock of granitic composition, with more than 65 per cent total silica, and over 20 per cent quartz. White muscovite mica may form as large sheets, over 6cm (2½in) long, within the rock mass. There is also some feldspar, and biotite. The name pegmatite generally refers to rocks of acid composition, but the term applies to any igneous rock of very coarse grain size.

- **TEXTURE** Pegmatites owe their very coarse grain size to slow cooling. Large crystals, some several feet long, may be found.
- **ORIGIN** Forms deep below the Earth's surface, in plutonic environments. Cooling of magma is slow, and often associated with late-stage fluids, which may carry some of the rarer chemical elements into the rock mass.

grey quartz

large, glittering, muscovite mica crystals

Classification	Acid	Occurrence	Pluton, Dyke, Sill	Colour	Light

Group Igneous	Origin Intrusive	Grain size Very coarse	Crystal shape Euhedral

TOURMALINE PEGMATITE

This rock has an acid composition, similar to
that of granite, with well over 20 per cent
quartz, and more than 65 per cent total
silica. A high proportion of grey
quartz, pink K-feldspars, and dark
biotite mica may be present. The
dark, prismatic crystals are the
borosilicate mineral, tourmaline.
• TEXTURE Consists of very
coarse-grained crystals. Some
of the larger crystals in this
specimen are 5–6cm (2–2½in)
long. Most are euhedral (good
crystal shape). The
tourmaline forms coarse,
striated prismatic crystals.
• ORIGIN Tourmaline pegmatite
forms in large intrusions, and also
in dykes or sills. The rock is created
by the slow cooling of magma at
a considerable depth in the
Earth's crust.

dark,
prismatic
tourmaline crystals

pink orthoclase
feldspar

Classification Acid	Occurrence Pluton, Dyke, Sill	Colour Light

Group Igneous	Origin Intrusive	Grain size Medium	Crystal shape Anhedral, Euhedral

GRANOPHYRE

This rock has an acid composition, with
more than 20 per cent quartz, and a total
silica content of over 65 per cent. It
contains both K-feldspars and plagioclase feldspars, mica, and amphibole.
When ferro-magnesian minerals are
present in granophyre, they give the
rock a darker colour.
• TEXTURE This is a medium-
grained rock but can be porphyritic,
characterized by a texture formed by
an intergrowth of feldspars and quartz
– called granophyric – and a finer
version of graphic texture found in
some granites. The texture is best
seen with a magnifying glass, or viewed
under a microscope.
• ORIGIN The rock
occurs on the margins
of large plutonic,
intrusive masses, and
also in hypabyssal
intrusions.

ferro-magnesian
minerals give
dark colour

similar-sized
grains

Classification Acid	Occurrence Pluton, Dyke	Colour Light, Medium

Group Igneous	Origin Intrusive	Grain size Coarse	Crystal shape Anhedral, Euhedral

PINK GRANODIORITE

This is a plutonic rock generally
consisting of quartz, plagioclase, and
lesser amounts of alkali feldspar.
Minor constituents of pink
granodiorite may be hornblende,
biotite, or pyroxene.
• TEXTURE A medium- to
coarse-grained rock, with well-
formed crystals.
• ORIGIN Forms in many
types of igneous intrusions.
This is probably the commonest rock of the granite family.

*hornblende •
crystals*

Classification Intermediate	Occurrence Pluton, Dyke	Colour Light, Medium

Group Igneous	Origin Intrusive	Grain size Coarse	Crystal shape Anhedral, Euhedral

WHITE GRANODIORITE

The total silica content of this
rock is lower than that of granite,
being between 55 and 65 per cent. This
light form of granodiorite contains a
high proportion of grey quartz and white
feldspar. Dark mica and hornblende
give the rock a speckled appearance.
• TEXTURE A coarse-grained rock,
white granodiorite has well-formed
crystals. Some of the interstitial
quartz may be anhedral.
• ORIGIN Forms in many
types of igneous intrusions.

light feldspar •

*dark •
ferro-magnesian
minerals*

Classification Intermediate	Occurrence Pluton	Colour Light

Group Igneous	Origin Magma	Grain size Coarse	Crystal shape Anhedral, Euhedral

DIORITE

A rock of intermediate composition, diorite has
55 to 65 per cent total silica content. Essentially
composed of plagioclase feldspar (oligoclase or
andesine), and hornblende. Biotite mica, and
pyroxene may also occur in diorite.
• TEXTURE The grain size of diorite is
medium to coarse (sometimes pegmatitic). It may
be equigranular, or porphyritic with phenocrysts
of feldspar or hornblende.
• ORIGIN Forms as independent intrusions,
such as dykes, but usually
comprises parts of major
granitic masses.

*light plagioclase •
feldspar*

Classification Intermediate	Occurrence Pluton, Dyke	Colour Medium, Dark

Group Igneous	Origin Intrusive	Grain size Coarse	Crystal shape Euhedral

SYENITE

A coarse-grained plutonic rock generally devoid of quartz (up to 10 per cent quartz in quartz syenites), syenite is a light-coloured rock, often confused with granite. An intermediate rock, with total silica between 55 and 65 per cent, principally formed of alkali feldspar, and/or sodic plagioclase, usually associated with biotite, amphibole, or pyroxene.

amphibole

• **TEXTURE** A coarse-grained rock, with all minerals visible to the naked eye, and with grains generally the same size. It is sometimes porphyritic – where larger crystals are enclosed by a finer-grained matrix. Crystals are mainly anhedral to euhedral.
• **ORIGIN** Usually forms in minor intrusions, dykes, and sills often associated with granites.

Classification Intermediate	Occurrence Pluton, Dyke	Colour Light, Dark

Group Igneous	Origin Intrusive	Grain size Coarse	Crystal shape Euhedral

NEPHELINE SYENITE

This rock has the typical intermediate igneous rock composition of 55 to 65 per cent total silica content. It contains a high proportion of feldspar, amphibole, and mica. Pyroxene can sometimes be present. Nepheline syenite contains the feldspathoid mineral, nepheline, from which its name is derived. There is no quartz present in this rock.

• **TEXTURE** This syenite is coarse-grained; the minerals can be seen clearly without a magnifying glass. The crystals generally have the same grain size (equigranular). This rock can sometimes be pegmatic.
• **ORIGIN** Nepheline syenite forms from the crystallization of magmas that are often associated with highly alkaline rocks. These are rocks which contain minerals rich in sodium and potassium.

dark patches of ferro-magnesian minerals

coarse-grained texture

Classification Intermediate	Occurrence Pluton, Dyke	Colour Light, Dark

Group Igneous	Origin Intrusive	Grain size Coarse	Crystal shape Euhedral

GABBRO

A basic rock in which quartz is rare. Gabbros are poorer in silica than granites (about 50 per cent by weight). Gabbro is composed essentially of calcic plagioclase, pyroxene (usually augite), and olivine and magnetite.
• TEXTURE Gabbro is a coarse-grained and equigranular rock.
• ORIGIN Forms in major plutonic intrusions, which are commonly layered.

light plagioclase feldspar

coarse grain size

dark pyroxene

Classification Basic	Occurrence Pluton	Colour Medium

Group Igneous	Origin Intrusive	Grain size Coarse	Crystal shape Euhedral

LAYERED GABBRO

A basic rock composition as in gabbro. The main minerals are calcium-rich plagioclase and pyroxene, with olivine and magnetite also present. Layering, defined by alternate layers of light and dark coloured minerals, varies from a metre to a few centimetres in thickness, and is due to gravity settling.
• TEXTURE A coarse-grained rock, with euhedral crystals.
• ORIGIN Forms in basic plutonic intrusions, sometimes as major structures (lopoliths).

alternating layers

light plagioclase feldspar

dark ferro-magnesian minerals and magnetite

Classification Basic	Occurrence Pluton	Colour Medium

Group Igneous	Origin Intrusive	Grain size Coarse	Crystal shape Euhedral

LARVIKITE

A variety of augite syenite, larvikite is an intermediate rock consisting of feldspar, pyroxene (usually Ti – augite), mica, and amphibole. It contains minor amounts of nepheline and olivine. Dark to light grey in colour, the feldspars usually display a distinctive schiller.
• TEXTURE This is a coarse-grained rock. In this specimen, the mafic minerals are seen to form in clots.
• ORIGIN Forms in relatively small intrusions, such as sills.

coarse-grained rock

mass of greyish feldspar crystals with ferro-magnesian minerals in between

Classification Intermediate	Occurrence Pluton	Colour Light, Dark

Group Igneous	Origin Intrusive	Grain size Coarse	Crystal shape Anhedral, Euhedral

OLIVINE GABBRO

This rock has a basic composition, with a total silica content of less than 55 per cent. Quartz occurs only rarely. The high content of ferro-magnesian minerals gives the rock a dark colouring. It is of higher density than the granitic rocks. Olivine gabbro contains plagioclase feldspar (a calcium-rich variety), pyroxene, and olivine. Magnetite is generally present in small amounts.

• **TEXTURE** A coarse-grained rock, the crystals, which are mostly euhedral, are over 5mm (³⁄₁₆ in) and easy to see with the naked eye. The grains are all of similar size, though gabbros can be porphyritic – having larger crystals surrounded by a finer matrix.

• **ORIGIN** Forms in plutonic environments, often in stocks, sills, and other sheet-like intrusions.

plagioclase
• *feldspar*

• *abundance of olivine evident as dark greenish patches*

Classification Basic	Occurrence Pluton, Dyke, Sill	Colour Medium, Dark

Group Igneous	Origin Intrusive	Grain size Coarse	Crystal shape Anhedral, Euhedral

LEUCOGABBRO

Basic in composition, leucogabbro has a total silica content of less than 55 per cent. It is lighter than other gabbros, because of a high percentage of plagioclase feldspar. This is usually associated with the clinopyroxene, augite. Olivine and magnetite can also sometimes be present.

• **TEXTURE** This is a coarse-grained rock. The crystals are over 5mm (³⁄₁₆in) in diameter, and can easily be seen with the naked eye.

• **ORIGIN** This rock forms in plutonic environments, often in major intrusions. During crystal-lization, crystals and liquid may be separated under the influence of gravity. The tapping off of the liquid fraction can lead to the formation of a variety of rock types, a process known as fractional crystallization.

• *white plagioclase feldspar*

dark • *pyroxene, equal in quantity to feldspar*

Classification Basic	Occurrence Pluton	Colour Medium, Light

Group Igneous	Origin Intrusive	Grain size Coarse	Crystal shape Anhedral, Euhedral

BOJITE

A plutonic rock consisting of plagioclase feldspar (labradorite), brown hornblende, minor augite, and biotite. The brown hornblende is thought to be primary. A common accessory mineral is iron oxide (magnetite). Bojite is often visually striking, with patches and streaks and a layering of mafic minerals.

• **TEXTURE** Coarse-grained, with crystals greater than 5mm (³⁄₁₆in) in diameter. Grains are of the same size, but dark minerals tend to be in patches and layers.

• **ORIGIN** Forms in plutonic environments, at considerable depth in the Earth's crust.

recognizable patches of different coloured minerals

coarse-grained texture

patches of iron-rich alteration

Classification Basic	Occurrence Pluton	Colour Dark

Group Igneous	Origin Intrusive	Grain size Coarse	Crystal shape Anhedral, Euhedral

ANORTHOSITE

A rock of basic composition, the total silica content is less than 55 per cent, and quartz is virtually absent. Anorthosite comprises at least 90 per cent plagioclase feldspar (labradorite-bytownite). Other minerals in the rock include olivine, pyroxene, and iron oxides. Garnet sometimes forms in reaction rims around pyroxene.

• **TEXTURE** Generally coarse-grained, granular, and light in colour, these rocks may have a parallel alignment of dark minerals.

• **ORIGIN** Forms in plutonic environments, in stocks, dykes, and sheet-shaped intrusions. It is often associated with gabbros in layered sequences, and has been shown to form part of the Moon's surface.

mass of light plagioclase feldspar crystals

ferro-magnesian minerals

coarse grain size

Classification Basic	Occurrence Pluton	Colour Light

Group Igneous	Origin Intrusive	Grain size Medium	Crystal shape Anhedral, Euhedral

DOLERITE

A rock of basic composition, with
a total silica content of less
than 55 per cent; the quartz
content is usually lower than
10 per cent. Dolerite consists
of calcium-rich plagioclase
feldspar, and pyroxene – often
augite – with some quartz, and
sometimes magnetite and olivine.
(If olivine is present it is known as
olivine dolerite; if quartz is present
it is called quartz dolerite.)
• TEXTURE A medium-grained
rock, with crystals between 0.5–5mm
(1/64– 3/16 in) in diameter. Euhedral or
subhedral crystals of plagioclase are
embedded in pyroxene crystals.
• ORIGIN This rock usually forms as
dykes and sills in basaltic provinces. It
may also occur as dyke or sill swarms –
hundreds of individual intrusions
associated with a single igneous centre.

plagioclase
feldspar

pyroxene

Classification Basic	Occurrence Dyke, Sill	Colour Dark

Group Igneous	Origin Intrusive	Grain size Medium	Crystal shape Anhedral, Euhedral

NORITE

Similar to gabbro, this is a rock of basic
composition with less than 55 per cent total
silica. Norite is composed of plagioclase
feldspar and pyroxene. Importantly, it is a
variety of gabbro, in which orthopyroxene is
dominant over clinopyroxene. Olivine may
be present in some varieties of the rock.
Biotite mica, hornblende, and
cordierite can sometimes also
occur in this rock.
• TEXTURE A coarse-grained rock,
which is granular in texture, norite
often shows a layered structure.
• ORIGIN Forms by the freezing
of magma in a plutonic environment. Norite is associated with
larger basic igneous bodies,
and is often found in layered
igneous intrusions; different
rock types may form within one
intrusion by a separation of their
mineral content, often due to the
effects of gravity settling.

light plagioclase
feldspar

dark
ferro-
magnesian
minerals

Classification Basic	Occurrence Pluton	Colour Dark

Group Igneous	Origin Intrusive	Grain size Medium	Crystal shape Anhedral, Euhedral

TROCTOLITE

A variety of gabbro, troctolite has a total silica content of less than 55 percent. It is composed essentially of highly calcic plagioclase and olivine, with virtually no pyroxene. The olivine is often altered to serpentine. Troctolite is generally dark grey, often with a mottled appearance.
• **TEXTURE** This is a medium- to coarse-grained rock, with many crystals about 5mm (³⁄₁₆in) in diameter. The grains are generally of a similar size.
• **ORIGIN** This rock forms in a plutonic environment, where the magma cools slowly. Troctolite is usually associated with gabbros or anorthosite, sometimes in layered complexes.

grey coloured plagioclase feldspar

mottled appearance

Classification Basic	Occurrence Pluton	Colour Dark

Group Igneous	Origin Intrusive	Grain size Medium	Crystal shape Euhedral

DUNITE

A rock of ultrabasic composition, dunite contains less than 45 per cent total silica and no quartz. It is made up almost entirely of olivine, which gives the rock its recognizable greenish or brownish colouring. The alternative name, olivinite, refers to its mineral composition. Chromite occurs in this rock as an accessory mineral.
• **TEXTURE** A medium-grained rock, with crystals 0.5–5mm (¹⁄₆₄–³⁄₁₆in) in diameter. The texture of dunite is granular and sugary.
• **ORIGIN** Forms in a plutonic environment. Small volumes of ultra-basic rocks are often formed as cumulates during the differentiation of basic rocks. Minerals in some dunites are often crushed, and they may be emplaced in a near solid state due to earth movements. This can produce a mass of ultrabasic rock from a magma that is otherwise of basic composition.

greenish colouring from olivine

typical sugary texture

Classification Ultrabasic	Occurrence Pluton	Colour Dark, Medium

Group Igneous	Origin Intrusive	Grain size Coarse	Crystal shape Anhedral, Euhedral

SERPENTINITE

This is a plutonic rock with an ultrabasic composition, with less than 45 per cent total silica. It is composed almost entirely of serpentine minerals, such as antigorite and chrysotile. Relics of olivine are often present. Other ferro-magnesian minerals such as garnet, pyroxene, hornblende, and mica are also commonly found, as are chromite or chrome spinels. It is dark in colour, with areas of black, green, or red.

• **TEXTURE** A coarse- to medium-grained rock, in which most crystals are easy to see with the naked eye. This is a compact, often banded rock, commonly veined by fibrous serpentine.

• **ORIGIN** Occurs as dykes, stocks, and lenses. Serpentinites are formed by the serpentinization of other rocks, principally peridotite. It commonly occurs in folded metamorphic rocks, probably from altered olivine-rich intrusions.

easily seen, coarse-grain crystals

dark colouring

patches of different colour

Classification Ultrabasic	Occurrence Orogenic belts	Colour Dark

Group Igneous	Origin Intrusive	Grain size Coarse	Crystal shape Anhedral, Euhedral

PYROXENITE

This is an ultramafic, plutonic rock with less than 45 per cent total silica. As the name suggests, it is composed almost entirely of one or more pyroxenes. Some biotite, hornblende, olivine, and iron oxide may also be present. The light-coloured crystals in pyroxenite are of feldspar in very small amounts.

• **TEXTURE** Pyroxenite is a coarse- to medium-grained rock. It has a granular texture, with well-formed crystals sometimes forming layers. The texture can easily be seen with the naked eye.

• **ORIGIN** Pyroxenite forms in small, independent intrusions that are usually associated with gabbros or other types of ultrabasic rock.

dark colouring

granular texture

pyroxene minerals

Classification Ultrabasic	Occurrence Pluton	Colour Dark

Group Igneous	Origin Intrusive	Grain size Coarse	Crystal shape Euhedral

KIMBERLITE

An ultrabasic rock consisting of major amounts of serpentinized olivine. It is associated with phlogopite, ortho- or clino-pyroxene, carbonate, and chromite. Pyrope garnet, rutile, and perovskite may also be present. Kimberlite is dark in colour.
• TEXTURE This is a coarse-grained rock, often with a porphyritic texture. Kimberlite often has a brecciated appearance.
• ORIGIN Forms in pipes and other igneous bodies which are steep-sided and intrusive. The pipes are usually less than a kilometre in diameter. Kimberlite pipes are the primary source of diamonds, and are mined, especially in South Africa, for their high diamond content.

crystals of ferro-magnesian minerals

dark matrix

Classification Ultrabasic	Occurrence Hypabyssal, Pluton	Colour Dark

Group Igneous	Origin Intrusive	Grain size Coarse	Crystal shape Anhedral, Euhedral

GARNET PERIDOTITE

A rock with less than 45 per cent total silica content, garnet peridotite is composed only of dark minerals: feldspar is virtually absent, olivine is essential, as is garnet. Pyroxene and/or hornblende are often present.
• TEXTURE This is a coarse- or medium-grained rock, with garnets set into a granular matrix. The garnets may vary in size from very small grains to larger patches over 5mm (⅕in) in diameter.
• ORIGIN Garnet peridotite forms in intrusive dykes, sills, and stocks, and is sometimes associated with large masses of gabbro, pyroxenite, and anorthosite. It is found in basalts and as xenoliths in high-grade metamorphic rocks. It is possible for garnet peridotite to have been derived from the Earth's mantle.

smaller patches of red garnet

typical greenish colour produced by olivine

Classification Ultrabasic	Occurrence Pluton, Dyke, Sill	Colour Dark

Group Igneous	Origin Extrusive	Grain size Fine	Crystal shape Anhedral

RHYOLITE

These are extrusive rocks with the same general composition as granite. Like granites, these rocks are often rich in quartz and alkali feldspars. Unlike granites, glass is often one of the major components in rhyolite. Biotite mica is usually present.

• **TEXTURE** A fine-grained acid, volcanic rock which may have phenocrysts giving a porphyritic texture. The matrix crystals are too small to be seen with the naked eye, and the rapid cooling of the lava causes glass to be formed. Rhyolite may also have vesicles and amygdales.

• **ORIGIN** These rocks erupt from volcanoes with explosive violence, and are the result of the cooling of viscous lava. These lavas may plug the volcano's vent, causing a build up of gaseous pressure.

porphyritic texture

phenocrysts include quartz

Classification Acid	Occurrence Volcano	Colour Light

Group Igneous	Origin Extrusive	Grain size Fine	Crystal shape Anhedral

BANDED RHYOLITE

bands of different colours

A group of rocks similar in composition to granites. Quartz, feldspar, and mica, along with glass, are the major components of banded rhyolite, while hornblende may also be present.

• **TEXTURE** A fine- or very fine-grained rock, in which the minerals are too small to be seen with the naked eye. Flow banding is common in rhyolites, and is defined by swirling layers of different colour and texture. These rocks may also have a spheroidal texture formed by radial aggregates of needles composed of quartz and feldspar.

• **ORIGIN** Formed by the rapid cooling of lava, leading to the formation of minute crystals or glass. The magma is highly viscous.

hard, flinty appearance

Classification Acid	Occurrence Volcano	Colour Light, Medium

Group	Igneous	Origin	Extrusive	Grain size	Fine	Crystal shape	Anhedral, Euhedral

DACITE

A volcanic rock of intermediate composition. Quartz and plagioclase feldspar are the major constituents in dacite, with minor amounts of biotite and/or hornblende or pyroxene.
• **TEXTURE** Dacite is a fine-grained rock, though it can have a porphyritic texture. The crystals formed can vary from anhedral to euhedral.
• **ORIGIN** Although a volcanic rock, dacite can also occur in small intrusions.

porphyritic texture •

Classification	Intermediate	Occurrence	Volcano	Colour	Light, Medium

Group	Igneous	Origin	Extrusive	Grain size	Very fine	Crystal shape	Anhedral

OBSIDIAN

This is a silica-rich volcanic rock. With glass as its main component, obsidian is sometimes defined as being a glassy volcanic rock, with less than 1 per cent water content in its structure.
• **TEXTURE** Glassy, obsidian may contain rare phenocrysts of quartz and feldspar. It breaks with a very sharp conchoidal fracture which has been exploited since Palaeolithic times for making cutting tools.
• **ORIGIN** Volcanic, formed by the very rapid cooling of viscous acid lava.

glass, rather than crystals • *of minerals*

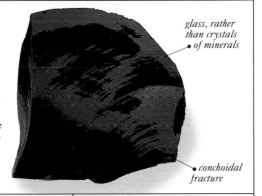

conchoidal fracture •

Classification	Acid	Occurrence	Volcano	Colour	Dark

Group	Igneous	Origin	Extrusive	Grain size	Very fine	Crystal shape	Anhedral

SNOWFLAKE OBSIDIAN

Like obsidian, this rock is composed of a high percentage of glass rather than crystals. The characteristic pale "snowflakes" on its surface are patches where the glass has become devitrified around distinct centres.
• **TEXTURE** This is an extremely fine-grained rock. It also displays micro-crystalline patches of white colour.
• **ORIGIN** A volcanic rock, snowflake obsidian is formed from lava that has cooled rapidly.

black, glassy matrix •

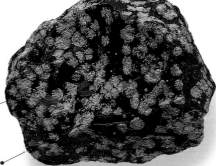

white "snowflakes" •

Classification	Acid	Occurrence	Volcano	Colour	Dark

Group Igneous	Origin Extrusive	Grain size Very fine	Crystal shape Anhedral

PITCHSTONE

This rock has a composition equivalent to a wide range of other volcanic rocks. It is essentially a volcanic glass, and it contains a few phenocrysts. Pitchstone is usually very dark in colour, and has a lustre similar to that of tar or pitch.
• TEXTURE Although the proportion of glass content in pitchstone is very high, it contains more crystalline material than obsidian. It may also be spotted or flow-banded. Even under microscopic examination, the crystals in pitchstone appear to be poorly formed.
• ORIGIN The rock forms as the result of very sudden solidification of lava, especially in dykes and flows. The large quantity of glass contained in pitchstone is a result of its rapid cooling history.

tar-like surface

fine-grained, crystals

Classification Acid to basic	Occurrence Volcano, Dyke, Sill	Colour Dark

Group Igneous	Origin Extrusive	Grain size Very fine	Crystal shape Anhedral

PORPHYRITIC PITCHSTONE

porphyritic texture

A very dark and glassy rock in appearance, porphyritic pitchstone is usually of acid composition, although, as in the case of pitchstone, the chemistry is variable. Some pitchstones are rich in phenocrysts, generally of quartz, feldspar, and pyroxene. Some authorities distinguish between pitchstone and obsidian by the water content of the rocks: pitchstone has as much as 10 per cent, while obsidian usually contains less than 1 per cent.
• TEXTURE Because of the two stages in its rapid cooling history, porphyritic pitchstone contains phenocrysts of feldspar, which are set into the fine-grained matrix.
• ORIGIN Forms in lava flows, and small sills and dykes, often near to granitic masses. In both these situations, the lava solidifies rapidly, giving the crystals no time to grow – hence the glassy appearance.

light phenocrysts

Classification Acid to basic	Occurrence Volcano, Dyke, Sill	Colour Dark

| Group Igneous | Origin Extrusive | Grain size Medium | Crystal shape Anhedral, Euhedral |

LAMPROPHYRE

A group of rocks of variable composition. They are characterized by being strongly porphyritic in mafic minerals, typically biotite, amphibole, and pyroxene – any feldspar (whether alkali or plagioclase feldspar) is confined to the matrix. Accessory minerals include hornblende, calcite, sphene, and magnetite.

• TEXTURE Medium-grained, this group of rocks is typically porphyritic. Both biotite and hornblende phenocrysts give the rocks a distinctive appearance.

• ORIGIN Forms in minor intrusions, and in dykes and sills. The rocks often show signs of hydrothermal alteration. They can be associated with a variety of other igneous rocks, such as granites, syenites, and diorites.

• *porphyritic texture*

| Classification Acid to basic | Occurrence Dyke, Sill | Colour Medium |

| Group Igneous | Origin Extrusive | Grain size Fine | Crystal shape Anhedral, Euhedral |

ANDESITE

An intermediate volcanic rock, andesite usually has 55 to 65 per cent total silica content. Plagioclase feldspar (andesine or oligoclase) is the most significant constituent, along with pyroxene, amphibole, and biotite mica.

• TEXTURE A fine-grained, often porphyritic rock. The phenocrysts set into the matrix are usually white tabular feldspar crystals, or biotite, hornblende, or augite.

• ORIGIN This rock forms as lava flows from andesitic volcanoes, which are second only in abundance to basalt. Andesitic volcanoes are often associated with sub-duction zones, as in the Andean mountains of South America.

• *phenocrysts of light plagioclase feldspar*

• *fine-grained groundmass*

| Classification Intermediate | Occurrence Volcano | Colour Medium |

Group Igneous	Origin Extrusive	Grain size Fine	Crystal shape Anhedral, Euhedral

AMYGDALOIDAL ANDESITE

This is an intermediate volcanic rock which is usually porphyritic. Amygdaloidal andesite consists of plagioclose feldspar (frequently zoned labradorite-oligoclase), pyroxene, and/or biotite. The rock matrix tends to be a medium-coloured grey, rather than the black of basalt.
• TEXTURE This rock has a fine-grained matrix although it may often be porphyritic. Many small, rounded vesicles are visible on the rock surface. These vesicles are left after gas bubbles have escaped from the lava. Infilled vesicles are known as amygdales, and are commonly infilled by the zeolite group of minerals. The cavities are widened by the growth of minerals.
• ORIGIN Amygda-loidal andesite forms from the rapid cooling of lava, that has been erupted from a gas-rich volcanic eruption.

small gas bubble cavities, infilled with minerals

fine-grained matrix

Classification Intermediate	Occurrence Volcano	Colour Medium

Group Igneous	Origin Extrusive	Grain size Fine	Crystal shape Anhedral, Euhedral

PORPHYRITIC ANDESITE

This rock has the same composition as andesite. It is an intermediate rock with 55 to 65 per cent total silica. Plagioclase feldspar is an important constituent, as are pyroxene, amphibole, and biotite mica. Andesite is usually a darker-coloured volcanic rock than rhyolite, though it is lighter than basalt.
• TEXTURE The matrix is fine-grained, and the crystals can be studied in detail only under a microscope. Larger phenocrysts of feldspar and pyroxene are set into the matrix. This texture indicates that some crystals grew in the magma below the Earth's surface, and that, on eruption, the lava solidified rapidly.
• ORIGIN Porphyritic andesite forms as lava flows usually associated with andesitic volcanoes.

fine-grained matrix

euhedral phenocrysts set into the matrix

Classification Intermediate	Occurrence Volcano	Colour Medium

Group	Igneous	Origin	Extrusive	Grain size	Fine	Crystal shape	Anhedral, Euhedral

TRACHYTE

These are volcanic rocks with a total silica content of between 55 to 60 per cent. Trachytes are rich in alkali feldspar and also carry either nepheline or small amounts of quartz (less than 10 per cent). Dark minerals, such as the pyroxene, aegerine, are present in small amounts, though trachytes are usually light in colour.

• TEXTURE A fine-grained rock, usually porphyritic. Feldspar microcrystals exhibit flow structure.

• ORIGIN Trachytes form as lava flows, and narrow dykes and sills.

minute crystals in matrix

small phenocrysts

Classification	Intermediate	Occurrence	Volcano	Colour	Medium

Group	Igneous	Origin	Extrusive	Grain size	Fine	Crystal shape	Anhedral, Euhedral

PORPHYRITIC TRACHYTE

This rock has a similar composition to trachyte, and has 55 to 65 per cent total silica. Dominantly composed of alkali feldspar, some quartz and oligoclase feldspar may be present, as well as pyroxene, hornblende, and biotite mica.

• TEXTURE This rock has a fine-grained matrix, and euhedral phenocrysts are common, giving the porphyritic texture.

• ORIGIN Formed by the cooling of lava.

black phenocrysts, give a porphyritic texture

Classification	Intermediate	Occurrence	Volcano	Colour	Medium

Group	Igneous	Origin	Extrusive	Grain size	Medium	Crystal shape	Euhedral

RHOMB PORPHYRY

A rock of intermediate chemistry, rhomb porphyry is often called microsyenite. It has 55 to 65 per cent total silica content, and up to 10 per cent quartz. The main minerals are alkali feldspar with hornblende, pyroxene, and biotite mica.

• TEXTURE This rock derives its name from the distinctive rhombic shape of the cross section of its feldspar phenocrysts.

• ORIGIN Occurs as lava flows and dykes.

plagioclase feldspar phenocrysts

medium grained matrix

Classification	Intermediate	Occurrence	Dyke, Sill	Colour	Medium

Group Igneous	Origin Extrusive	Grain size Fine	Crystal shape Anhedral, Euhedral

BASALT

A basic volcanic rock consisting of calcic-plagioclase feldspar and pyroxene, basalt is the most abundant of all lava types. Apatite and magnetite are nearly always present, while olivine may also occur.
• **TEXTURE** A fine-grained rock, basalt has crystals which are both euhedral and anhedral. The crystals, however, are not easy to see, even with a magnifying glass.
• **ORIGIN** Forms by the cooling of highly-mobile basaltic lavas. Because of their fluidity, they may form very thick lava sheets. Basalt occurs widely in continental areas, and is the principal rock of the ocean floor. One of the best studied active basaltic volcanoes, Mauna Loa, forms much of the island of Hawaii.

dark coloured, fine-grained crystals

Classification Basic	Occurrence Volcano	Colour Dark

Group Igneous	Origin Extrusive	Grain size Fine	Crystal shape Anhedral, Euhedral

PORPHYRITIC BASALT

This rock is of a similar basic composition to basalt. It contains between 45 and 55 per cent total silica, and less than 10 per cent quartz. Plagioclase – usually calcium-rich – and pyroxene make up the bulk of the rock. Olivine and magnetite may also be present.
• **TEXTURE** This is a fine-grained rock, with phenocrysts set into the matrix. These phenocrysts are usually of olivine (green), pyroxene (black), or plagioclase (white-grey). The resulting porphyritic texture indicates two stages in the cooling of the lava.
• **ORIGIN** Erupted from volcanoes in oceanic areas. Basalt is a non-viscous lava and flows for great distances. The lava flows may form lava plateaux extending over thousands of square kilometres.

fine-grained matrix

large phenocrysts of pyroxene

Classification Basic	Occurrence Volcano	Colour Dark

Group Igneous	Origin Extrusive	Grain size Fine	Crystal shape Anhedral

AMYGDALOIDAL BASALT

A basic volcanic rock with a total silica content of 45 to 55 per cent. Calcium-rich plagioclase feldspar and pyroxene are the main minerals. Olivine and magnetite are other minerals that are frequently associated with amygdaloidal basalt.

• TEXTURE Numerous amygdales (small, rounded gas-bubble cavities infilled with minerals) are characteristic of some basalts. Zeolites and quartz – often in the form of agate – are common minerals.

• ORIGIN This rock is formed by the cooling of lava.

numerous rounded amygdales •

rusty weathering of iron minerals •

Classification Basic	Occurrence Volcano	Colour Dark

Group Igneous	Origin Extrusive	Grain size Fine	Crystal shape Anhedral, Euhedral

VESICULAR BASALT

This rock has a very similar composition to that of basalt, with calcic-plagioclase feldspar and pyroxene being the essential minerals. Olivine and magnetite are also usually present in vesicular basalt.

• TEXTURE The surface may be covered with empty, gas-bubble cavities called vesicles. The matrix is fine-grained, often porphyritic. If the cavities are infilled with minerals, vesicular basalt becomes an amygdaloidal basalt.

• ORIGIN Forms from the cooling of basaltic lava.

rounded cavities •

Classification Basic	Occurrence Volcano	Colour Dark

Group Igneous	Origin Extrusive	Grain size Fine	Crystal shape Anhedral, Euhedral

SPILITE

A basic rock with a silica content averaging 40 per cent, spilite occurs as pillow lavas. A distinctive feature of this rock is that the plagioclase feldspar is albite (Na-rich). The pyroxene content in spilite is often altered to chlorite, although augite sometimes remains.

• TEXTURE A fine-grained rock with infilled gas-bubble cavities. Amygdales are sometimes visible, set in the rock matrix.

• ORIGIN Found in underwater lava flows and in pillow lava, formed on the ocean floor.

pale green amygdales, set in fine-grained matrix •

Classification Basic	Occurrence Volcano	Colour Dark

Group Igneous	Origin Pyroclastic	Grain size Coarse	Crystal shape Fragments

AGGLOMERATE

A consolidated or unconsolidated, coarse, pyroclastic rock material, agglomerate may be composed of both volcanic and country rock fragments that are completely unsorted.
• **TEXTURE** The size of the particles varies considerably: the rock texture often consists of angular to sub-rounded fragments set into a finer-grained matrix. The lava particles are vesicular, sometimes spindle-shaped.
• **ORIGIN** This rock generally accumulates in volcanic craters, or on the flanks of a volcano. Agglomerate consists of lava fragments and blocks of country rock that have been caught up with the volcanic activity, and have erupted with the lava through a volcanic vent. Usually associated with other extrusive deposits such as tuff.

many rock fragments held together in fine matrix

Classification Acid to basic	Occurrence Volcano	Colour Medium

Group Igneous	Origin Pyroclastic	Grain size Fine	Crystal shape Fragments

LITHIC TUFF

This is a pyroclastic rock (tuff) in which lithic fragments are more abundant then either crystal or vitric (glassy) fragments.
• **TEXTURE** A fine-grained rock, tuff consists of consolidated volcanic fragments which are usually less than 2mm (½in) in diameter. Lithic tuff contains a variety of crystalline rock fragments which may be of rhyolitic, trachytic, or andesitic composition.
• **ORIGIN** This rock forms as a deposit from volcanic ash blown into the atmosphere. Lithic tuff sometimes accumulates underwater, when strata may develop. Grading of these layers may take place, and the tuff can have a variety of structures associated with sedimentation, including layering and banding. From very explosve eruptions, ash is often carried many kilometres into the atmosphere. Wind systems then carry the ash to settle a long way from the original volcano. When this happens, the dust particles, blown high into the atmosphere, may cause beautiful sunsets.

small fragments of lava and ash cemented together

fine-grained matrix

Classification Acid to basic	Occurrence Volcano	Colour Medium

Group Igneous	Origin Extrusive	Grain size Fine	Crystal shape Anhedral, Euhedral

CRYSTAL TUFF

mass of fine crystals

This is a variety of tuff in which crystal fragments are more abundant than either lithic, or vitric fragments. Most tuffs are mixtures of lithic, vitric, or crystal fractions. The minerals present in crystal tuff usually include feldspars, and pyroxenes, as well as amphiboles.
• TEXTURE This is a fine- to medium-grained rock, with masses of crystals set into an ash matrix. The crystals are often euhedral.
• ORIGIN Forms when ashes are blown out from volcanoes during eruption. Previously formed crystals are separated from lava, and may accumulate on land or underwater. When underwater deposition occurs, tuff becomes stratified and takes on the features of a sedimentary rock.

• dark colour due to ferro-magnesian mineral content

Classification Acid to basic	Occurrence Volcano	Colour Medium

Group Igneous	Origin Extrusive	Grain size Fine	Crystal shape Anhedral

PUMICE

• typically elongated vesicles

This is a light, porous rock with the composition of rhyolite. It may contain a variety of minute crystals of silicate minerals, such as feldspar and ferro-magnesians, and also has a considerable amount of glass.
• TEXTURE Pumice usually tends to be used as a textural term – applied to vesiculated lavas that may resemble froth or foam. This rock has a highly scoriaceous texture, with many hollows and cavities. The vesicles may join to form elongated passages and tubes throughout the rock. Zeolites may fill these cavities. The density of pumice is so low that it can easily float in water.
• ORIGIN Forms as frothy lavas associated with rhyolitic volcanic eruptions. When erupted into the sea, patches may drift for great distances. Pumice can also be formed by land bound volcanic eruptions.

• hollow, gas-bubble cavities or vesicles

Classification Acid to basic	Occurrence Volcano	Colour Medium

Group Igneous	Origin Extrusive	Grain size Fine	Crystal shape Anhedral

IGNIMBRITE

This is a hard, volcanic tuff consisting of crystal and rock fragments in a matrix of glass shards which are usually welded together. This welding, in some cases, may lead to the original texture, shown by the glass shards, being lost. Ignimbrite has a similar composition to rhyolite.

• **TEXTURE** It is often a fine-grained rock with a banded structure. In the field, you may see wavy flow-banding through the outcrop. The glass shards in the rock are often curved where they have formed around gas bubbles in the original frothy flow of ash, tuff, and lava droplets.

• **ORIGIN** Forms as a deposit from a rapidly moving, turbulent, ignited cloud of gas called a *nuée ardente*. Associated with especially violent eruptions, producing clouds of incandescent gas and lava drops. These flow from volcanic eruptions at great speed, close to the ground.

shard glass

pale coloured acid rock with darker patches

Classification Acid	Occurrence Volcano	Colour Light, Medium

Group Igneous	Origin Extrusive	Grain size Fine	Crystal shape Anhedral

BREADCRUST VOLCANIC BOMB

rough surface texture

Volcanic bombs usually have the composition of the lava erupted by a particular volcano. The lava clots have a high silica content with a high proportion of quartz. Clots from intermediate composition lavas have a silica content of 55 to 65 per cent. Basic volcanoes are mainly non-explosive, and bombs are less likely to form.

• **TEXTURE** Breadcrust volcanic bombs have a fine-grained crust and may show coarser crystals within. The crust may be marked and cracked because of the force of impact with the ground. They may contain small fragments of country rock, torn from around the volcanic pipe.

• **ORIGIN** Volcanic bombs are small to large molten lava clots that have been ejected from a volcano by violent eruption, and have landed on the Earth. The lava clots are usually made of viscous lava, which cools on the outside during flight, forming a skin that cracks on impact of landing to produce the "breadcrust" surface. The bombs may sometimes measure over 1 metre (3ft) in diameter. When they land in volcanic ash, these bombs will often form a crater.

fine-grained crystals

Classification Acid to basic	Occurrence Volcano	Colour Dark

Group Igneous	Origin Extrusive	Grain size Fine	Crystal shape Anhedral

ROUNDED SPINDLE BOMB

Spindle bombs usually have the composition of the lava
erupted by a particular volcano, whether it be andesite
or basaltic. However, they also tend to be associated
with acidic and other intermediate lava volcanoes.
These rocks are often rich in silica, and
contain minerals such as quartz, feldspar,
mica, and some ferromag-nesian
minerals, such as hornblende.
• **TEXTURE** These rocks are
composed of fine-grained
crystals, which need microscopic examination. The shape
results from the molten lava
clot twisting during flight.
• **ORIGIN** Rounded
spindle bombs form
as molten lava clots
thrown from violently
erupting volcanoes.

*twisted
shape*

*rough, slaggy,
vesicular surface*

dark colour

Classification Acid to basic	Occurrence Volcano	Colour Medium

Group Igneous	Origin Extrusive	Grain size Fine	Crystal shape Anhedral

ROPY LAVA

*folded, rope-like
surface*

This rock tends to be formed from basic
volcanic eruptions, and is usually of a basaltic
composition. It contains a high proportion of
plagioclase feldspar and augite, and small amounts of
iron oxide. Such a composition gives ropy lava a dark
colour and a high specific gravity.
• **TEXTURE** These lavas are often highly
vesicular, which means that they contain
many gas bubble cavities. The cavities can
be filled, at a subsequent time, by a variety
of minerals, including quartz, calcite, and
zeolites. The rock is described as amygdaloidal when the cavities are filled.
• **ORIGIN** Ropy lava forms when mobile
lava flows from basic volcanoes and
continues to move beneath a relatively
solid, but plastic, crust. Basaltic lavas
with a low silica content and a high
gas content are usually very mobile. The flowing lava causes
the crust to stretch, thus making
folds and rope-shaped patterns.
In Hawaii, where ropy lava is
common, it is called *pahoehoe*,
an accepted geological term.

*dark colour, but
weathered surface is
paler and brownish*

Classification Basic	Occurrence Volcano	Colour Dark

METAMORPHIC ROCKS

METAMORPHIC ROCKS form from the alteration of a pre-existing rock. Contact metamorphism is caused by direct heat, and the resulting rock is usually crystalline. Regional metamorphism is due to heat and pressure, and produces foliation, or cleavage, in rocks where the minerals have been aligned due to pressure and recrystallization. Dynamic metamorphism is associated with the alteration of rocks along major thrust zones (fault planes).

Group Metamorphic	Origin Mountain ranges	Grain size Fine	Classification Regional

GREEN SLATE

A low-grade metamorphic rock, slate is derived from clay (shale) pelitic rocks. Green slate is formed from quartz, some feldspar, and mica. The presence of chlorite gives this slate its green colour.
• **TEXTURE** Fine-grained with grains of a similar size. The grain size is too fine to be seen without a microscope.
• **ORIGIN** Forms when fine-grained sediments, such as clay or volcanic ash, undergo regional metamorphism. Minerals like mica and chlorite become aligned, giving a perfect, or slaty, cleavage.

many small dark patches of carbon and pyrite

greenish colour across cleavage surface

Pressure Low	Temperature Low		Structure Foliated

Group Metamorphic	Origin Mountain ranges	Grain size Fine	Classification Regional

BLACK SLATE

This rock is formed from pelitic sediments – clays, mudstones, shales, and fine-grained tuff. It contains clay minerals, quartz, mica, and feldspar. Organic matter as graphite and pyrite give black slate its dark colour.
• **TEXTURE** This is a fine-grained rock. It has the characteristic perfect, slaty cleavage produced by the alignment of flaky minerals, such as mica, which makes it easy to split into parallel-sided slabs.
• **ORIGIN** Forms when fine-grained, pelitic sediments, such as mudstones or shales, undergo regional metamorphism at low temperatures and low pressures.

dark colour

small, raised pyrite porphyroblasts

fine grain size

Pressure Low	Temperature Low		Structure Foliated

Group Metamorphic	Origin Mountain ranges	Grain size Fine	Classification Regional

SLATE WITH PYRITE

Formed from pelitic sediments, as with other slates, this rock is composed of quartz, clay minerals, chlorite, mica, and feldspar. As its name suggests, there is also pyrite present. The pyrite can be either finely disseminated small crystals, or larger porphyroblasts (distinct crystals) set in a fine-grained matrix. The pyrite is often in the form of cubic crystals.

• **TEXTURE** This slate is fine-grained, with only the pyrite porphyroblasts visible to the naked eye. The fine-grained matrix can be studied in detail only under a microscope. Like other slates, this rock is characterized by its perfect, slaty, cleavage, which has resulted from the alignment of flaky minerals due to pressure conditions.

• **ORIGIN** This rock forms under low temperature and low pressure conditions. The distinct pyrite crystals grow in response to this regional metamorphism.

small pyrite crystal set in the surface

fine-grained matrix

Pressure Low	Temperature Low	Structure Foliated

Group Metamorphic	Origin Mountain ranges	Grain size Fine	Classification Regional

SLATE WITH DISTORTED FOSSIL

This rock contains minerals associated with the original pelitic sediments from which it was formed. Quartz, clay minerals, and mica, with feldspar and chlorite, are the main minerals in this slate. There may also be minute crystals of pyrite. Fossils can be preserved in the slates formed from fossiliferous shales, because the metamorphic grade is low.

• **TEXTURE** Fine-grained rock, with a few porphyroblasts of pyrite.

• **ORIGIN** Fossiliferous slate forms by the low-grade regional metamorphism of shales. Fossils, such as this brachiopod, can survive in identifiable form but may be distorted due to shear metamorphism which produces rock cleavage.

fine-grained matrix

distorted fossil

pyrite crystal

Pressure Low	Temperature Low	Structure Foliated

Group Metamorphic	Origin Mountain ranges	Grain size Medium	Classification Regional

PHYLLITE

Derived from low-grade metamorphosed
sediments, phyllites are comparable with
slates but are not restricted in pre-
metamorphic terms to very fine clays.
Quartz and feldspars are more abundant
than in shales. Mica and chlorite are
essential constituents, imparting a
characteristic sheen, and a grey or
green colour to the rock.
• **TEXTURE** This is a foliated
rock of fine- to medium-grain size.
Phyllite may have small, distinct
crystals (porphyroblasts) of garnet set
into the wavy foliation. This foliation
results from the alignment of mica and
chlorite under low to moderate pressure.
Phyllites often show small-scale folding.
• **ORIGINS** Forms from pelitic sediments,
during low to moderate pressure, and low
temperature regional metamorphism.

pale greyish green colouring

"sheen" on surfaces, due to high mica and chlorite content

Pressure Low, Moderate	Temperature Low		Structure Foliated

Group Metamorphic	Origin Mountain ranges	Grain size Medium	Classification Regional

GARNET SCHIST

The group of rocks known as schist are
characterized by the presence of visible
flaky or tabular minerals aligned in a
cleavage. Garnet schist is rich in the
micas, biotite and muscovite, with
quartz and feldspar also present. The
usually well-shaped crystals of garnet
are about 5mm (³⁄₁₆in) in diameter,
and have grown in the rock during
pressure and temperature changes.
The garnet is usually the reddish
variety (almandine).
• **TEXTURE** A medium- to
coarse-grained rock. A schistosity is always well-developed
due to the parallel alignment of
micas. The rock may often show
small-scale folding.
• **ORIGIN** Forms in conditions
of medium-grade, regional metamorphism, at deeper levels than
phyllite. The pressure is moderately high, and temperature has
been influential in changing
the rock's original character.

dark coloured rock

wavy foliation

red garnet porphyroblasts

mica gives glittery, silvery sheen

Pressure Moderate	Temperature Low to moderate		Structure Foliated

Group Metamorphic	Origin Mountain ranges	Grain size Medium	Classification Regional

FOLDED SCHIST

This rock contains quartz, feldspar, biotite, and muscovite mica. Folded schist is characterized by small-scale folds accentuated by glittering, mica crystals.

- **TEXTURE** A medium-grained rock, the constituent minerals are often segregated into distinct bands. Schistosity, a wavy foliation caused by the rock splitting along planes of weakness, is emphasized by the mica crystals.
- **ORIGIN** Formed by moderate pressures and low to moderate temperatures very deep in the crust within fold mountain belts. Folded schist is typical of mountain-forming belts.

dark biotite

pale muscovite

wavy folds picked out by mineral bands

Pressure Moderate	Temperature Low to moderate	Structure Foliated

Group Metamorphic	Origin Mountain ranges	Grain size Medium	Classification Regional

MUSCOVITE SCHIST

This is a rock rich in silvery muscovite mica. The mica is aligned on the planes of wavy foliation within the rock. Muscovite schist also contains quartz and feldspar, and some biotite mica. Garnet and chlorite minerals may also be present in the rock.

- **TEXTURE** A medium-grained rock with mica crystals 2–3mm (⅟₁₆–⅛in) in size. The schistosity, or wavy foliation, may be emphasized by bands rich and poor in muscovite.
- **ORIGIN** Muscovite schists form from pelitic rocks under conditions of medium-grade regional metamorphism, where pressures are moderate, and temperature influences low to moderate. Such conditions typically lead to the alteration of mud- and clay-based rocks. Other rocks are also affected by this metamorphism, but these tend to show less foliation.

silvery mica on foliation

Pressure Moderate	Temperature Low to moderate	Structure Foliated

Group Metamorphic	Origin Mountain ranges	Grain size Medium	Classification Regional

BIOTITE SCHIST

This rock contains a high proportion of mica, along with quartz and feldspar. It is especially rich in biotite mica, which gives it a darkish colouring. Compositionally, biotite schist is very similar to the pelitic sediments from which it developed during metamorphism.
• **TEXTURE** A medium-grained rock, with crystals that are visible to the naked eye. Biotite schist is, however, best studied with a hand lens. This specimen shows the dark flakes of mica aligned with the foliation.
• **ORIGIN** Forms during medium-grade regional metamorphism of pelitic sediments, and other rocks, but these may not become foliated.

quartz

high proportion of mica

wavy foliation from alignment of flaky minerals

Pressure Moderate	Temperature Low to moderate	Structure Foliated

Group Metamorphic	Origin Mountain ranges	Grain size Medium	Classification Regional

KYANITE SCHIST

The bulk of this rock is composed of quartz, feldspar, and mica though it is characterized by the mineral kyanite. Kyanite forms sky-blue porphyroblasts of bladed habit which lie parallel to the foliation, or as clusters of crystals. It is often folded. Other minerals can be garnet and staurolite. The overall colour is greyish, but may be darker.
• **TEXTURE** A medium- to coarse-grained rock, the crystals are easy to see with the naked eye. These are always schistose but may also be gneissose.
• **ORIGIN** Found in the central high-grade part of metamorphic belts, under moderate to high pressure and temperate regimes. This rock is associated with sillimanite and staurolite schists. Kyanite is one of the minerals used by geologists to map metamorphic zones. Each zone is defined according to a mineral formed under certain pressure-temperature conditions.

grey rock with foliated structure

dark mica

grey quartz

blue bladed kyanite

medium- to coarse-grained

Pressure Moderate	Temperature Moderate to high	Structure Foliated

Group Metamorphic	Origin Mountain ranges	Grain size Coarse	Classification Regional

GNEISS

A metamorphic rock characterized by compositional banding of metamorphic origin is known as gneiss. Feldspar and quartz are abundant, while muscovite, biotite, and hornblende are also commonly present. Other rocks characteristic of high-grade regional metamorphism, such as pyroxene and garnet, may also occur.

• TEXTURE A medium- to coarse-grained rock, characterized by discontinuous, alternating light and dark layers. The presence of quartz and feldspar help to form the lighter layers which tend to have a granular texture. The darker layers of ferro-magnesian minerals tend to be foliated.

• ORIGIN This rock forms from the high-grade regional metamorphism of any pre-formed rock. The minerals are segregated into bands as a result of high temperatures and pressures. Gneisses may be either be meta-sediments or meta-igneous rocks, and occur in association with migmatites and granites. Gneiss is thought to comprise much of the lower continental crust.

dark and light coloured foliated bands

pale feldspar

dark mica

Pressure High	Temperature High		Structure Foliated, Crystalline

Group Metamorphic	Origin Mountain ranges	Grain size Coarse	Classification Regional

FOLDED GNEISS

As with other gneisses, this rock is composed of segregated bands: the lighter bands are rich in quartz and feldspar; the dark bands are made up of ferro-magnesian minerals, such as hornblende and biotite mica. In folded gneiss these bands are often very obvious. The composition may be very similar to that of granite.

• TEXTURE A coarse-grained rock, with all the minerals easy to see with the naked eye. The folded structure is emphasized by the segregation of the minerals, and gives the impression that parts of the rock had been plastic when formed.

• ORIGIN Folded gneiss is formed under conditions of high-grade regional metamorphism. All rock types, such as sediments, sandstones and shales, and igneous rocks, including dolerite and granite, may become gneisses under these conditions.

pale quartz and feldspar

dark hornblende and biotite mica

folded, separate bands of pale and dark minerals

Pressure High	Temperature High		Structure Foliated, Crystalline

Group Metamorphic	Origin Mountain ranges	Grain size Coarse	Classification Regional

AUGEN GNEISS

These are metamorphic rocks of granite
composition that contain large lens-shaped
crystals ("eyes" or "augen") of feldspar in a
banded matrix of quartz, feldspar, and micas.
• **TEXTURE** A coarse-grained rock, the
gneissose banding is somewhat displaced
by the augen structure.
• **ORIGIN** Augen gneiss
forms in the highest
temperature and
pressure zones of
regional metamorphism.

dark and light banding

larger eye-shaped patches of feldspar

Pressure High	Temperature High	Structure Foliated, Crystalline

Group Metamorphic	Origin Mountain ranges	Grain size Coarse	Classification Regional

GRANULAR GNEISS

High proportions of light grey quartz, white and
pink feldspar, and light and dark mica make up
this rock. Amphibole and pyroxene may be
present. The composition is often granitic.
• **TEXTURE** The crystals are streaked
out into typical gneissose banding, with
dark and light bands. The texture is
granular with interlocking crystals.
• **ORIGIN** Forms in very
high-grade metamorphic
environments deep in
the Earth's crust.

alternating bands of dark and light minerals

Pressure High	Temperature High	Structure Foliated, Crystalline

Group Metamorphic	Origin Mountain ranges	Grain size Coarse	Classification Regional

MIGMATITE

These are mixed metamorphic rocks
consisting of a schist or gneissose component, and a granitic component
forming as layers or pods. Migmatite
may approach granite in composition.
• **TEXTURE** A coarse-grained rock
with a granular texture, it often shows
banding like gneiss. The
various components may
display schistosity.
• **ORIGIN** Forms on a
regional scale in areas of
high-grade metamorphism.

small-scale folds

light mineral band

dark and light coloured components

dark basic material

Pressure High	Temperature High	Structure Foliated, Crystalline

Group Metamorphic	Origin Base of crust	Grain size Coarse	Classification Regional

ECLOGITE

A rock predominantly composed of
pyroxene (green variety, omphacite)
and red garnet. Kyanite crystals may
sometimes occur in eclogite.
• TEXTURE A medium- to coarse-
grained rock which may be banded.
• ORIGIN Formed under highest
temperature and pressure conditions, at
considerable depth in
the Earth's crust.
Found in association
with perditites and
serpentinites.

greenish pyroxene

red garnet

foliated texture

Pressure High	Temperature High	Structure Foliated, Crystalline

Group Metamorphic	Origin Base of crust	Grain size Coarse	Classification Regional

GRANULITE

This rock has a characteristically high content of pyroxene, and either diopside or
hypersthene. Garnet, kyanite, biotite,
quartz, and feldspar may also be present.
• TEXTURE These are tough, massive,
coarse-grained rocks which may be
banded, but are not usually schistose.
• ORIGIN Believed to be formed at very
high temperatures and
pressures. Found in
ancient continental
shield areas.

*pale, distinct
crystals set in
finer matrix*

Pressure High	Temperature High	Structure Crystalline

Group Metamorphic	Origin Mountain ranges	Grain size Coarse	Classification Regional

AMPHIBOLITE

This rock is dominantly formed of amphibole,
commonly hornblende, but sometimes actinolite or tremolite. Feldspar, pyroxene, chlorite,
epidote, and garnet are also often present.
• TEXTURE This is a coarse-grained rock. A
well-developed foliation or schistosity may be
present. Porphyroblasts, particularly of garnet,
may also be present.
• ORIGIN Medium- to high-
grade rocks, amphibolites are
formed mostly from the
metamorphism of igneous
rocks such as dolerites.

*amphibole
crystals*

Pressure High	Temperature High	Structure Foliated, Crystalline

Group Metamorphic	Origin Contact aureoles	Grain size Fine, Coarse	Classification Contact

GREEN MARBLE

This rock is composed essentially of calcite, derived from the original limestone, but may contain lesser amounts of dolomite. Other minerals formed from impurities in the limestone may include brucite, olivine, tremolite and serpentine – all of which can give the otherwise whitish rock a greenish colouring.

• **TEXTURE** This is a crystalline rock which, when looked at through a hand lens, but especially under a microscope, is seen to have a mosaic of interlocking and fused crystals of calcite. The original limestone would probably have contained fossils, but these will have been lost during the metamorphic recrystallization.

• **ORIGIN** This rock results from the thermal metamorphism of limestone around igneous intrusions.

green veins of calc-silicate minerals

crystalline texture

Pressure Low	Temperature High	Structure Crystalline

Group Metamorphic	Origin Contact aureoles	Grain size Fine, Coarse	Classification Contact

BLUE MARBLE

Composed essentially of calcite, which forms the original limestone, but may contain lesser amounts of dolomite. If the limestone is impure, new minerals develop when the rock is recrystallized due to thermal metamorphism. The new minerals can include forsterite, wollastonite, serpentine, brucite, diopside, and tremolite. The blue colouring, which makes this marble attractive is due mainly to the diopside in its composition.

• **TEXTURE** A crystalline rock, with a mosaic of fused calcite crystals, just visible with a magnifying glass. Other minerals are set into the matrix.

• **ORIGIN** Forms when limestone is intruded by igneous rock. The heat from such events causes recrystallization of the calcite, thus destroying original structures in the limestone, and leads to the formation of new minerals.

pale coloured calcite

blue patches from diopside

crystalline texture

Pressure Low	Temperature High	Structure Crystalline

Group Metamorphic	Origin Contact aureoles	Grain size Fine, Coarse	Classification Contact

GREY MARBLE

Unlike other marbles, this rock forms from
relatively pure limestones, and therefore few
calc-silicate minerals develop. Grey marble
is a calcite-rich rock which, when studied
under a microscope, is seen to contain a
small amount of wollastonite, brucite,
tremolite, serpentine, or diopside.
• **TEXTURE** This is a crystalline
rock, with interlocking calcite crystals,
forming a pale, soft rock. The sugary
surface can be scratched easily with a
knife blade. Marbles will effervesce in
a weak hydrochloric acid solution – this
is a very useful test.
• **ORIGIN** Forms in the metamorphic
aureoles of igneous rocks, where limestone
has been heated and recrystallized,
especially near granite intrusions.

*crystalline
texture*

Pressure Low	Temperature High		Structure Crystalline

Group Metamorphic	Origin Contact aureoles	Grain size Fine, Coarse	Classification Contact

OLIVINE MARBLE

This rock contains a very high percentage
of calcite, which is recrystallized from the
original pre-metamorphic limestone.
Other minerals are produced as a
result of metamorphic conditions,
the most important of which is
olivine. This mineral occurs in the
marble as greenish-brown
granular crystals in the matrix.
• **TEXTURE** A rock with
a crystalline texture,
olivine marble is formed
from an interlocking
mass of calcite crystals.
It differs from the
original limestone, in
which the calcite grains
may have pore spaces
between them. Fossils
occur only rarely in
marble, because the
calcite is recrystallized.
The olivine crystals are
granular in texture.
• **ORIGIN** This rock is formed
when limestone is thermally metamorphosed by the intrusion of igneous rock.

*individual crystals
of olivine*

*• greenish
brown olivine*

• calcite matrix

Pressure Low	Temperature High		Structure Crystalline

Group Metamorphic	Origin Contact aureoles	Grain size Fine	Classification Contact

CORDIERITE HORNFELS

A rock that contains a variety of minerals, the final assemblage depends on the composition of the original rock, and on the temperature conditions of metamorphism. Cordierite hornfels is usually a dark-coloured rock, and contains quartz, mica, and cordierite, which develop during metamorphism.

• **TEXTURE** A fine- to medium-grained crystalline rock, it contains porphyroblasts of cordierite, which are often several centimetres in diameter. Without foliation, the original sedimentary structures are usually destroyed by metamorphic recrystallization. The equigranular composition of the rock causes it to be tough and splintery in texture.

• **ORIGIN** Forms in contact metamorphic aureoles, which occur in rocks close to large igneous (often granite) intrusions. Contact metamorphic aureoles grade outwards into lower grade rocks such as spotted slate.

dark grey, fine-grained rock

Pressure Low	Temperature High	Structure Crystalline

Group Metamorphic	Origin Contact aureoles.	Grain size Fine	Classification Contact

PYROXENE HORNFELS

Tough, fine grained, dark-coloured rock, essentially composed of quartz, mica and pyroxene. Pyroxene in the hornfels often occurs as porphyroblasts. Some of the other minerals may not be visible to the naked eye, as all primary sedimentary structures are destroyed by recrystallization. Hornfels lacks planar structures and its colouration can also be greyish, greenish, or black.

• **TEXTURE** This is a fine- to medium-grained rock, with an even grain size. Porphyroblasts of pyroxene, cordierite or andulusite are often developed. The high degree of recrystallization that has occured removes any original sedimentary structures.

• **ORIGIN** Pyroxene hornfels forms in the innermost part of contact metamorphic aureoles, where the temperature is highest. These are formed by thermal metamorphosis following granite intrusion.

dark coloured pyroxene crystals

Pressure Low	Temperature High	Structure Crystalline

Group Metamorphic	Origin Contact aureoles	Grain size Fine	Classification Contact

GARNET HORNFELS

This is generally a dark-coloured rock.
Garnet hornfels has reddish patches and
crystals of garnet set into the matrix. It
also contains quartz, mica, and feldspar,
and metamorphic minerals, such as
cordierite and andalusite.
• TEXTURE This is a fine- to medium-
grained rock, with a tough, splintery
texture. The distinct garnet crystals give
garnet hornfels a porphyroblastic texture.
• ORIGIN Forms in the contact aureoles
of large igneous intrusions. These can be
formed of granite, syenite, and gabbro.

*red garnet
porphyroblasts*

*flinty
texture*

Pressure Low	Temperature High	Structure Crystalline

Group Metamorphic	Origin Contact aureoles	Grain size Fine	Classification Contact

SPOTTED SLATE

This is a black, greenish or grey rock with
dark spots. The spots may be metamorphic
minerals, such as cordierite or andalusite.
This rock also has in its composition
many of the original non-metamorphic
minerals, such as quartz and mica.
• TEXTURE Same structures as slate
with a good cleavage. This rock is
characterized by the presence of
spots, which are often indistinct.
• ORIGIN Forms in the peri-
meter zones of contact aureoles,
often grading into hornfels.

*dark greyish cordierite
crystals*

*small,
dark spots*

Pressure Low	Temperature High to moderate	Structure Crystalline

Group Metamorphic	Origin Contact aureoles	Grain size Fine	Classification Contact

CHIASTOLITE HORNFELS

A grey or brownish rock, this hornfels contains
minerals such as quartz and mica, with
andalusite and cordierite. The thin-bladed
crystals that stand out from the matrix are of
chiastolite, a variety of andalusite.
• TEXTURE This rock consists of fine-
grained crystals of even size. Porphyroblasts
of andalusite sometimes form, with fine
dark-grained inclusions known as chiastolite,
which are cross shaped in section.
• ORIGIN Forms close to the
igneous intrusion that provides
the heat for metamorphism.

bladed chiastolite

*rhombic
chiastolite*

Pressure High	Temperature Moderate to high	Structure Crystalline

| Group Metamorphic | Origin Contact aureoles | Grain size Medium | Classification Contact |

METAQUARTZITE

This rock contains well over 90 per cent quartz, giving it a pale, almost sugary, appearance. It is formed from quartz-rich sandstones. At high magnification, minerals such as mica and feldspar along with iron oxides, may be seen.

• **TEXTURE** A fine- to medium-grained rock, its texture is very even, with the quartz crystals fused to form a tough crystalline rock. The texture is thus very different from that of the original arenaceous (sandy) sediment, in which there would have been pore spaces between the grains.

• **ORIGIN** Metaquartzite forms both by contact metamorphism of sand-stone near a large igneous intrusion, and by regional metamorphism.

crystalline texture

very high percentage of quartz

| Pressure Low | Temperature High | Structure Crystalline |

| Group Metamorphic | Origin Contact aureoles | Grain size Fine, Coarse | Classification Contact |

SKARN

While containing a variety of minerals, skarn is essentially calcite-rich. Skarn may contain olivine, periclase, wollastonite, diopside, garnet, serpentine, tremolite, and other minerals that are typical of metamorphosed limestones. The garnet is commonly grossular. Ore minerals may also be present such as pyrite, sphalerite, galena, and chalcopyrite.

• **TEXTURE** With a grain size that is fine to medium to coarse, skarn has euhedral crystals of a number of minerals. The associated minerals may often concentrate into patches and nodules in the rock.

• **ORIGIN** The complex mineral assemblages found in skarns are the result of its formation from the contact metamorphism of limestone, usually by granite or syenite intrusions. Impurities in the limestone, as well as fluids from intrusions, cause the formation of various minerals. Ore deposits, including copper, manganese, and molybdenum, which are of sufficient size to be of economic use, are often found in skarns.

typical veined and banded structure

much pale calcite

dark mineral bands

| Pressure Low | Temperature High | Structure Crystalline |

Group Metamorphic	Origin Contact aureoles	Grain size Fine	Classification Contact

HALLEFLINTA

This is a rock containing a variety of minerals related to its original pre-metamorphosed composition as a volcanic tuff. Halleflinta, therefore, contains quartz, and has been enriched with silica during metamorphism. It is frequently pale-coloured, and can vary from brown to pink, green, grey, or yellowish brown.
• TEXTURE Halleflinta is a fine grained rock – a microscope is needed to study its mineral composition. Texture is even, with a flinty, crystalline appearance. This rock breaks with a sharp, splintery fracture. It may show a layered structure related to the original stratification of the volcanic tuff. Porphyroblastic textures with large, isolated crystals are sometimes found.
• ORIGIN Forms by the contact metamorphism of tuffs, which have usually been impregnated by secondary silica. It is often associated with hornfels.

brownish, flinty rock

splintery fracture

high proportion of quartz

Pressure Low	Temperature High		Structure Crystalline

Group Metamorphic	Origin Thrust zones	Grain size Fine	Classification Dynamic

MYLONITE

The minerals contained in mylonite vary depending on the rocks being subjected to metamorphic alteration. Mylonite contains two main groups of material: one is derived from fragments of rock, called "rock flour", and the other consists of minerals that have crystallized at, or soon after, metamorphism. The rock can be dark or light-coloured.
• TEXTURE This is a rock that has been destroyed by deformation, and the particles streaked out into small lenses and patches. It tends to be fine-grained. However, in some coarser specimens, the streaked-out structure may be visible, and the surfaces may have lineations on them.
• ORIGIN Forms when large scale thrust faults develop. The rocks near the thrust plane suffer great shearing stress and are fragmented and drawn out in the direction of thrust movement. This occurs during earth movements associated with mountain formation.

foliation

pale mylonite with small scale contortions

Pressure Shearing stress	Temperature Low		Structure Streaked out

SEDIMENTARY ROCKS

SEDIMENTARY rocks are formed at the earth's surface, mostly on the sea bed. The rocks have layers that are often visible to the naked eye. Detrital sediments result from weathering, erosion, and accumulation of particles from rocks already formed. Organic sediments are composed of fossils and material derived from once living organisms. Chemical sediments are formed from chemical precipitation of material such as rock salt and calcite.

Group Sedimentary	Origin Marine, Freshwater	Grain size Very coarse

QUARTZ CONGLOMERATE

This rock contains many light coloured quartz fragments set in a much finer matrix. The matrix usually comprises sand or silt, small rock fragments, and iron oxides often cemented by silica or calcite.
• **TEXTURE** The large grains are rounded; the matrix may be angular or rounded. Quartz conglomerates rarely contain fossils because of their coarse nature, and the often turbulent conditions associated with their formation. Bedding structures are seldom seen in small samples.
• **ORIGIN** Forms where there is sufficient energy to move large fragments of material. This includes beaches and river systems.

large fragments of quartz

fine sandstone matrix

Classification Detrital	Fossils Very rare	Grain shape Rounded

Group Sedimentary	Origin Marine, Freshwater	Grain size Very coarse

POLYGENETIC CONGLOMERATE

Containing a great variety of different materials, polygenetic conglomerates can have fragments derived from igneous, metamorphic, and sedimentary rocks, as well as particles of individual minerals. The fragments can be cemented by a variety of minerals, including quartz, iron oxides, and calcite.
• **TEXTURE** The grains in a polygenetic conglomerate are rounded, or sub-rounded, by the action of water. There may be some smaller angular fragments in the matrix between the large grains.
• **ORIGIN** Forms in high energy environments, such as powerful water currents, which are able to move the very large fragments of rock.

large sub-rounded fragment

Classification Detrital	Fossils Very rare	Grain shape Rounded

Group Sedimentary	Origin Transitional, Water	Grain size Very coarse

LIMESTONE BRECCIA

This is a rock that contains fragments of limestone, usually set in a fine-grained matrix cemented with calcite. Other minerals such as quartz may be present in limestone breccia, as may fragments of other rocks.
• TEXTURE The grains are large and angular in contrast to the rounded fragments in conglomerate. The individual fragments in limestone breccia may contain fossils.
• ORIGIN Found in transitional environments near continental margins. Limestone breccia may form as deposits at the base of cliffs. As water seeps through the cliff and the accumulated scree, it deposits lime that will cement together the fragments.

dark, angular fragments of limestone

finer matrix

Classification Detrital	Fossils Invertebrates	Grain shape Angular

Group Sedimentary	Origin Transitional, Water	Grain size Very coarse

BRECCIA

Fragments of breccia are angular, and may be of any type of igneous, metamorphic, and sedimentary rock. These fragments are set together in a fine- to medium-grained matrix of salt or sand.
• TEXTURE Bedding structures are usually visible only on a large scale in the field. Fossils are uncommon in such rocks. The large fragments of rocks and minerals in breccia are angular, and the surrounding matrix material is also angular.
• ORIGIN Forms as scree at the base of cliffs. Breccia has a similar origin to limestone breccia, but the fragments in it are not calcareous. The accumulation of the large, angular fragments can take place in a number of environments, especially where mechanical weathering is active.

angular fragments showing no preferred orientation

grey siliceous fragments

yellowish matrix

Classification Detrital	Fossils Uncommon	Grain shape Angular

Group Sedimentary	Origin Glacier, Ice sheet	Grain size Fine

BOULDER CLAY

This rock consists of angular and some rounded pebbles, varying in size, and set in a fine, unconsolidated matrix. The rock types may be of any size, set together in a clay or sandy matrix. The glacial fragments included in the boulder clay are called glacial erratics. These are fragments carried away from their place of origin by the glacier. Fragments of breccia can be of some assistance to geologists in helping them to work out the general direction of ice movement.
• **TEXTURE** The fragments in boulder clay are mainly angular. The rock is made up of various unsorted materials, ranging from clay size to boulder size.
• **ORIGIN** Boulder clay usually forms as a deposit from melting glaciers and ice sheets.

angular rock fragment •

• brown, fine-grained clay

Classification Detrital	Fossils Rare	Grain shape Angular

Group Sedimentary	Origin Continental	Grain size Fine

LOESS

This is a yellowish or brownish clay made up of very small angular particles of quartz, feldspar, calcite, and other minerals and rock fragments.
• **TEXTURE** Loess is a fine-grained aeolian clay, and it is porous and earthy. It is poorly cemented which makes it crumbly. The grains may be rounded because of wind action, and bedding is difficult to determine.
• **ORIGIN** Forms by the winds blowing out from glaciated regions. Loess is deposited by the wind, and the material is probably derived from foliated regions. Wind-deposited loess is found in thick layers, especially in China, but also in areas of Western Europe.

yellowish colouring due • to presence of limonite

powdery texture •

Classification Detrital	Fossils Rare	Grain shape Rounded, Angular

Group Sedimentary	Origin Marine, Freshwater, Cont.	Grain size Medium

SANDSTONE

These are rocks predominantly made up of quartz grains, but often accompanied by feldspar, mica or other minerals. Grains may be cemented by silica, calcite, or iron oxides.

- **TEXTURE** Sandstone is a medium-grained rock. The grains are usually well-sorted (grains all of a similar size). The grains can either be angular (gritstone) or rounded (sandstone).
- **ORIGIN** Sandstones are extremely common rocks which form in a great variety of geological situations. The majority of sandstones, however, are accumulated in either water, usually marine, or as wind-blown deposits in arid continental areas.

numerous grains of quartz make up the matrix

fine stratification

Classification Detrital	Fossils Invertebrates, Vertebrates, Plants	Grain shape Angular, Rounded

Group Sedimentary	Origin Marine	Grain size Medium

GREENSAND

This is a quartz sandstone which contains a few per cent of the glauconite (a green-coloured mineral which forms only under marine conditions). Small quantities of detrital mica, feldspar and rock fragments are usually cemented by calcite. The glauconite may well have formed in place (authigenic), and occurs as flaky grains.

- **TEXTURE** Greensand is a medium-grained rock, with the majority of the grains being angular. The sediment is well-sorted.
- **ORIGIN** Greensand forms in a marine environment. The constituent mineral glauconite, a potassium iron silicate, may be used to help in radiometric age-dating.

glauconite gives green colouring

Classification Detrital	Fossils Invertebrates, Vertebrates, Plants	Grain shape Angular

Group Sedimentary	Origin Continental, Marine	Grain size Medium

RED SANDSTONE

These are rocks predominantly formed by quartz grains but also accompanied by some mica and feldspar. The red coloration is due to coatings of hematite over the sand grains. Hematite is an iron oxide, derived by the oxidation of iron-rich minerals swept in from a source area.

• **TEXTURE** This is a well-sorted sediment, and the grains may be angular or rounded. Red sandstone often displays sedimentary structures including cross-bedding, ripple marks and desiccation cracks.

• **ORIGIN** Forms as continental deposits, where iron may be oxidized. Red sandstone also commonly forms in shallow marine environments.

rounded grains

iron oxide gives red colour

well-sorted sediment

Classification Detrital	Fossils Invertebrates, Vertebrates, Plants	Grain shape Angular, Rounded

Group Sedimentary	Origin Continental	Grain size Medium

MILLET-SEED SANDSTONE

A quartz sandstone with conspicuous rounding of the grains, producing what is known as a millet-seed texture. The rock may also contain some feldspar and rock fragments, but mica is usually absent. There is often a thin coating of iron oxides to the grains.

• **TEXTURE** This is a very well-sorted sediment, with the quartz grains all the same size. The grains are rounded, and are of medium size. Fossils are very rare.

• **ORIGINS** Millet-seed sandstone forms in arid environments. The quartz sand grains are rounded by the action of the wind. In the field, large-scale dune bedding may be a feature of this rock, indicating continental deposition.

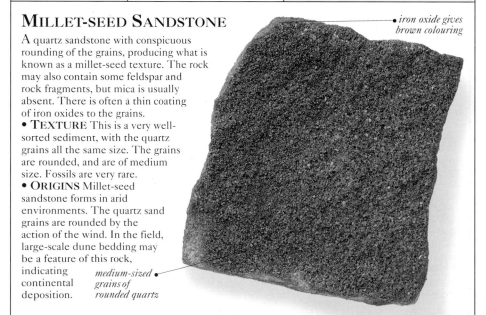

iron oxide gives brown colouring

medium-sized grains of rounded quartz

Classification Detrital	Fossils Rare	Grain shape Rounded

Group Sedimentary	Origin Marine, Freshwater	Grain size Medium

MICACEOUS SANDSTONE

A rock containing abundant quartz, but also considerable amounts of mica. It may also contain detrital feldspar and rock fragments. On the bedding planes, the surfaces where the sand is deposited, there are many small, glittering, flakes of mica. These can be muscovite, biotite mica, or both.
• TEXTURE This rock is well-sorted and medium-grained. The majority of the grains are angular, the mica occurring typically as flakes.
• ORIGIN Mica is a rare mineral in continental, wind-deposited sandstones, because its flaky habit causes it to be blown away. Its presence in micaceous sandstone suggests water deposition, in either lakes and rivers, or the sea.

patches of iron oxide on surface

many small mica flakes

Classification Detrital	Fossils Invertebrates, Vertebrates, Plants	Grain shape Angular, Flattened

Group Sedimentary	Origin Marine, Freshwater	Grain size Medium

LIMONITIC SANDSTONE

angular grains cemented with limonite

dark brown colouring due to limonite

Rich in quartz grains, limonitic sandstone may contain small rock fragments, and minerals such as feldspar and mica. The presence of the iron mineral "limonite" – from which the rock gets its name – may give it a yellowish or dark brownish colouring.
• TEXTURE This is a well-sorted sediment, with most of the grains the same size. The fragments are angular and coated with limonite, which acts as a cement. As with other sandstones, bedding surfaces may be discernible, although this may not be particularly obvious in a hand specimen.
• ORIGIN Limonitic sandstone can form in a number of different environments, including marine and freshwater.

well-sorted sediment

Classification Detrital	Fossils Invertebrates, Vertebrates, Plants	Grain shape Angular

Group Sedimentary	Origin Marine, Freshwater	Grain size Medium

PINK ORTHOQUARTZITE

As with all orthoquartzites, this rock is a sandstone with a quartz content greater than 95 per cent. The rocks are composed almost entirely of quartz grains with a silica cement. With a magnifying glass other minerals may occasionally be visible, including some feldspar or rock fragments. Fossils in ortho-quartzite are very rare.

• **TEXTURE** This is a medium-grained, well-sorted rock with a crystalline appearance.

• **ORIGIN** As orthoquartzites contain very little feldspar, they are said to be mature rocks. This is because the long-term processes of weathering, erosion, and deposition have removed virtually all the less resistant materials from the source rocks, and quartz becomes the dominant mineral.

crystalline appearance

high quartz content

Classification Detrital	Fossils Rare, Invertebrates	Grain shape Angular

Group Sedimentary	Origin Marine, Freshwater	Grain size Medium

GREY ORTHOQUARTZITE

Compositionally the same as pink orthoquartzite, the grey colouring of this rock comes from the constituent quartz grains. It contains over 95 per cent quartz. The cement is also quartz, and this binds the grains very firmly. Orthoquartzite may be difficult to distinguish from metaquartzite (metamorphosed quartz sandstones), though the occasional presence of fossils can help in identification. There are also stratification and other sedimentary structures, such as cross or graded bedding in orthoquartzite. These are not usually evident in metaquartzite.

• **TEXTURE** This is a rock of medium-grain size, and it is usually well-sorted.

• **ORIGIN** This rock forms in marine and freshwater environments and is subject to much erosion and weathering. With so much quartz present, this, as with other ortho-quartzites, is known as a mature sediment.

medium-grained quartz

Classification Detrital	Fossils Rare, Invertebrates	Grain shape Angular

Group Sedimentary	Origin Marine	Grain size Medium, Fine

GREYWACKE

This rock contains abundant quartz-
feldspar, and rock fragments. The
matrix is of clay, chlorite, quartz, and
pyrite, but the minerals are too small to
be seen with the naked eye.
• **TEXTURE** Individual units of
greywacke have a poorly sorted nature,
with a great variety of different grain
sizes apparent. Larger fragments
typically contain sharply angular grains
in a finer-grained matrix.
• **ORIGIN** These rocks are marine sediments. They may form from a slurry of
sediment deposited in
deep ocean environ-
ments from fast-
moving currents.
When this is the case,
the rocks may exhibit
a variety of sedi-
mentary features.

*angular
frgaments* •

poorly sorted •

*fine-grained
matrix* •

Classification Detrital	Fossils Rare	Grain shape Angular

Group Sedimentary	Origin Marine, Freshwater	Grain size Medium

ARKOSE

A medium- to coarse-grained
rock which is pinkish to pale
grey in colour. Although
predominantly made up of
quartz, feldspar can contribute
as much as a third of the rock. Constituents are
usually well-sorted and partially rounded.
Together with mica flakes, they are cemented
in a calcritic or ferruginous cement.
• **TEXTURE** The grains in this rock are
angular and usually well-sorted.
• **ORIGIN** Forms in marine and freshwater
environments and continental deposits. Arkose
is said to be an immature rock because of its
high feldspar content. The sediment that
forms this rock must be deposited rapidly or
in an arid environment to prevent the
feldspar from decomposing. The effect of a
long process of chemical weathering,
erosion, and deposition would be to alter
and decompose the feld-
spar. Most arkoses are
terrestrially derived from
granite disintegration.

*high
percentage
of pinkish
feldspar* •

quartz grains •

Classification Detrital	Fossils Rare	Grain shape Angular

Group Sedimentary	Origin Marine, Freshwater, Cont.	Grain size Coarse, Medium

QUARTZ GRITSTONE

This rock contains over 75 per cent quartz, and some feldspar and mica. There can also be small rock fragments of varying types, depending on the rocks in the source area from which the sediment is derived. The cementing mineral may be quartz, and a yellowish coating of limonite on the grains might be evident.

• **TEXTURE** This is a coarse- to medium-grained rock. The grains are fairly well-sorted, and angular in shape. Gritstones are sometimes poorly cemented, and the individual grains can often be rubbed off with the fingers.

• **ORIGIN** Forms in a number of different environments, ranging from marine and freshwater, to continental. Most gritstones are formed in water, often in river systems and deltas. In all these places, a reasonable amount of energy is needed to carry the coarse particles.

well-sorted sediment

high percentage of quartz

Classification Detrital	Fossils Invertebrates, Vertebrates, Plants	Grain shape Angular

Group Sedimentary	Origin Marine, Continental	Grain size Coarse, Medium

FELDSPATHIC GRITSTONE

This rock contains a high percentage of quartz, but also has as much as 25 per cent feldspar. Mica is present, and there are small rock fragments derived from the source area. Feldspathic gritstone has a similar composition to arkose, which is its fine-grained equivalent. It is a brownish coloured rock, and may take on a pinkish tinge when pink orthoclase feldspar is present. A cement of quartz or iron oxide may bind the grains together.

• **TEXTURE** This is a coarse- to medium-grained rock. The grains are angular, although the feldspar may have flattened faces where it has broken along cleavage planes. It is well-sorted and most of the grains are of the same size.

• **ORIGIN** Forms by rapid deposition in transitional environments. Feldspar decomposes during protracted weathering.

medium grain size

feldspar grains visible

Classification Detrital	Fossils Invertebrates, Vertebrates, Plants	Grain shape Angular

Group Sedimentary	Origin Marine	Grain size Fine

BLACK SHALE

This, and other shales, consists of a mixture of clay minerals together with detrital quartz, feldspar, and mica. Black shales are rich in carbonaceous matter, and pyrite and gypsum commonly occur. The pyrite content may result from the rock forming under reducing conditions in deep, still water. This mineral may occur as cubic crystals on bedding planes, and fossils in black shale are often replaced by pyrite.

• TEXTURE This is a very fine-grained rock, with mineral grains invisible, except under a microscope. It is finely laminated, and splits easily along the bedding planes, sometimes revealing flattened fossils.

• ORIGIN Forms as a clay deposit in deep marine environments. The fossils in black shale are often marine creatures, such as molluscs.

fine laminations

cracks due to shrinkage

Classification Detrital	Fossils Invertebrates, Vertebrates, Plants	Grain shape Angular

Group Sedimentary	Origin Marine, Freshwater	Grain size Fine

FOSSILIFEROUS SHALE

Compositionally similar to other shales, fossiliferous shale may also have a high calcite content derived from the fossils it contains. As well as complete fossils, it will also have detrital fossil fragments.

• TEXTURE Because of its fine grain size, shale can preserve a variety of fossils with very fine detail. Fossil brachiopods may be present. Fossils commonly found in shales include molluscs, such as ammonoids, bivalves and gastropods. There are also arthropods such as trilobites, and graptolites – delicate structures which are not found in coarser rocks. Plants and vertebrates may also be present.

• ORIGIN Usually forms under relatively shallow marine conditions. Fossiliferous shale can also be found under freshwater conditions. The nature of the fossils found in the rock are usually a good indicator of the environment in which the rock was formed.

many fossil brachiopods

shale matrix

Classification Detrital	Fossils Invertebrates, Vertebrates, Plants	Grain shape Angular

Group Sedimentary	Origin Marine, Freshwater	Grain size Fine

SILTSTONE

This rock contains more quartz, than either mudstones or shales. Siltstones are commonly laminated, due to variations in grain size, organic content, or amounts of calcium carbonate.
• **TEXTURE** This is a fine-grained sediment. The individual rock fragments and mineral grains in siltstone are too small to be visible to the naked eye.
• **ORIGIN** Siltstone forms by the compaction of sediment of silt grade which may have accumulated in a variety of environments, both marine and freshwater. The fossil content may be a guide to the precise environment of deposition. Because of the presence of feldspar, and other minerals besides quartz, siltstone is said to be immature. A long-term weathering process would decompose feldspar and other material, leaving the quartz grains.

uneven fracture

fine-grained sediment

Classification Detrital	Fossils Invertebrates, Vertebrates, Plants	Grain shape Angular

Group Sedimentary	Origin Marine, Freshwater	Grain size Fine

MUDSTONE

This rock consists of a mixture of clay minerals together with detrital quartz, feldspar and mica. Iron oxides are also often present.
• **TEXTURE** Mudstone is a very fine-grained rock, and the grains cannot be seen with the naked eye. It shares many characteristics with shale and may contain fossils, though it has less well-defined lamination compared to shale.
• **ORIGIN** Mudstone forms in a variety of environments resulting from the deposition of mud in, for example, oceans and freshwater lakes. Studying the fossils contained in a specimen of mudstone, and comparing them with the lifestyles of related modern organisms, can help to identify the type of environment in which the rock was formed.

fine-grained rock

curved fracture

Classification Detrital	Fossils Invertebrates, Plants	Grain shape Angular

Group Sedimentary	Origin Marine, Freshwater	Grain size Fine

CALCAREOUS MUDSTONE

As its name suggests, this rock is similar to mudstone but it also has a high calcite content. Detrital quartz, feldspar and quartz may also be present. Fossils are not uncommon. It is often light coloured.
• **TEXTURE** A very fine-grained rock, in which the particles cannot be seen with the naked eye. The grains are much the same size, but recrystallization may change their original shape. The rock may break in a distinctive way, with a subconchoidal fracture. Because of the high calcite content, it will effervesce when tested with cold hydrochloric acid.
• **ORIGIN** Forms in marine and freshwater conditions. Being very fine-grained, calcareous mudstone is easily transported by water into sea and lakes where it may accumulate with some sand, silt and other calcerous organisms.

calcite vein •

curved •
fracture

Classification Detrital	Fossils Invertebrates, Plants	Grain shape Angular

Group Sedimentary	Origin Marine, Freshwater, Cont.	Grain size Fine

CLAY

This rock is very rich in clay minerals (from where it gets its name), together with detrital quartz, mica and feldspar.
• **TEXTURE** The grain size is so fine that the individual minerals cannot be seen, even with a microscope. Clays often have a characteristic smell, and the grains absorb water to become plastic.
• **ORIGIN** Clay forms in many different environments. It can occur in deep and shallow marine conditions (fossils of oysters are evident in clays from marine environments), in lakes, and as a continental sediment. Glacial clays develop from the powdering of rock by ice action. Clay minerals are formed by the decay and alteration of certain silicate minerals, such as feldspars, under chemical weathering. Fossils are often well preserved in clay because of its very fine grain size.

very fine grains •

these mollusc shells suggest •
marine environment

Classification Detrital	Fossils Invertebrates, Vertebrates, Plants	Grain shape Angular

Group Sedimentary	Origin Marine, Freshwater	Grain size Fine

RED MARL

This rock is a sediment intermediate between clay and limestones, and includes gradations between calcareous clays and muddy limestones. The calcareous matter should range between 40–60 per cent, with detrital quartz, clay and silt particles. The red colouring is due to the presence of iron oxide.

• **TEXTURE** Because marl is such a fine-grained rock, it can be examined in detail only under a microscope. The grains are well formed and may be cemented by calcite.

• **ORIGIN** Marls are often found in shallow lakes with much vegetation. They are also associated with evaporite deposits formed in saline basins. In this case they may be interbedded with gypsum and rock salt.

curved fracture

fine-grained rock

reddish-brown colour

Classification Detrital	Fossils Invertebrates, Vertebrates, Plants	Grain shape Angular

Group Sedimentary	Origin Marine, Freshwater	Grain size Fine

GREEN MARL

As with its red counterpart, green marl is an intermediate sediment between the clays and the limestones. It differs only in colour, with the greenish colouring due to the presence of minerals such as glauconite and chlorite. Green marl also has a high calcite content.

• **TEXTURE** Green marl is a fine-grained rock. The individual particles can be seen only under a microscope. The calcite present causes the rock to effervesce when it is tested with cold dilute hydrochloric acid.

• **ORIGIN** This rock forms in marine and freshwater conditions. When glauconite is present in green marl, it indicates that the rock would have formed in a marine environment.

fine-grained sediment

Classification Detrital	Fossils Invertebrates, Vertebrates, Plants	Grain shape Angular

Group Sedimentary	Origin Marine, Salt lakes	Grain size Crystalline

ROCK SALT

This rock is essentially composed of halite, together with impurities of clay minerals and iron oxides. The rock is often coloured reddish-brown when iron oxides are present.
• **TEXTURE** Rock salt is usually massive and coarsely crystalline, sometimes forming as distinct cubic crystals. Under pressure, the rock salt may be caused to flow forming salt plugs that intrude other strata.
• **ORIGIN** Forms from saline waters, such as salt lakes, in a sequence which includes other evaporites – minerals such as dolomite and gypsum.

orange-brown crystals •

Classification Chemical	Fossils None	Grain shape Crystalline

Group Sedimentary	Origin Marine, Salt lakes	Grain size Crystalline

ROCK GYPSUM

This rock normally occurs as massive gypsum (hydrated calcium sulphate).
• **TEXTURE** Coarse to fine in texture, this crystalline rock shows a fibrous habit. It may also show bedding which is often strongly distorted. Rock gypsum is usually interbedded with sandstones, marls, and limestones. A soft rock, it can be scratched easily with a fingernail.
• **ORIGIN** Forms in evaporite rock sequences in association with dolomite rocks and marl, and the minerals anhydrite, halite, and calcite.

• crystalline rock

• vitreous lustre

• uneven fracture

Classification Chemical	Fossils None	Grain shape Crystalline

Group Sedimentary	Origin Marine, Salt lakes	Grain size Crystalline

POTASH ROCK

This rock is essentially a mixture of sylvite and halite. The crystalline sylvite is a pale grey colour when it is pure, while orange-red sylvite gets its colour from iron oxide staining.
• **TEXTURE** This is a crystalline rock. Potash occurs with other minerals in strata containing rock salt, gypsum, and dolomite.
• **ORIGIN** Deposited from saline waters, potash rock forms in a sequence that includes evaporites such as dolomite, marl, and mudstone.

rough, partly dissolved surface •

iron impurities give reddish colouring •

Classification Chemical	Fossils None	Grain shape Crystalline

Group Sedimentary	Origin Marine	Grain size Coarse

PISOLITIC LIMESTONE

This rock is similar to oolitic limestones, but contains larger and more irregular structures up to pea-size, known as pisoliths. These pisoliths are formed of calcite precipitated around a nucleus, such as a sand grain, or a fragment of shell. The cementing material is calcite.

• **TEXTURE** This limestone is a coarse-grained rock, with pisoliths all of much the same size. The pisoliths can often be flattened, unlike the spherical ooliths. Fossils are common and include many invertebrates.

• **ORIGIN** Pisolitic limestone forms in moderately shallow marine conditions, similar to those where oolite forms. Such environments favour the precipitation of calcite. These conditions were common during the past, especially during the Mesozoic era.

calcite matrix

pisoliths may be flattened

pale, cream-coloured calcium carbonate-rich rock

Classification Chemical	Fossils Invertebrates	Grain shape Rounded

Group Sedimentary	Origin Marine	Grain size Medium

OOLITIC LIMESTONE

Containing a high degree of calcium carbonate, oolitic limestone may also contain small amounts of quartz and other detrital minerals. Fossil fragments are common.

• **TEXTURE** Rock essentially composed of closely packed ooliths is called oolite. Ooliths are spheroidal or ellipsoidal structures built of concentric layers – usually composed of calcite. The rounded ooliths are easy to see with the naked eye on the typically light-coloured rock matrix.

• **ORIGIN** Forms in warm, shallow, and strongly agitated marine conditions. The constant action of tides, currents, and waves encourages the precipitation of calcium carbonate around quartz grains.

medium-grained, rounded ooliths set in calcite cement

pale-coloured matrix

Classification Chemical	Fossils Invertebrates	Grain shape Rounded

Group Sedimentary	Origin Marine	Grain size Fine

CHALK

This is a very pure limestone formed of calcite, and containing only small amounts of silt or mud. It consists mainly of the tests of micro-organisms, such as coccoliths and foraminifera, which cannot be seen without the aid of a microscope. Macrofossils, which can be seen with the naked eye, are often present, and these include molluscs, such as ammonites and bivalves, brachiopods, and echinoderms. Chalk may contain detrital material, mainly quartz, as well as other mineral fragments.
• **TEXTURE** A very fine-grained, powdery, soft rock. It effervesces strongly when in contact with cold, dilute hydrochloric acid.
• **ORIGIN** Formed in marine conditions during the Cretaceous period. During this period, the continental shelves, where the chalk was deposited, were below a much greater depth of sea water than today. The small amount of detrital material suggests that nearby continental areas were low-lying and arid.

soft, white, powdery texture

almost pure calcite rock composed of micro-fossils

Classification Chemical	Fossils Invertebrates, Vertebrates	Grain shape Rounded, Angular

Group Sedimentary	Origin Marine	Grain size Fine

RED CHALK

A fine-grained calcareous rock, red chalk gets its colour from a detrital component of iron oxide (hematite). It may also contain scattered quartz pebbles. Many of the minute grains in red chalk are microfossils, such as coccoliths. Macrofossils, including belemnites, ammonites, bivalves, and echinoderms, are frequently present in red chalk.
• **TEXTURE** The grain size is small, and the individual particles are too minute to be detected, except with a microscope.
• **ORIGIN** Thought to be formed under slow marine deposition, the red colouring agent hematite may be derived from a nearly lateritic land surface. A study of the fossils in red chalk will give a much more detailed indication of the environment of deposition.

reddish colouring due to iron oxide

calcite grains

small veins and patches of calcite

Classification Chemical	Fossils Invertebrates	Grain shape Rounded

Group Sedimentary	Origin Marine	Grain size Coarse

CRINOIDAL LIMESTONE

This rock is essentially formed of calcite as fine or larger crystals. These may have been derived from animal skeletons such as crinoid plates. Ossicles of crinoid stems are conspicuous ingredients of this rock.

• **TEXTURE** The large fragments in the rock are the broken stems of crinoids. These may be long, cylindrical pieces, as well as single, rounded ossicles. They are bound in a matrix of massive calcite, with a calcite cement.

• **ORIGIN** This limestone is formed in marine conditions, and takes its name from crinoids – a group of sea-dwelling creatures related to starfish and sea urchins. Crinoids' presence in coral limestone suggests that they inhabited shallow marine environments. Crinoids are not the only fossils that are commonly found in crinoidal limestone; it can be rich in brachiopods, molluscs, and corals.

pale greyish pink rock with much fragmented calcite

mass of broken crinoid stems

Classification Chemical	Fossils Invertebrates	Grain shape Angular, Rounded

Group Sedimentary	Origin Marine	Grain size Fine

CORAL LIMESTONE

This limestone is almost entirely formed from the calcareous remains of fossil coral. The individual structures are called corallites, and they are held in a matrix of lime-rich mud. As well as a high proportion of calcite, this mud, now limestone, contains small amounts of detrital material such as clay and quartz.

• **TEXTURE** The texture is determined by the type of coral preserved in the rock. The matrix of this limestone is fine-grained.

• **ORIGIN** These rocks form in marine conditions, and by studying the individual corals it may be possible to give more precise details of the environment. Most coral limestone forms on the continental shelf. Though these rocks are rich in coral, they can also contain other shallow water marine invertebrates, including brachiopods, cephalopods, gastropods, and bryozoans.

overall pink-grey colour of calcite

mass of coral held in lime mud matrix

Classification Chemical	Fossils Invertebrates	Grain shape Angular

Group Sedimentary	Origin Marine, Freshwater	Grain size Medium, Fine

SHELLY LIMESTONE

A general name for calcareous rocks containing a high proportion of fossil shells. This limestone can contain a great variety of brachiopod and bivalve shells. The rock matrix is usually cemented by calcite. Any brownish colouring the rock exhibits may be due to detrital minerals and iron oxides.
• **TEXTURE** The matrix of this rock is medium- or fine-grained, and has angular fragments.
• **ORIGIN** These limestones are essentially of marine origin although a very few of them may also form in freshwater environments. As with many of the rocks that contain fossils, it is often possible to discover the actual environment in which a specimen formed by a careful study of the fossils found within the shelly limestone.

many grey calcite brachiopod shells

brownish colouring from iron oxides

shells set in calcite-rich matrix

Classification Chemical	Fossils Invertebrates	Grain shape Angular

Group Sedimentary	Origin Marine	Grain size Fine

BRYOZOAN LIMESTONE

The percentage of calcite in bryozoan limestone is very high. This rock also contains a very small amount of detrital material, such as quartz and clay. These detrital materials may give the rock a colouring that is darker than the pale grey of purer limestone. Essentially, bryozoan limestone is lime mud characterized by the net-like structures of fossil bryozoans.
• **TEXTURE** The lime mud that forms the matrix is fine-grained, and even-textured.
• **ORIGIN** This rock forms in marine conditions. It commonly originates in calcareous reef deposits, where the bryozoans, such as *Fenestella*, help to bind the mounds of reef sediment. Besides bryozoans, the reef environment also supports a wealth of other organisms, and these limestones are rich in molluscs, brachiopods, and other marine invertebrates.

high percentage of calcium carbonate

small, net-like bryozoans within a lime mud

Classification Chemical	Fossils Invertebrates	Grain shape Angular

Group Sedimentary	Origin Freshwater	Grain size Medium, Fine

FRESHWATER LIMESTONE

Less common than marine limestone, the freshwater variety is distinguished by the nature of the fossils contained in it, connected to freshwater environments. As with other limestones, this rock has a high proportion of calcium carbonate and it can also contain detrital quartz and clay.

• TEXTURE The calcareous matrix is crystalline, and binds the rock together. This rock consists essentially of a calcareous mud, with a number of coiled gastropod shells. The chief way to determine if a limestone is marine or freshwater is by identifying the fossils. The high calcite content causes the rock to effervesce when it comes into contact with cold, dilute hydrochloric acid.

• ORIGIN This limestone forms in freshwater lakes with a high lime content, and is unusual in the stratigraphic record.

lime mud matrix

many non-marine gastropod shells

calcite is main mineral

Classification Chemical	Fossils Invertebrates, Plants	Grain shape Angular

Group Sedimentary	Origin Marine	Grain size Fine

NUMMULITIC LIMESTONE

This rock contains a very high percentage of calcium carbonate, mainly in the form of whole and fragmented, circular-shaped shells of foraminiferid fossil called *nummulites*. These are cemented together with calcite. In common with other biogenic limestones, which are composed largely of one type of fossil, other fossils can be found in nummulitic limestone. It may also contain some detrital material, usually quartz.

• TEXTURE The matrix of this limestone is fine-grained, whereas the whole fossil can measure up to about 2 cm (¾ in) in diameter and vary somewhat in size.

• ORIGIN This rock is formed under marine conditions, and is commonly found in localized areas. The Egyptian pyramids are made of this particular limestone.

fine matrix

fossil nummulites

Classification Chemical	Fossils Invertebrates	Grain shape Crystalline

Group Sedimentary	Origin Marine	Grain size Medium, Fine

DOLOMITE

The name of a rock and also a mineral, the rock contains a high proportion of dolomite from which it gets its name. Detrital minerals and secondary silica (chert) are also present. While the mineral dolomite is magnesium carbonate, dolomite rocks are usually darker than other limestones (often creamy brown). Dolomites also tend to be less fossilferous than other limestones, possibly because of the recrystallization that has often taken place during their formation.
• **TEXTURE** It has an even crystalline texture. Dolomite masses are often compact and earthy.
• **ORIGIN** These rocks forms in marine environments. Most dolomites are believed to be of secondary origin, replacing original limestones.

fine-grained matrix

even texture

dolomite-rich

Classification Chemical	Fossils Invertebrates	Grain shape Crystalline

Group Sedimentary	Origin Continental	Grain size Fine

TUFA

Principally composed of calcite (calcium carbonate), impurities of iron oxides are responsible for tufa's distinctive yellow and red coloration. Calcrete is a name given to the pebbly form of tufa. This is a porous and usually non-bedded deposit. Travertine is a more dense and banded form of tufa.
• **TEXTURE** This is a crystalline material and may have pebbles and grains of sediment caught up in it.
• **ORIGIN** The rock forms when calcium carbonate is precipitated from lime-rich waters. This may occur on cliffs, in caves, and on quarry faces, especially in lime-stone regions. Plants and mosses are often covered with tufa, and so preserved as crusty, lime-rich fossils. Such preservation is very rapid, and modern organisms can become encrusted in a matter of months in favourable conditions.

noticeable lack of any bedding

crusted, porous structure

Classification Chemical	Fossils Plants, Invertebrates	Grain shape Crystalline

Group Sedimentary	Origin Continental	Grain size Crystalline

TRAVERTINE

Consisting of almost pure calcium carbonate, travertine may also contain some detrital quartz and clay. Fossil material is virtually absent. Travertine is a very light-coloured rock, unless it contains iron compounds or other impurities, which can give it colouring. Travertine deposits are rounded, botryoidal (resembling a grape structure), and often banded structures.
• **TEXTURE** This rock is formed of small crystals of calcite which bind together other sediment particles. In many situations travertine occurs in strata. The rock is often bedded.
• **ORIGIN** Travertine is frequently associated with springs rising from deep-seated sources. This results in many hot springs, especially in volcanic regions, giving rise to travertine by the deposition of solid calcium carbonate.

iron minerals give slight staining

porous, spongy texture

Classification Chemical	Fossils Rare	Grain shape Crystalline

Group Sedimentary	Origin Continental	Grain size Crystalline

STALACTITE

Sedimentary structures formed of calcium carbonate, stalactites are sometimes coloured by impurities, such as iron oxide.
• **TEXTURE** These crystalline structures occur in the shape of pendants grown from the roofs of caves, especially in limestone regions. While stalactites are long, slender forms, the corresponding structures - stalagmites - that grow up from the cave floor are stumpy and shorter. The two sometimes join together to form calcite columns.
• **ORIGIN** These structures form by inorganic precipitation of calcium carbonate, from waters seeping through fractures in the roofs of caves. When carbon dioxide is released and the lime-rich waters meet the air, lime is deposited, while evaporation of the water speeds up the process. Lime-rich water, dropping from the end of a stalactite, results in the formation of a stalagmite.

pale calcite

pendent-shaped

Classification Chemical	Fossils None	Grain shape Crystalline

Group Sedimentary	Origin Continental	Grain size Medium, Fine

BANDED IRONSTONE

These rocks, ferruginous cherts, show a marked banded structure. The banding mainly consists of alternate layers of chert and siderite, or hematite in which considerable recrystallization has taken place. Magnetite and pyrite may also occur in the iron-rich bands of the rock.

• TEXTURE Banded ironstones are fine- to medium-grained rocks.

• ORIGIN Mostly formed in the Precambrian, between 2000 and 3000 million years ago. It is open to interpretation whether or not banded ironstones were deposited by precipitation in enclosed lakes or basins. They do, however, occur in many sedimentary environments, from shallow and intertidal to deep water situations. There is evidence from some areas that these rocks formed in marshes and waterlogged mudflats, and some geologists suggest that organic activity was important in helping the carbonate and sulphide association to be precipitated. The possibility of organic involvement is of considerable interest, because at the time of formation only very primitive organisms existed on the earth.

alternating grey and red layers of chert and iron-rich material

prominent banding

Classification Chemical	Fossils None	Grain shape Crystalline

Group Sedimentary	Origin Marine	Grain size Medium

OOLITIC IRONSTONE

This rock consists of closely packed ooliths variably replaced by siderite and other iron minerals. Quartz, feldspar, and other detrital minerals may be present. The rock may have originally been lime-rich, and replacement has converted the lime to iron minerals. The ooliths, which give the rock its name, are small and rounded as they are in oolitic limestone.

• TEXTURE Detrital grains in the rock may be angular. Calcite is a common cement between the ooliths.

• ORIGIN Forms in marine environments; the rock may undergo change shortly after deposition, or it may be deposited already rich in iron.

dark red, iron-rich colouring

rounded ooliths form body of rock

Classification Chemical	Fossils Invertebrates	Grain shape Rounded, Angular

| Group Sedimentary | Origin Continental | Grain size Medium, Fine |

BITUMINOUS COAL

shiny patches •

The action of pressure on the rock lignite leads to the formation of bituminous or "household" coal. It is hard, brittle and has a high carbon content. This rock has alternating shiny and dull layers, and may contain some recognizable plant material. It is dirty to handle.
• TEXTURE It is even-textured, with the appearance of being fused material. Bituminous coal breaks into cube-like fractures due to its structure – two sets of joints at right angles.
• ORIGIN It forms by the accumulation of peat and subsequent changes, due to pressure and heat burial – water being driven off.

dull patches •

| Classification Chemical | Fossils Plants | Grain shape None |

| Group Sedimentary | Origin Continental | Grain size Medium, Fine |

ANTHRACITE

uneven • surfaces

conchoidal • fracture

This differs from other coals because of its extremely high content of carbon with a correspondingly low proportion of volatile matter. Normally an unbanded type of coal.
• TEXTURE It is more glassy and cleaner to handle than bituminous coal. Anthracite ignites at much higher temperatures compared to other coals.
• ORIGIN Forms by accumulation of peat. It is suggested that the increase of pressure and especially heat has caused volatiles to be driven off – thus forming a higher grade of coal.

dark, shiny • matrix

| Classification Chemical | Fossils Plants | Grain shape None |

| Group Sedimentary | Origin Continental | Grain size Medium, Fine |

LIGNITE

This is a brown-coloured coal, having a carbon content that is between peat and bituminous coal. Lignite still has a large amount of visible plant material in its structure and is friable.
• TEXTURE Less compact than other coals, lignite has a high moisture content and is crumbly. It also contains more volatiles and impurities.
• ORIGIN A type of low-rank coal most commonly found in Tertiary and Mesozoic strata where changes have not occured to the vegetable matter. Lignite also occasionally results from shallow burial of peat.

plant fragments •

crumbly surface •

| Classification Organic | Fossils Plants | Grain shape None |

Group Sedimentary	Origin Continental	Grain size Medium, Fine

PEAT

This rock represents the initial stage in the modification of plant material to lignite and bituminous coal. Peat is dark brown to black in colour, and contains about 50 per cent carbon, as well as much volatile material. It is crumbly and easily broken in the hand.

• **TEXTURE** There are many plant fragments visible in peat, often including large roots. It is frequently high in water, and breaks unevenly when dry. Peat is a soft rock.

• **ORIGIN** Forms from the deposition of plant debris on forest floors, in fens, or on moorland. The large deposits of coal, now used for fuel, were originally forest peat. Much of the vegetable matter in the peat that accumulates today is mosses, rushes, and sedges. The deposits may be many metres thick. By decay and reconstruction, the bottom layers of peat banks become compacted, darkened and hardened, while the carbon content increases.

plant fragments

crumbly surface

Classification Chemical	Fossils Plants, Invertebrates	Grain shape None

Group Sedimentary	Origin Marine	Grain size Medium, Fine

JET

Due to its high carbon content, jet is classified as a type of coal. It is a compact substance found in bituminous shales, and it produces a brown streak. Jet has a conchoidal fracture and it is hard enough to take a good polish. It rarely forms in geographically extensive seams.

• **TEXTURE** When examined in close detail, jet shows woody tissue structures. It has a vitreous lustre, which has been exploited for making ornaments and jewellery.

• **ORIGIN** The formation of jet has been open to debate. It is generally believed that this black, coal-like rock developed in marine strata from logs and other drifting plant material, which then became waterlogged and sank into the muds of the sea. It is found in rocks of marine origin, unlike other forms of coal which form from plant matter accumulated on the land surface.

bedded structure

vitreous lustre

Classification Chemical	Fossils Plants	Grain shape None

Group Sedimentary	Origin Marine	Grain size Fine

CHERT

This occurs as siliceous nodules or sheets, especially in sedimentary rocks such as limestone and among lavas. Chert is usually greyish in colouring.
• **TEXTURE** It is composed of crypto-crystalline silca, and its components can be seen only under a microscope. Chert breaks with an uneven to subconchoidal fracture. It is a hard rock that cannot be scratched with a knife.
• **ORIGIN** Chert is formed from the accumulation of silica, possibly in a colloidal form on seabeds. The silica may well come from organic sources.

fine grain size

subconchoidal fracture

Classification Chemical	Fossils Invertebrates, Plants	Grain shape Crystalline

Group Sedimentary	Origin Marine	Grain size Fine

FLINT

The term flint is used principally for siliceous nodules in the Chalk of western Europe. It is a hard, compact substance with an homogenous appearance and breaks with a conchoidal fracture. Its flakes were used as tools by primitive peoples.
• **TEXTURE** Consists entirely of silica. Crypto-crystalline silica in flint appears to be derived from organic opal from contained sponge spicules.
• **ORIGIN** Occurs as bands and nodular masses in fine-grained limestones, especially Chalk. Flint frequently contains fossils.

sharp edges

conchoidal fracture

Classification Chemical	Fossils Invertebrates	Grain shape Crystalline

Group Sedimentary	Origin Continental	Grain size Crystalline

AMBER

This rock is the fossil resin of extinct coniferous trees. Amber is soft and has a resinous or subvitreous lustre. It varies from transparent to translucent. Insects and small vertebrates which were trapped in the original sticky resin are sometimes found fossilized in amber. Amber is frequently used to make jewellery.
• **TEXTURE** When broken, amber has a conchoidal fracture.
• **ORIGIN** Forms from the resin of coniferous trees, and is found in sedimentary deposits.

conchoidal fracture

resinous lustre

Classification Biogenic	Fossils Vertebrates, Invertebrates	Grain shape None

Group Sedimentary	Origin Post depositional	Grain size Crystalline

SEPTARIAN CONCRETION

Concretions are often formed of the same material as the host sediment, but are cemented (concreted) together by silica, carbonate minerals, or iron oxides. Septarian concretions have radiating and polygonal internal patterns of veins – usually of calcite.

• **TEXTURE** The structure is one of radiating and concentric cracks, in a tough outer shell. When opened, this internal veined structure is apparent.

• **ORIGIN** It may form by the segregation of minerals during diagenesis (the processes that turn soft, muddy material into rock), and their concentration around a nucleus, which may be a grain of sediment or even a fossil. After formation of the concretion, the cracks known as septa may develop during shrinkage.

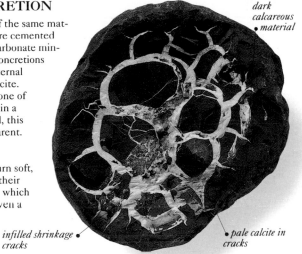

dark calcareous material

infilled shrinkage cracks

pale calcite in cracks

Classification Chemical	Fossils Invertebrates	Grain shape Crystalline

Group Sedimentary	Origin Post depositional	Grain size Crystalline

PYRITE NODULE

These rocks occur as spherical, botryoidal, or cylindrical nodules, formed by the bronzy yellow mineral, pyrite. On weathered surfaces, the nodules usually have a yellow-black colouring. Becomes black or brownish yellow. Pyrite nodules are commonly found in shales and mudstones.

• **TEXTURE** The internal structure of these rounded nodules reveal acicular crystals radiating from a central nucleus. Nodules can be a great variety of shapes, such as tubular or ovoid. These nodules may even take on an almost organic appearance.

• **ORIGIN** Pyrite nodules commonly form in shales, clays, and other pelitic rocks, which are themselves rich in pyrite. Also commonly found in the Chalk. Pyrite nodule formation is not fully understood, but precipitation of pyrite around a central nucleus seems a possible explanation.

silvery yellow acicular pyrite crystals

outer surface dull and weathered

internal radiating structure

brownish coating

Classification Chemical	Fossils Rare	Grain shape Crystalline

Group Meteorite	Origin Extra terrestrial	Grain size/Crystalline Crystalline

STONY IRON

Stony iron meteorites are composed of about 50 per cent metal, and 50 per cent silicate material. The metallic content is nickel-iron alloy. The silicate components are minerals recognized in many rocks on Earth, and include olivine, pyroxene, and plagioclase feldspar.

• **TEXTURE** These are rock-like objects, and have a surface showing various components, including crystals. The silicate minerals, such as olivine, may be removed by weathering, giving the surface a pitted appearance.

• **ORIGIN** These are rare meteorites and only about 4 per cent of known meteorites are in this group. Stony iron meteorites help geologists to understand how certain elements combine with iron or silica during the process of melting and vein formation. They give an insight into planets with an iron-rich core and a silicate outer shell.

• *rough surface with alteration due to ablation*

• *cavities on surface*

Classification Stony Iron	Shape Angular, Rounded	Composition Silicate, Metal

Group Meteorite	Origin Terrestrial	Grain size/Crystalline Glass

TEKTITE

These are silica-rich glass objects that were once believed to be meteorites. However, their distribution on the Earth, and their chemistry, have now led scientists to suggest that they may not in fact have an extra-terrestrial origin. Tektites actually have a composition not unlike that of some volcanic rocks. These rocks have a high silica content, and are also rich in oxides of potassium, calcium, and aluminium.

• **TEXTURE** The rocks are small in size, usually about 200–300g (7–10oz) in weight, and have a disc or ovoid shape. Their surface may be smooth or rough.

• **ORIGIN** A matter of debate, but tektites may result from the melting of terrestrial rocks on the impact of a meteorite. It seems unlikely that they were fired towards the Earth from a large volcano on the Moon, as has been suggested in the past.

typical rounded • shape

• *smooth surface*

• *indentations*

Classification Tektite	Shape Rounded	Composition Silicate

Group Meteorite	Origin Extra-terrestrial	Grain size/Crystalline Crystalline

CHONDRITE

These rocks form the largest group of meteorites classified as stones. Chondrites contain silicate minerals, mostly pyroxene and olivine, and small amounts of plagioclase feldspar. There is also a small proportion of nickel-iron.

• **TEXTURE** These meteorites have a structure consisting of chondrules, which are small, spherical grains. The overall shape of chondrite varies, but many are rounded or even dome-shaped. Angular specimens are those that have fragmented on impact.

• **ORIGIN** How chondrites form is not certain, but their chemistry seems to represent the mantle material of planet-forming bodies, planetesimals. This type of meteorite gives the oldest radiometric date yet obtained from rocky material – 4,600 million years – a figure generally accepted as the date of the formation of the Solar system.

crystalline, rocky texture

crust around edges showing features of melting on entry into the Earth's atmosphere

Classification Chondrite	Shape Rounded	Composition Silicate, Metal

Group Meteorite	Origin Extra-terrestrial	Grain size/Crystalline Crystalline

ACHONDRITE

These rocks vary from chondrites in both structure and composition. Achondrites contain a high proportion of silicate material, similar to that found in rocks on the Earth. This includes pyroxene and olivine, as well as plagioclase feldspar. However, the composition of achondrites is more variable than that of chondrites, and they generally contain very little metallic iron.

• **TEXTURE** The structure is coarser-grained than chondrites, and they lack chondrules.

• **ORIGIN** As achondrites resemble the rocks found in the mantle and basaltic crust of the Earth, their origin may possibly be volcanic. These rocks also could have originated on planet-forming bodies, called planetesimals.

rough surface

much silicate material including pyroxene and olivine

medium to coarse grains

Classification Achondrite	Shape Angular, Rounded	Composition Silicate

GLOSSARY

TECHNICAL EXPRESSIONS have been avoided wherever possible, but a limited use of them is essential in a book of this nature. The terms listed below, many of which are peculiar to minerals and rocks, are defined in a concise manner. Some definitions have been simplified and generalized in order to avoid obscure language, and involved examples have been left out. Words that appear in bold type in the definitions are explained elsewhere in the glossary. Many key words are also fully explained with colour photographs in the introduction section of the book.

• **ACCESSORY MINERAL**
The mineral constituents of a rock that occur in such small amounts that they are disregarded in the definition and chemistry.

• **ACICULAR**
Needle-shaped mineral habit.

• **ACID ROCK**
Igneous rock with over 65% total silica and over 20% quartz.

• **ADAMANTINE**
Very bright mineral **lustre** similar to that of diamond.

• **AEOLIAN**
Term applied to deposits arranged by the wind. Some features of sedimentary rocks, such as dune bedding, are aeolian structures.

• **AMPHIBOLE GROUP**
Group of common rock-forming minerals, often with complex composition but mostly **ferro-magnesian** silicates.

• **AMYGDALE**
Secondary in-filling of a **vesicle** in an igneous rock. Minerals that occur as amygdales include quartz, calcite, and the zeolite group.

• **ANHEDRAL**
Poorly formed crystal.

• **ARENACEOUS**
Sedimentary rocks that have either been derived from sand or that contain sand.

• **AUREOLE**
Area around an igneous **intrusion**, where contact metamorphism of the original **country rock** has occurred.

• **BASAL CLEAVAGE**
Cleavage that is parallel to the basal crystal plane of a mineral.

• **BASIC ROCK**
Igneous rock that contains between 45% and 55% total silica. These have less than 10% quartz and are rich in **ferro-magnesian minerals**.

• **BATHOLITH**
Very large, irregularly-shaped mass of igneous rock formed from the **intrusion** of magma at great depth.

• **BEDDING**
Layering of sedimentary rocks. Beds or strata are divided by bedding planes.

• **BLADED**
Blade-shaped habit in minerals.

• **CLAY MINERALS**
Alumino-silicate group of minerals, common in sedimentary rocks.

• **CLEAVAGE**
The way certain minerals break along planes related to their internal atomic structure.

• **CONCORDANT**
Following existing rock structures.

• **CONCHOIDAL**
Curved or shell-like fracture in many minerals and some rocks.

• **CONCRETION**
Commonly discrete, rounded nodular rock masses formed and found in beds of shale or clay.

• **COUNTRY ROCK**
Rock surrounding an igneous **intrusion** or below a lava flow.

• **CRYPTOCRYSTALLINE**
Crystalline, but very fine-grained. Individual components need to be viewed under a microscope.

• **DENDRITIC**
Having a tree-like habit.

• **DETRITAL**
Group of sedimentary rocks formed essentially of fragments and grains derived from pre-existing rocks.

• **DISCORDANT**
Cuts across existing rock structures.

• **DULL LUSTRE**
Lustre with little reflectiveness.

• **DYKE**
Sheet-shaped igneous **intrusion**. Cuts across existing rock structures.

• **EARTHY**
Non-reflective, mineral **lustre**.

• **ESSENTIAL MINERAL**
The mineral constituents of a rock that are necessary to classification and name.

• **EUHEDRAL**
Crystal that shows good faces.

• **EVAPORITE**
Mineral or rock formed by the evaporation of saline water.

• **FELDSPATHOID MINERAL**
Group of minerals similar in chemistry and structure to the feldspars, but with less silica.

• **FERRO-MAGNESIAN MINERAL**
Mineral rich in iron and magnesium. These are dense, dark-coloured silicates, such as the olivines, pyroxenes, and amphiboles.

• **FOLIATED**
Laminated, parallel orientation or segregation of different minerals.

• **FOSSIL**
Any record of past life preserved in the crustal rocks. As well as bones and shells, fossils can be of footprints, excrement, and borings.

• **GLASSY TEXTURE**
In igneous rock, where glass forms because of speed of cooling.

• **GRADED BEDDING**
Sedimentary structure where coarser grains gradually give way to finer grains upwards through a bed.

• **GRANULAR**
Having grains, or in grains.

• **GRAPHIC TEXTURE**
Rock texture resulting from the regular intergrowth of quartz and feldspar.

• **GROUNDMASS**
Also called matrix. Mass of rock in which larger crystals may be set.

• **HACKLY**
Mineral fracture that has a rough surface with small protuberances, as on a piece of cast iron.

- **HEMIMORPHIC**
Crystal that has different facial development at each end.
- **HOPPER CRYSTAL**
Crystal with faces that are hollowed as in the "stepped" faces of some halite crystals.
- **HYDROTHERMAL VEIN**
Fracture in rocks in which minerals have been deposited from hot magmatic emanations rich in water.
- **HYPABYSSAL**
Minor intrusions at relatively shallow depths in the Earth's crust.
- **INCLUSION**
A crystal or fragment of another substance enclosed in a crystal or rock.
- **INTERMEDIATE ROCK**
Igneous rock with between 65% and 55% total silica.
- **INTRUSION**
A body of igneous rock that invades older rock. This may be by forceful intrusion or by magmatic sloping.
- **LACCOLITH**
Mass of intrusive igneous rock with dome-shaped top; usually flat base.
- **LAMELLAR**
In thin layers or scales, composed of plates or flakes.
- **LUSTRE**
The way in which a mineral shines because of reflected light.
- **MAGMA**
Molten rock that may consolidate at depth or be erupted as lava.
- **MASSIVE**
Mineral habit of no definite shape.
- **MATRIX** *see* **Groundmass.**
- **METALLIC LUSTRE**
Like that of fresh metal.
- **METASOMATIC**
Process that changes composition of a rock or mineral by the addition or replacement of chemicals.
- **METEORIC WATER**
Water derived from, or in, the atmosphere.
- **MICROCRYSTALLINE**
Small crystal size that is only detectable with a microscope.
- **OOLITH**
Individual, spheroidal sedimentary grains from which oolite rocks are formed. Usually calcareous with a concretic or radial structure.
- **OROGENIC BELT**
Region of the Earth's crust that is, or has been, active, and in which fold mountains are, or were, formed.

- **OSSICLE**
Fragment of the stem of a crinoid, a group of creatures within the phylum *Echinodermata.*
- **PELITIC**
Sediment made of mud or clay.
- **PILLOW LAVA**
Masses of lava formed on sea-bed, shaped like rounded pillows.
- **PHENOCRYST**
Relatively large crystal set into the **groundmass** of an igneous rock to give a **porphyritic** texture.
- **PISOLITH**
Pea-sized sediment grain with concentric internal structure.
- **PLACER DEPOSIT**
Deposit of minerals often in alluvial conditions, or on a beach, formed because of their high specific gravity or resistance to weathering.
- **PLATY HABIT**
Mineral habit with flat, thin crystals.
- **PLUTON**
Mass of igneous rock that has formed beneath the surface of the Earth by consolidation of magma.
- **PORPHYRITIC**
Igneous rock **texture** with relatively large crystals set in the **matrix.**
- **PORPHYROBLASTIC**
Metamorphic rock **texture** with relatively large crystals set into rock **matrix,** i.e. garnets in schist.
- **PSEUDOMORPH**
A crystal with the outward form of another species of mineral.
- **PYROCLAST**
Detrital volcanic material that has been ejected from a volcanic vent.
- **RADIOMETRIC DATING**
A variety of methods by which absolute ages for minerals and rocks can be obtained by studying the ratio between stable (or radioactive) daughter products and their parent elements.
- **RECRYSTALLIZATION**
Formation of new mineral grains in a rock while in the solid state.
- **RESINOUS LUSTRE**
Having the reflectivity of resin.
- **RETICULATED**
Having a network, or net-like, structure.
- **ROCK FLOUR**
Very fine-grained rock dust, often the product of glacial action.
- **SALT DOME**
Large intrusive mass of salt.

- **SCHILLERIZATION**
Brilliant play of bright colours, often produced by minute rod-like intrusions of, for example, iron oxide, in certain minerals.
- **SCHISTOSITY**
Variety of foliation that occurs in medium, coarse-grained rocks. Generally the result of **platy** mineral grains.
- **SCORIACEOUS**
Lava or other volcanic material that is heavily pitted with hollows and empty cavities.
- **SCREE**
Mass of unconsolidated rock waste found on a mountain slope or below a cliff face, derived by weathering.
- **SECONDARY MINERAL**
Any mineral that has subsequently formed in a rock due to secondary processes.
- **SILL**
Concordant, sheet-shaped igneous **intrusion.**
- **SLATY CLEAVAGE**
Structure in some regionally metamorphosed rocks, allowing them to be split into thin sheets.
- **TEXTURE**
Size, shape, and relationships between rock grains or crystals.
- **THRUST PLANE**
Type of fault (break in the rocks of the crust) that has a low angle plane of movement, where older rock is pushed over younger rock.
- **TWINNED CRYSTALS**
Crystals that grow together, with a common crystallographic surface.
- **ULTRABASIC ROCK**
Igneous rock having less than 45% total silica.
- **VEIN**
Sheet-shaped mass of mineral material; usually cuts through rock.
- **VESICLE**
Gas-bubble cavity in lava, left as a hole after the lava solidifies.
- **VITREOUS LUSTRE**
Having the lustre of broken glass.
- **VOLCANIC PIPE**
Fissure through which lava flows.
- **WELL SORTED**
In sedimentary rock, when all the grains are much the same size.
- **ZEOLITE**
Group of hydrous alumino-silicates. Characterized by their easy and reversible loss of water.

INDEX

ACKNOWLEDGMENTS

The author would like to thank the following people for their help with the production of this book: "My wife, Helen, has worked tirelessly throughout the project. She has checked the factual content and read the proofs with meticulous attention to detail. Without her help and encouragement, the work would have taken many more months to complete. My elder son, Daniel, has been a great help on the occasions when I have not fully understood the workings of my wordprocessor, and Emily, my daughter, provided the photograph for the back flap of the jacket. Adam, my other son, has tried to help me relax now and then with games of indoor cricket and golf. I must also thank Stella Vayne, Gillian Roberts, Mary-Clare Jerram, and James Harrison for their editorial work; Dr. George Rowbotham, of Keele University, for answering numerous mineralogical questions; and Dr. Robert Symes, of the Natural History Museum, for his expert help."

Dorling Kindersley would like to thank: David Preston, Marcus Hardy, Susie Behar, Irene Lyford, Gillian Roberts, and Sophy Roberts for their invaluable editorial work; Arthur Brown, Peter Howlett of Lemon Graphics, and Alastair Wardle for additional design; Michael Allaby for compiling the index; The Right Type for additional text film output.

The author and publisher are greatly indebted to the Natural History Museum for making available for photography most of the rocks and minerals illustrated, and Alan Hart of the Mineralogy department for selecting the specimens.

PICTURE CREDITS
All photographs are by Harry Taylor except for: Chris Pellant *(top right)*, 16 *(bottom left)*, 17 *(bottom)*, 18 *(bottom left and right)*, 19 *(top right and bottom left)*, 30 *(bottom left and right)*, 31 *(bottom left)*, 32 *(bottom left)*, 33 *(top right (3) and middle)*, 34 *(top right)*, 35 *(top right and bottom left)*, 37 *(middle left)*, 38 *(bottom left)*, 39 *(middle left and right)*; Colin Keates *(Natural History Museum)* 17 *(top, right, and middle)*, 24 *(bottom right)*, 25 *(lower middle, bottom left and right)*; C.M. Dixon/ Photosources 26 *(bottom)*. Line illustrations by Chris Lyon; airbrushing by Janos Maffry; colour illustrations, 7, 30, and 31 by Andy Farmer; and endpaper illustrations by Caroline Church.